ORTHODOXY IN MASSACHUSETTS
1630–1650

Perry Miller was born in Chicago in 1905. He received a Ph.B. in 1928 and a Ph.D. in 1931 from the University of Chicago. He began his long association with the Harvard University faculty in 1931, becoming professor of American literature in 1946. During World War II he served as a captain and then as a major with the U. S. Army, E.T.O. He has taught at Leiden University, Netherlands, and Tokyo University, Japan, and has served as a member of the Institute of Advanced Study, Princeton, New Jersey. At present he lives and teaches in Cambridge, Mass.

Among the author's other books are THE PURITANS (with T. H. Johnson), THE NEW ENGLAND MIND (2 volumes), JONATHAN EDWARDS, ROGER WILLIAMS, THE RAVEN AND THE WHALE, and ERRAND INTO THE WILDERNESS.

Orthodoxy In Massachusetts

1630-1650

BY PERRY MILLER

WITH A NEW PREFACE BY THE AUTHOR

BEACON PRESS   BEACON HILL   BOSTON

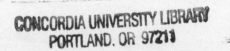

For

PERCY HOLMES BOYNTON
MAGISTRO ET AMICO

Acknowledgments

PERHAPS the greatest pleasure of scholarship, from the standpoint of the student, is the long list of friends he acquires by the simple process of making them his benefactors. Of this long list I wish in particular to memorialize the various important contributions of Professors Percy Holmes Boynton, Napier Wilt, T. V. Smith, and William E. Dodd of the University of Chicago, Professors Kenneth Ballard Murdock, Samuel Eliot Morison, and Francis Otto Matthiessen of Harvard University, and Professor Stanley T. Williams of Yale University. To the Library of Yale University I am indebted for access to the Dexter Collection, to the Boston Public Library for access to the Prince Collection, to the Congregational Library of Boston for generously placing at my disposal its remarkable collection of seventeenth century tracts, and to Mr. Julius H. Tuttle and to the Massachusetts Historical Society for much valuable assistance. Mr. D. H. Mugridge offered very helpful criticism and Mr. Raymond P. Stearns helped materially with the Dutch backgrounds. Without the aid of Mr. Alfred Stern and Mrs. Moïse Dreyfus this research could never have been undertaken. And finally I am indebted to my wife for a vast amount of patient labor, without which the volume could never have materialized.

P. M.

CAMBRIDGE, MASSACHUSETTS
October 1, 1933

Contents

Contents

Foreword

UPON the verge of publication I am fully conscious that in the work to be offered I have treated in a somewhat cavalier fashion certain of the most cherished conventions of current historiography. I have attempted to tell of a great folk movement with an utter disregard of the economic and social factors. I lay myself open to the charge of being so very naïve as to believe that the way men think has some influence upon their actions, of not remembering that these ways of thinking have been officially decided by modern psychologists to be generally just so many rationalizations constructed by the subconscious to disguise the pursuit of more tangible ends.

In part I might take refuge behind the contention that a specialized study is, after all, specialized, that other aspects of the story can easily be found in other works. The field of intellectual or religious history may, I presume, be considered as legitimate a field for research and speculation as that of economic and political. But I am prepared actually to waive such a defense and hazard the thesis that whatever may be the case in other centuries, in the sixteenth and seventeenth certain men of decisive importance took religion seriously; that they often followed spiritual dictates in comparative disregard of ulterior considerations; that those who led the Great Migration to Massachusetts and who founded the colony were predominantly men of this stamp. It has not been part of my conscious intention either to defend or to blame them, to praise or to condemn their achievement. I have simply endeavored to demonstrate that the narrative of the Bay Colony's early history can be strung upon the thread of an idea.

Immediately this statement is made I encounter such authoritative rebuttal as that of Mr. James Truslow Adams, who in *The Founding of New England* has expressed his conviction that "four out of five" immigrants had no particular sympathy with the ecclesiastical aspirations of the leaders and submitted to the régime of the elders for the sake of free land and economic opportunity. For those who desire more detailed discussion on the value of this hackneyed statement of proportions I commend the delightful appendix to Professor Samuel Eliot Morison's *Builders of the Bay Colony*. No one, of course, can doubt that the hope of material advantage played a tremendous part in tempting people to colonial shores and in shaping their life in the new scenes. I do not venture to determine in exactly what ratio the two sorts of motives operated in New England, but I do believe the story as I have offered it must be considered prerequisite to the forming of any just and full estimate.

Hitherto any such complete estimate of the colony's religious life has encountered two principal obstacles which it has been my hope to level. First, there has been, so far as I can discover, no concerted attempt to realize the continuity of thought extending from the initial stages of English Puritanism to the peculiar institutions of New England. By and large, American historians have begun their studies with the landing upon these coasts, and they have almost taken for granted what the textbooks pronounce to have been the intellectual baggage already at hand. Undoubtedly the crucial moment in the religious history of Massachusetts was the founding of the church at Salem in 1629. Let us look at the histories. One after another they have stumbled over the seeming inconsistencies of a people who in England emphatically proclaimed that they were not Separatists and who yet in America apparently turned precisely about and adopted the ecclesiastical discipline of schismatics. To them the obvious explanation has always seemed to be the influence of Plymouth. If this be true, then indeed how can we have much respect for the intellectual development of these people when they did not seem to know where they stood or what they wanted, when the determination of their gravest problem lay at the chance mercy of a medical visit from Deacon Fuller? But if, on the other hand, the action at Salem can be seen to be the outcome of a long and matured program, the deliberate achievement of an objective deliberately sought after, then the religious history of the Massachusetts Colony is seen in an entirely different light. Then we need a new interpretation, which, in explaining the founding of the church of Salem and the other early churches, will not have to take refuge in citing the mystical declaration of Scotch Baillie that "the free aire of a new world" suddenly inspired the settlers to cast off the shackles of episcopacy. The Congregational polity resulted from an elaborate preparation; it was based upon a complex body of Biblical exegesis that could not be mastered on a single voyage, long as voyages then were. However free the "aire" of a new world might be, it could not at once offer what seemed to be an authoritative explanation for Matthew xviii: 17, or for any other of the texts upon which the organization was based.

The new interpretation, then, has had to begin far back in the previous century. It has had to distinguish the various intellectual streams and trace them to their convergence in the single pool of New England orthodoxy. It has had, at perhaps too great a length, to insist that the ecclesiastical issues as they existed in England in 1630 be defined as much as possible from a contemporary point of view. In the course of its researches into "background" the study has offered at least one "new" contribution to New England's history: it has presented a certain school of ecclesiastical thinkers as the specific source of the New England Way, and by analyzing the thought of this school has endeavored to depict what was the actual inheritance of John Cotton and his colleagues. Though I fear that Chapter IV makes dreary reading, still the metaphysics I have therein attempted to describe seems to me fundamental to any right comprehension of what the leaders and at least a large number of the settlers of Massachusetts and Connecticut considered their *raison d'être*. And I hasten to add that this "discovery" of what I believe to be the keystone of New England thought is not entirely original with me; the germinal idea I found in Professor George Lyman Kittredge's short "Note on Dr.

William Ames" [1] and in the pages of that excellent work, Champlin Burrage's *Early English Dissenters in the Light of Recent Research*. My work has in reality been a development of the hints I have received from these scholars.

The second quarrel I have with many of my predecessors has been over what seems to be their inveterate tendency to discuss the history of early Massachusetts from points of view which, however stimulating, are relevant only to their own particular time. Here I part company with those writers, generally ministers, whom Mr. Adams has placed in "a less critical day," as well as with the economic and social historians of the type of which Mr. Adams is himself an eminent example. The New England student of the nineteenth century, raised in the tradition of the land, has done admirable work; and this volume could never have been written without the aid supplied by Henry Martyn Dexter's *The Congregationalism of the Last Three Hundred Years* and Williston Walker's *The Creeds and Platforms of Congregationalism*. But quite naturally such men have seen the events of the past primarily in reference to their own present; they have praised what they thought good and palliated what they thought bad. And they have ever felt called upon to justify; they have had no desire to throw over their preoccupations in order to see seventeenth century issues merely with the eyes of seventeenth century men. Mr. Adams, however, has gone to another extreme. Setting aside the creed and the platform as the queer monomania of one fifth of the colony,

1. Colonial Society of Massachusetts, *Publications*, XIII, 60–69.

he too has always passed judgment, but in his case in the
name of the enlightened insight of modern social science.
In the latter chapters of my work, having previously
tried to ascertain what were the religious objectives of
the settlers, I have wished to illustrate the directions in
which the realization was sought, what problems were
encountered, and what changes in the philosophy were
wrought by success or failure. For that reason I have
allowed the men themselves to speak as often as possible
and perhaps overlarded my text with quotations.
There are not, I believe, any particular factual novelties
in these portions, but I hope that the new orientation
will make some contribution to a more complete realization of what New England "Puritanism" meant — at
least in the beginning.

PREFACE TO THE
BEACON PRESS EDITION

In 1928, as a graduate student at the University of Chicago, I unaccountably found John Winthrop's *Journal* exerting upon me a baneful spell. I resisted manfully, as long as I could, but Governor Winthrop irresistibly lured me to the brink of commitment, and so I threw myself from the precipice of twentieth-century prejudice into the maelstrom of his epoch.

One of my most revered instructors tried to prevent me. This, he said, was an *ignis fatuus*. All the hay of New England Puritanism had been threshed. I would wreck my career, even before it commenced, crawling through the dry stubble hoping to pick up stray gleanings.

His counsel was generous and, furthermore, seemed at that time the soul of prudence. Some perversity of temper would not let me yield. Another beloved teacher, Percy Holmes Boynton, encouraged me to risk the try. Without him, I would have faltered. As I now look back on that academic drama, I realize that he was working on the principle which always made his tuition exciting: namely, that a student should be given enough rope to hang himself, if this he was resolved to do. Wherefore I dedicated the book to him. Wherefore I have endeavored to accord the same privilege to my own students.

Having been offered by the Beacon Press the opportunity of reissuing *Orthodoxy in Massachusetts* (long since out of print), I first strove to rewrite my "Foreword" of 1933. I had to surrender: I could not make the original version pertinent to 1959 without abjectly confessing that it concealed an original cowardice. (So I let it stand, as the record of an evasion, that it may warn other beginners.)

I had commenced my work within an emotional universe dominated by H. L. Mencken. My contemporaries and I came of age in a time when the word "Puritan" served as a comprehensive sneer against every tendency in American civilization which we held reprehensible — sexual diffidence, censorship, prohibition, theological fundamentalism, political hypocrisy, and all the social antics which Sinclair Lewis, among others, was stridently ridiculing. Because I too had been an adolescent campaigner in this anti-Puritan rebellion, I dared not profess, even in a sentence, that I considered the intellect of Puritans worth serious examination. In consequence, I excused myself by pleading in that "Foreword" that I stood for the cause of intellectual history against the perspective which then was, more glibly than today, termed social and economic. It is a pleasure now to purge my bosom of the poisonous stuff which for a quarter of a century has been festering there.

I may say without boasting that the book has gradually wrought an effect. I must thereupon acknowledge, as etiquette then prevented me from doing, my debt to Mr. Harold Murdock, in 1933 Director of the Har-

vard University Press. He perceived some value in
the manuscript and insisted upon printing it, though
the Press, along with all the country, was still in the
anguish of the Depression. As I remember, the book
did not receive a wide or an immediate response. But
I am proud to report that in the following years a
considerable amount of first-rate scholarship has been
devoted to this supposedly exhausted field of Puritanism. My tentative venture appears to have held up.
Much has been added to our knowledge in areas extending outside the restricted limits of this study; still,
no substantial objections have prevailed against the
central thesis. Since 1933 I have published many
things which I regret, but in this case I find no reason
to alter a word from the original phrases.

This I say despite the fact that lately I have become
aware in the intellectual community of a curious re-
luctance to accept it. This recalcitrance is bewildering,
if only because it arises from two completely incompatible quarters. The first can be quickly passed over;
it is a lingering sentimentality, generally displayed
among pietistic New Englanders, which clings to the
myth that Deacon Samuel Fuller of Plymouth first
instructed John Endecott at Salem about the principles
of Congregational polity. According to this tradition,
the system was then and there embraced by Massachusetts Bay, on the assumption that none of the
leaders had previously possessed the slightest notion
of what kind of churches they intended to erect. Several historians, having pretensions to sophistication,

cherish this tale with a zeal comparable to that of treasuring the story of George Washington and the cherry tree.

This kind of obstinacy has, I am happy to say, weakened with the passing of a generation brought up to regard the Fuller legend as gospel truth. A more serious problem is the rise of a new anti-intellectualism — no longer a Menckenesque hatred of the kill-joy Puritan, but rather a sullen hostility to the entire notion that ideas ever have consequences. From this derives the supposition that in the highly self-selected Great Migration the rank-and-file would not have had the wits to comprehend the exquisite theories of Cotton and Hooker, of Winthrop and *The Cambridge Platform*. I have shown myself the last to deny that the elaborate scheme of ideas imported in 1630 underwent rapid and often astonishing transformations, as it became adjusted to the unpredictabilities of the wilderness. But those who strive, as to me it seems they do, to escape all concept of the mind by playing down the majesty and coherence of Puritan thinking, level a barrage against early New England infinitely more Philistine — not to say more historically inaccurate — than the comparatively innocent fulminations in the 1920's of Mencken and James Truslow Adams.

The edition of 1933 contained a long "Bibliography." At that time, many of the titles were not familiar in American scholarship. Also, I wished to show off my erudition. Both these incentives are fortunately no longer operative. I am therefore replacing that list with a selective inventory of basic items, including later studies which have extended insights I chanced to attain in 1933. I have run original sources and secondary treatments into an alphabetical sequence, since all of these are equally essential for anyone who would undertake further exploration. A full bibliography of both sorts appears in my and Thomas Johnson's *The Puritans* (1938). For titles thereafter, either of books or articles, the student can most expeditiously consult the review sections and the annual bibliographies of *The New England Quarterly*.

PERRY MILLER

Cambridge, Massachusetts
February, 1959

ORTHODOXY IN MASSACHUSETTS

I

SUPREMACY AND UNIFORMITY

CONSIDERED purely in its legalistic aspects, Henry VIII's "reformation" of the Church of England was a relatively simple affair. A legislative enactment sufficed to prohibit appeals to Rome, because "by divers sundry old authentic histories and chronicles" it appeared the body spiritual of the realm was sufficient unto itself.[1] While the Pope was being ruled out the King was read in. At first, in 1531, the clergy surmised that he was supreme head of the Church "quantum per Christi legem licet";[2] then after three years of Henry's coaxing they unhesitatingly called him "the only supreme heed in erthe of the Churche of England."[3] Convocation and Parliament soon passed such legislation as was required to remove the last vestiges of Papal control, and Parliament in 1536 placed the final seal upon its work by enacting that the oath of supremacy be taken by all subjects.[4]

The apparent simplicity of these manœuvers is, however, deceptive. Henry's assertion of a princely control over the Church was not entirely an inspiration of the

1. Henry Gee and William John Hardy, *Documents Illustrative of English Church History*, pp. 187–188.
2. Felix Makower, *Constitutional History and Constitutions of the Church of England*, pp. 49, 252 n. 2.
3. *Ibid.*, pp. 55–56, 252 n. 4.
4. *Ibid.*, pp. 51–52, 253; Gee and Hardy, *op. cit.*, p. 197.

moment. Pope and Emperor in the Middle Ages had been theoretically partners in the task of maintaining the Church in unity both of doctrine and of ritual, for which reason the Emperor had been expected to wield a sword against heretics and schismatics.[1] When the Empire began to fade, kings took the imperial rôle; and, reversing the maxim *divide et impera*, kings obtained for themselves a greater power over the Church than the Emperor ever enjoyed. For two hundred years before Henry VIII princes had been striving for the right to appoint bishops, had been curtailing ecclesiastical courts and combating Papal interference in their government — as the Statutes of Provisors and Praemunire illustrate. Henry's reformation gained for England hardly any more independence than France secured without officially breaking from Rome. By merely extending the powers of ecclesiastical supervision that they already possessed, princes of reformed countries, or town councils of the cities, were eminently fitted to become the virtual and, if necessary, the titular governors of their churches. They might take the step in various fashions and go to various lengths, but in each instance they went upon the assumption that a ruler was duty bound to protect, encourage, and oversee the church of his land. The principle of *cujus regio, ejus religio* did not for a moment imply the allowance of dissenting church organizations within the national frontiers. "The key to the political thought of the time," says Professor McIlwain, "is the fact that all men still held the medieval conception of the necessity of uniformity, though

1. Gee and Hardy, *op. cit.*, pp. 231, 242–244.

diversity had in fact come into existence." [1] The larger medieval conception of all Europe welded into a vast whole was shattered, but within the nations there was a complete carry-over of the medieval philosophy of unity. By the joining of Church and Commonwealth under the civil power, it seemed that the ancient antagonism of the spiritual and temporal was to be reconciled forever. The Church, by being resolved into compact national units, was at last to thrive as Isaiah had predicted, under the loving care of "nursing fathers and nursing mothers." [2]

The princes' endeavor to bring the Church under their sceptres was heartily encouraged by the leaders of the Reformation. The rulers not only rendered service as patrons or protectors, or by holding over-zealous followers in check, but their very existence was necessary to Protestant theology. With their revolt against "salvation by works" the reformers brought a renewed emphasis upon the doctrine of original sin. Society to them could, therefore, be only another example of human depravity. If men gave the reins to every natural impulse, declared Calvin, "there would certainly not be an individual in the world, whose actions would not evince all the crimes" of which human nature is capable.[3] Man, therefore, had to be subjected to earthly powers, and magistracy was an institution of the just Divinity Himself. Luther, recoiling from the Peasants' Revolt, cried that the sword of the worldly power would always

1. *Political Works of James I*, p. xvii.
2. J. W. Allen, *The History of Political Thought in the Sixteenth Century*, pp. 13–14.
3. *Institutes*, bk. ii, chap. iii, par. 3.

have to be red and bloody because the world would ever be wicked.[1] Obedience to the magistrate, taught Calvin, should be profound, sincere, and voluntary, "because the obedience which is rendered to princes and magistrates is rendered to God, from whom they have received their authority." "It is impossible," he continued, "to resist the magistrate without, at the same time, resisting God himself."[2] Indeed, resistance was wrong even if the ruler were heathen or tyrannical. "Those who rule in an unjust and tyrannical manner are raised up by Him to punish the iniquity of the people."[3] If the fact that the Emperor did wrong, wrote Luther to the Elector of Saxony in 1530, were a reason why subjects might revolt against him, there would be an end to government in this world, "for every subject could allege that his ruler was acting against God."[4]

The reformers' position may easily be explained. In all religious leaders in the sixteenth century there is no characteristic more pronounced than their several convictions that the revolt from Rome was neither to stop short of their own particular position nor to be carried beyond it. When unable to direct Christendom, they contented themselves with striving to mould the national religions closer to their hearts' desires. They held that the character of mankind necessitated control, and their original bias toward unity was accentuated by the motives which had inspired the religious insur-

1. *Werke*, xv, 302.
2. *Institutes*, bk. IV, chap. xx, pars. 22, 23.
3. *Ibid.*, par. 25; Allen, *op. cit.*, p. 10, chap. iv.
4. *Luther's Correspondence and Other Contemporary Letters*, ed. Preserved Smith and Charles Jacob, II, 519–520.

rection. The Deity Himself had commanded that all men's thoughts be turned toward redemption, and had prescribed certain ways and means. The Church could not accomplish this unaided by civil authority. The reformers envisaged a simple and plausible arrangement wherein they, the professional experts in Biblical knowledge, should teach the State its duties, and the State should silence contradiction. The highest function of the State, therefore, was the loving care of the Church, the maintenance of its external being in uniformity throughout the kingdom, and the physical support of its censures. In order that no reformed government should ever hesitate, the *Institutes* provided explicit instructions; civil government, we are told, exists

to cherish and support the external worship of God, to preserve the pure doctrine of religion, to defend the constitution of the church, to regulate our lives in a manner requisite for the society of men, to form our manners to civil justice, to promote our concord with each other, and to establish general peace and tranquillity. . . . Its objects also are that idolatry, sacrileges against the name of God, blasphemies against his truth, and other offenses against religion, may not openly appear and be disseminated among the people.[1]

In those countries whose religious inspiration was Genevan, this version of the theory was almost automatically incorporated into every creed: the Scotch Confession of 1560, for example, affirmed that "to Kings, Princes, Rulers and Magistrates . . . chieflie and most princi-pallie the conservation and purgation of the Religion apperteinis, so that not onlie they are appointed for Civill policie, bot also for maintenance of the trew Re-

1. Bk. iv, chap. xx, pars. 2, 3.

ligioun." [1] But even before Calvin's heyday the English
Reformation had recognized these same principles. The
King had assumed the actual headship, and had thereby
become, in the words of the great Genevan himself, a
person whom God had commissioned "to serve as his
lieutenant in ordering and maintaining the kingdom of
Jesus Christ in England." [2] The Act of Supremacy was
an assertion of the monarch's responsibility for the welfare of the Church, his duty of reforming its abuses and
punishing its adversaries, and was completely in accord
with the ruling assumption of the century. Its objectives were sanctioned by the past and blessed by contemporary theory. The act, said Stephen Gardiner,
wrought "no newly invented matter," but only intended "to haue the power perteinyng to a prince by
Goddes lawe to be the more clearely expressed." [3]

This civil supremacy was, consequently, the one thing
in the ecclesiastical situation that could be taken for
granted when Protestant Elizabeth succeeded her
Catholic sister in 1558. Her clergy were agreed upon no
definite policy, and Elizabeth herself was concerned
only that they should accommodate themselves to her
political ambitions. They could all agree that whatever
else was to happen, the sovereign should once more become "defender of the faith." The faith itself could be
defined later. So were passed the Acts of Supremacy and
Uniformity, which, in as broad and inclusive a fashion
as possible, incorporated the characteristic Protestant

1. Philip Schaff, *The Creeds of Christendom*, III, 475.
2. *Letters of John Calvin*, ed. Jules Bonnet, II, 340.
3. Stephen Gardiner, *Obedience in Church and State*, pp. 91–93.

theory of State and Church into the Church of England. With the Papal power once more expelled, all ecclesiastical authority, which had hitherto been used to reform the Church and correct errors, heresies, and schisms, was declared to be "for ever, by authority of this present Parliament . . . united and annexed to the imperial crown of this realm." [1] Officers in both State and Church were to swear upon oath that the Queen was the only supreme ruler, "as well in all spiritual or ecclesiastical things or causes, as temporal." [2] The ruler was no longer designated the "supreme head" but "supreme governor" of the Church: this phrase was more acceptable to both Catholics and Protestants, since, Burghley explained, the Crown thereby showed it was not challenging "authority and power of ministry of divine offices in the church," [3] — but Bishop Parkhurst's laconic comment was that the title of governor "amounts to the same thing." [4] The Act of Uniformity required ministers and laymen to use only the forms of the *Book of Common Prayer*; it exacted church attendance from all persons, and instructed the Church to execute "this good and wholesome law." [5] In order that there might be no mistake, Elizabeth issued her *Injunctions* in June, 1559, "intending the advancement of the true honour of Almighty God, the suppression of superstition throughout all her highness's realms and dominions, and

1. Gee and Hardy, *op. cit.*, pp. 442–446, 447.
2. *Ibid.*, p. 449.
3. *Ibid.*, pp. 438–439; W. H. Frere, *The English Church in the Reigns of Elizabeth and James I*, p. 39.
4. *Zurich Letters*, I, 29.
5. Gee and Hardy, *op. cit.*, pp. 458–467.

to plant true religion to the extirpation of all hypocrisy, enormities and abuses (as to her duty appertaineth)." [1] After recalling that "the queen's power within her realms and dominions is the highest power under God," she told the clergy to wear the garments that were prescribed, commanded her subjects to go to church on Sundays and to "forbear all vain and contentious disputations in matters of religion." [2] When a petition from the Continent asked indulgence for advocates of more extreme reformation, she replied in words that epitomize the whole situation: "It was not with her safety, honour, and credit, to permit diversity of opinions in a kingdom where none but she and her council governed." [3]

The policy thus enunciated continued to be basic in Elizabeth's government. For reasons of state the Queen might temporarily compound with dissenters, but she never lost sight of the ultimate ideal of uniformity. There were some, she declared in 1602, who insinuated that she had a purpose to grant a toleration of two religions in her domain. God, however, could not only witness "our innocency from such imagination, but how far it hath been from any about us to offer to our ears the persuasion of such a course, as would not only disturb the peace of the Church, but bring this our State into Confusion." [4] The Stuarts continued her policy. "I will haue one Doctrine and one discipline," announced

---

1. *Ibid.*, pp. 418–419.
2. *Ibid.*, pp. 432, 434, 435–436.
3. John Strype, *Annals of the Reformation* (Oxford, 1824), vol. 1, pt. 1, p. 128.
4. As quoted in Roland Green Usher, *Reconstruction of the English Church*, 1, 19.

James, "one Religion in substance, and in ceremonie," [1]
and his son was brought up to expect the same unanimity.

Quite naturally, therefore, the apologists for the
Church fully adhered to these political tenets. They,
too, accounted the magistracy of divine authorship.
"Princes are placed by God, and so not to bee displaced
by men: and subiectes threatned damnation by Gods
own mouth if they resist." [2] Obedience to princes was
still a duty, "yea, though they be wicked." [3] Kings,
said the 37th Article, were to rule "all estates and degrees committed to their charge by God, whether they
be Ecclesiastical or no;" [4] and they were to have care
of the Church, "for princes are nursing fathers of the
church, and keepers of both tables. Neither for any
greater cause hath God willed governments to exist,
than that there might be always some to maintain and
preserve religion and piety." [5] Assuredly, then, they
should enforce the religious uniformity required by the
Acts of 1559: "It must bee a consideration of great consequence, to further (by an absolute vnitie) the true
Religion: no examples being suffered that doe lead from
it." [6] The words "Compell them to come in" were
spoken "to Christian Princes, and are to them both a
warrant and a charge to represse schismes and heresies

1. William Barlow, *The Svmme and Svbstance of the Conference* (1604), p. 71.
2. Thomas Bilson, *The Trve Difference betweene Christian svbiection and vnchristian rebellion* (1585), sig. A5, recto.
3. John Jewel, "An Apology of the Church of England" (1564), *Works* (Parker Society, 1848), III, 74.
4. Edward Cardwell, *Synodalia*, I, 71.
5. Jewel, "Epistle to Scipio," *Works*, IV, 1125–1126.
6. William Covell, *A Modest and reasonable examination* (1604), p. 197.

with their Princely power, which they receiued from aboue." [1] To argue that ecclesiastical and civil government cannot be united in the same person, said Whitgift, is to spoil the civil magistrate "of the one half of his jurisdiction." [2] Indeed, the head and front of Laud's offending was no more than an over-passionate allegiance to this very creed: "The King's power is God's glory; and the honour of the subject is obedience to both." [3] In the light of his heritage he could see no alternative to the maintenance of religious unity: "Break unity once, and farewell strength." [4] When he defended himself in 1644, he instanced his labors in the interests of this ideal as in themselves sufficient excuse for his acts, "being still of opinion, that unity cannot long continue in the Church, where uniformity is shut out at the church door." [5]

Against this orthodox political creed the Puritans were the last persons in the world to take exception. If we were to consider merely detached statements of abstract principle from the writers of the time we should be puzzled to distinguish one party from the other; the whole system can be constructed as easily out of the pages of the Nonconformists as from the works of the Anglicans. Cartwright, for instance, was at one with Archbishop Whitgift in holding that magistrates were lawful and necessary institutions, and he affirmed that his followers obeyed them "in the Lord, and for the

1. Bilson, *op. cit.*, p. 132.
2. John Whitgift, *Works*, I, 21.
3. William Laud, *Works* (Library of Anglo-Catholic Theology), I, 79.
4. *Ibid.*, p. 66.
5. *Ibid.*, IV, 60.

Lord." [1] If the prince is wicked, said Udall, even if he commands things contrary to the word of God, his subjects are not to resist, "no, not so much as in thought: but with patience and humility to bear all the punishment laid upon them." [2] The Puritan party was no maintainer of "licentiousness and lewd liberty." [3] The authors of the *Admonition* wrote in 1572 that they abhorred from the bottom of their hearts all those sects "which rejecte magistrates, despise aucthoritie, bringe in equalitie amonge all men, and woulde have all things in common and no man to be riche." [4] The principle of the Supremacy did not in itself run counter to Puritan views: Cartwright pleaded in 1596, in all honesty, that he had taken the oath five or six times, and that "if there be doubt of any change of my judgement, I am ready to take th'oth againe." [5] Indeed, he could not refuse, for he, no less than Whitgift, held that magistrates were necessary to the Church, "that the use of them is more than of the sun, without which the world cannot stand." [6] A magistrate was as much bound by Puritan as by Anglican theory "to see that the laws of God, touching his worship, and touching all matters and orders of the Church, be executed and duly observed, and to see that every ecclesiastical person do that office whereunto he is appointed, and to punish those which fail in their office accordingly." [7] Equally acceptable

1. Cartwright, as quoted in Whitgift, *Works*, I, 79.
2. Strype, *Life and Acts of John Whitgift* (Oxford, 1822), II, 98–100.
3. Cartwright, *op. cit.*, I, 77.
4. *A Seconde Parte of a Register*, I, 87.
5. A. F. Scott Pearson, *Thomas Cartwright*, p. 336, App. XXX.
6. Cartwright, *op. cit.*, I, 20.
7. *Ibid.*, III, 295.

was the principle of enforced uniformity. Puritans, too, demanded that church attendance be made compulsory and that heretics be put to death.[1] "If this be bloody and extreme," declared Cartwright, "I am content to be so counted with the Holy Ghost."[2] Travers's *Full and plaine declaration* — which comes the nearest of any book to being the official platform of Elizabethan Puritanism — required civil magistrates "to set in order and establish the state of the Church by their authority, and to preserue and maintaine it according to Gods will being once established."[3] Sixty years of struggle did not bring to the Puritans, at the time of the migration to Massachusetts, any realization that this tenet should be questioned. English Puritans in Holland informed Charles I in 1628 that they had no wish to leave "every man to his owne liberty to use what Liturgie he pleaseth."[4] One of the most violent foes the hierarchy ever raised up, William Prynne, was still quoting the old dogma in 1629: "Kings, and temporall Magistrates, ought to bee the chiefe Defenders and Patrons of Religion; the suppressors of Haeresies, Idolatries, and false Doctrines: the principall Reformers of the Church." This, he was truthfully affirming, "is the positiue Resolution of all the Fathers, of all Protestant (and I thinke of most Popish) Diuines."[5]

1. *A Seconde Parte of a Register*, I, 169.
2. Cartwright, *op. cit.*, I, 116.
3. Walter Travers, *A full and plaine declaration of Ecclesiasticall Discipline* (Leyden, 1617), p. 103.
4. Champlin Burrage, *Early English Dissenters*, II, 267.
5. William Prynne, *The Church of Englands old Antithesis to New Arminianisme* (1629), sig. A3, recto.

II

DISCIPLINE OUT OF THE WORD

PROTESTANTISM, Troeltsch has said, "was, in the first place, simply a modification of Catholicism, in which the Catholic formulation of the problems was retained, while a different answer was given to them." [1] Just as the revolt from Rome did not entail any break with the political assumptions of the medieval Church, so it did not escape in its thinking the felt necessity for a final and absolute authority. Catholicism had replied to the question of where men should seek the answers to their spiritual controversies by indicating the infallible Church; Protestantism, equally predisposed to require a supreme arbiter, pointed to the infallible Bible. Scripture, said Calvin, "obtains the same complete credit and authority with believers . . . as if they heard the very words pronounced by God himself." [2] Once we have accepted the word of God, "we are attracted and inflamed to an understanding and voluntary obedience, but with a vigor and efficacy superior to the power of any human will or knowledge." [3] Before the bench of this incorruptible judge the reformers arraigned contemporary society and found it wanting. Their long protest and violent reaction against the manifold abuses of the

1. Ernst Troeltsch, *Protestantism and Progress*, p. 59.
2. *Institutes*, bk. 1, chap. vii, par. 1.
3. *Ibid.*, par. 5.

later medieval Church served to make their bibliolatry only the more fanatical, and to send them repeatedly to Scripture for the settlement of a lengthening list of disputes.

Inevitably they encountered the problem of what should be the proper external form of a reformed Church. Luther was able to find Biblical authorization only for dogma, preaching, and sacraments; in discipline anything seemed to him lawful which was not clearly antagonistic to Scripture. At this rate, it was quite permissible for the civil government to decide, and loyal subjects should accept the magistrate's decision. Calvin was remarkably indifferent to many minutiae of ceremony and government; in fact, in order to prove that the true Church had survived through the corruptions of the Papacy — a position he was compelled to assert to repel the charge of "novelty" — he too insisted that the essential criteria were preaching of God's word and legitimate administration of the sacraments. The precise organization was not so important but that the true Church could exist "without any visible form."[1] He felt that many external things were in themselves "indifferent"; we could omit or use them at our pleasure.[2] Still, when he devised a discipline for Geneva,[3] there were some features about which he felt that the Bible gave explicit directions, such as the process of excommunication and the lay eldership. These he described as part of "the order which it has been the Lord's

1. *Ibid.*, I, 33–34.
2. *Ibid.*, bk. III, chap. xix, par. 7.
3. Cf. *Ordonnances* of 1542, *Opera*, X^a 16–30.

will to appoint for the government of his Church." [1] As his disciples carried his teaching to other lands, they inevitably attempted to duplicate his church order. In the attempt to justify it, they sought warrants in the Bible, which seemed to offer them more plentifully than even the master had suspected. They finally produced a convincing body of disciplinary exegesis and began to advance the system as having been specifically and exclusively intended by Christ himself. All other organizations, ceremonies, regalias, laws, were now viewed as human inventions, designed at the instigation of Satan to lead the soul astray.

Henry VIII had put the Pope out of England, but he had retained the Papal organization, with its hierarchy, its ritual, and its regalia, and he had betrayed no intention of spoiling so excellent an administrative machine by tampering with its internal construction. But as Protestant sentiment took greater hold upon the nation, voices were raised here and there against the garments of Popery in which the Church was still disguised, and they cried aloud to the Scriptures. "Leave not," preached Bishop Hooper, "till the matter be brought unto the first, original, and most perfect church of the apostles. If thou find by their writings, that their church used the thing that the preacher would prove, then accept it; or else, not." [2] The issue was raised more clearly in the congregation of English exiles at Frankfort during the reign of Mary. John Knox desired them to follow "the order of Geneva . . . as an

1. *Institutes*, bk. iv, chap. iii, par. 1.
2. John Hooper, *Early Writings*, p. 83.

order most godly, and farthest off from superstitition," [1]
but the other leaders, Cox, Sandys, Grindal, refused because they felt bound in loyalty to the Prayer Book of
Edward VI. An agreement finally proved impossible,
and Knox's faction departed to the more congenial atmosphere of Geneva. All dispute, however, was momen-
tarily hushed by the accession of Elizabeth. The exiles
were happy to see Protestantism restored under any
circumstances, and the Genevan group itself took the
initiative in promising to abandon controversy if only
the Queen would guarantee that her church would agree
with other reformed churches "in unity of doctrine." [2]

The Establishment, with its genius for compromise,
easily succeeded in fulfilling this request. The Thirty-
Nine Articles as framed in 1563 were, as Fuller says,
"purposely couched . . . in general terms . . . to include
all such dissenters within the comprehensiveness of the
expressions." [3] They declared that Scripture contained
everything necessary for salvation, and advisedly
avoided more explicit description of the outward means.
The 17th Article, on predestination, stated merely the
Augustinian doctrine of election, but no Calvinist had
trouble in accepting it, because to him the doctrine of
election necessarily implied that of reprobation.[4] In-

1. William Whittingham, *A Brief Discourse of the Troubles begun at Frankfort in Germany* (ed. Edward Arber, London, 1907), p. 42.
2. Strype, *Annals of the Reformation* (Oxford, 1824), vol. I, pt. I, pp. 152,
153-154.
3. Thomas Fuller, *Church History of Britain*, bk. IX, sec. 6, par. 22; Frere,
The English Church in the Reigns of Elizabeth and James I, p. 97;
Arthur Jay Klein, *Intolerance in the Reign of Elizabeth*, pp. 94-99, 164-
166; Usher, *The Reconstruction of the English Church*, I, 200.
4. Strype, *op. cit.*, pp. 494 ff.

deed, if the Establishment had at first any theological tone, it was predominantly Calvinistic, as Whitgift demonstrated in the Lambeth Articles of 1595.[1] Cartwright never quarreled with the doctrine of the Church,[2] and the great Puritan manifesto, the *Admonition*, pronounced the "substance" of it "sound and good."[3] It was only with the time of Andrewes and Laud that the leadership of the Church was captured by a definite opinion with which the dissenters could quarrel theologically, and they were then joined by a number of loyal sons of the Establishment who were not essentially Puritans and who thought themselves only defending the faith of their fathers.

Upon the same spirit of compromise exemplified in its creed the Church determined its outward form. The Papal hierarchy was the only organization at hand, it offered some common ground both to Protestants and to Catholics, and there was no very coherent group to advocate any specific changes. But as the exiles came trooping back, it was obvious that some of them were restive. The keen eye of Cecil detected the issue; when the Council was still debating its course, he prophesied that the settlement would surely arouse two kinds of hostility, the Catholic and the Genevan, and that the latter would "call the alteration a cloaked papistry or a mingle mangle."[4] Many of the clergy were imbued with this spirit and frankly treated the in-

1. John Hunt, *Religious Thought in England from the Reformation to the End of the Last Century*, I, 91–94.
2. Pearson, *Thomas Cartwright*, p. 407.
3. W. H. Frere and C. E. Douglas, *Puritan Manifestoes*, p. 9.
4. Frere, *op. cit.*, p. 5.

stitution as a temporary expedient. "Our Gloss upon this text," wrote Sandys to Parker in April, 1559, concerning the vestment, "is that we shall not be forced to use them." [1] Elizabeth was annoyed, but she did not feel secure enough at first to force the issue. Even when she did, she characteristically refused to take the responsibility herself, and compelled the reluctant Parker to issue the *Advertisements* under his own authority.

The archbishop did what he could. Pointing out that all the Queen's subjects should be "knit together in one perfect unity of doctrine" and be "conjoined in one uniformity of rites and manners," he demanded in her name that the ministers stop arguing and wear the garments.[2] But he warned Cecil beforehand: "What tumult may follow, what speeches and talks like to rise in the realm . . . we leave it to your wisdom to consider." [3] He was not disappointed. A howl of protest went up. "These precise fools," he told the Queen, "would offer their goods and bodies to prison, rather than they would relent." [4] The *Advertisements* were designed to be the first step to complete uniformity; instead they created nonconformity,[5] and, as Bishop Horne at once recognized, divided the Church into two parties.[6] Dissent seemed only to thrive on Parker's

1. Matthew Parker, *Correspondence*, p. 65; cf. *Zurich Letters*, I, 74; Strype, *op. cit.*, pp. 500–505; R. W. Dixon, *History of the Church of England*, vol. v, chap. xxxv.
2. Gee and Hardy, *Documents Illustrative of English Church History*, pp. 467–468.
3. Parker, *op. cit.*, p. 268.
4. *Ibid.*, pp. 278–279.
5. William Pierce, *The Marprelate Tracts*, pp. xv–xviii.
6. *Zurich Letters*, I, 142.

attempts at repression, and its program expanded
rapidly to envisage not only reform of ceremonies, but
of the whole Establishment.[1] "I am inwardly afraid,"
wrote Cecil in 1566, "that if fear shall not stay this
riotous insolency, these rash young heads, that are so
soon ripe to climb into pulpits, will content themselves
with no limits, either in the Church or in the policy."[2]

All the rash young heads needed was a leader and a
platform. They found the first in Thomas Cartwright,
and Field and Wilcox wrote the platform in 1572 when
they published the *Admonition to Parliament*.[3] By this
date the "Puritan" party can be said to have appeared
fully armed upon the scene, and the long contest was
joined, which was to persist for well over the next half
century and to be as far from settlement in the days of
the Massachusetts Bay Company as at the moment of
its inception.

The word "Puritan" is one of those unfortunate terms
which have come to mean all things to all men. It is not
merely a modern source of confusion; even in the age of
which we are speaking there was no precise connotation.
"Concerning the name (*Puritan*) it is ambiguous, and
so it is fallacious."[4] At the beginning those who
scrupled at the liturgy and vestments were branded
"Puritans" in derision, but as their simple protest
gathered momentum, there "came forth an other sort,

1. G. W. Prothero, *Select Statutes*, p. 194.
2. Strype, *op. cit.*, p. 158.
3. *Ibid.*, vol. II, pt. I, pp. 183 ff.; *Cal. St. Pap., Dom., Eliz.*, vol. LXXXVI,
Nos. 45–48; Prothero, *Select Statutes*, p. 120; Sir Simonds D'Ewes,
Journals, p. 213.
4. Giles Widdowes, *The Schismatical Puritan* (1631), sig. A3 recto.

affirming that those matters touching Apparell, were but trifles, . . . but that there were greater things farre of more weight and importance . . . to be altered in a Church rightly refourmed." [1] With this larger Puritan objective in mind Udall put into the mouth of his fictitious bishop, Diotrephes, a trenchant definition of the party: "I meane them, that are not contented with the state, but mislike the gouernment of the Church, and would haue a new forme of gouernement." [2] As we shall use the word, therefore, we shall intend to signify strictly that group of men who wished to replace the hierarchy with another ecclesiastical system, and we shall take the liberty, for the time being, to understand by it the advocates specifically of Presbyterianism. At this time, however, the word was used more loosely. Any conspicuously pious person was apt to be dubbed Puritan by his more ribald contemporaries, so that even an Anglican author would admit that "all good behaviour is scorned of many, as a matter of *Puritanisme*, and so tearmed." [3] Many thus denominated were men who, as Nichols witnessed in 1602, merely objected to the use of certain ceremonies, or to subscription "beyond the statute," or who simply wanted to "heare sermons, talke of the scriptures, singe Psalmes together in priuate houses." [4] Not all such persons were hostile to the hierarchy if they might have their way in minor matters. But they were not the men who forced to the front

1. Thomas Cooper, *An Admonition to the People of England* (1589), p. 160.
2. *A Parte of a Register* (1590), p. 339.
3. John Burgess, *An answer rejoined to that much applauded pamphlet* (1631), p. 7.
4. Josias Nichols, *The Plea of the Innocent* (1602), p. 12.

the great questions over which the Establishment finally came to grief in the Civil Wars, and we can for the moment neglect them. It is to the movement for "discipline out of the Word" that we must look for the source of that energy which, after beating itself in vain for sixty years against the state Church, inundated the shores of another continent.

To begin with, the Puritan was sure that he had an unanswerable case. To him, Protestant church polity was every bit as important as Protestant theology; England had "divided and separated asunder the Doctrine and Discipline of the Gospell: two things which both by their owne nature, and also by the commandement of God are to be ioyned together." [1] Travers, the official spokesman for the party, stated the central contention with greatest clarity:

I affirme that Christ hath left us so perfect a rule and Discipline . . . which is common and generall to all the Church, and perpetuall for all times, and so necessary, that without it this whole society, and company, and Christian Commonwealth cannot well bee kept under their Prince and King Iesus Christ. [2]

Puritans were so absolutely persuaded they were fighting the Lord's battle that they never understood how any but the deliberate minions of Antichrist could oppose them. It was impossible for them to imagine that the Queen or the government had heard them, for if the sovereign were only once to consider their unanswerable arguments, she would necessarily become converted. The simplest and surest method of inaugurating the

1. Travers, *A full and plaine declaration of Ecclesiasticall Discipline* (Leyden, 1617), p. 103.
2. *Ibid.*, p. 5.

reformation of England always seemed to them to be a public debate: "Venture your byshopprickes vpon a disputation, and wee will venture our liues, take the challenge if you dare." [1] Puritans promised over and over again to abide by the results of such a meeting, but they were sure, indeed they knew, that any decision based upon the merits of the case could not possibly reject them.

For in Puritan eyes the hierarchy stood self-condemned. Its abuses were evident, its pomp and luxury, its pluralists and non-residents, its subjection to worldly interests. The contrast between the Church as it was and the Church as the Bible said it should have been was as plain as the nose on anybody's face: "The one parte being proude, pontificall and tyrannous: and the woorde of God for the other parte expresse and manifest, as if it pleased the state to examine the matters, it would be evident." [2] By 1572 Puritans were positive that the welfare of their own and the nation's souls demanded immediate action. The authors of the *Admonition* declared they had used gentle words too long: "the wound groweth desperate, and dead flesh hath overgrowne all, and therefore the wound had neede of a sharpe corsive and eatinge plaister. It is no tyme to blanch, nor to sewe cushens under mens elbowes, or to flatter them in their synnes." [3] And that a constantly applied "plaister" had not, by 1630, effected the desired cure was no discouragement to these self-appointed physicians.

1. John Udall, *A Demonstration of the truth of that Discipline* (ed. Edward Arber, 1895), p. 6.
2. Frere and Douglas, *Puritan Manifestoes*, p. 6.
3. *A Seconde Parte of a Register*, I, 89.

With such an institution as the Established Church they could never compromise.

The Puritans' campaign, thus, was essentially a crusade for what seemed self-evident righteousness. They were out to triumph or perish in the attempt. They might disguise their ultimate objective under occasional programs of lesser reforms in ceremony and ritual, but as long as the Biblical warrant for church polity remained their basic assumption nothing short of a Presbyterianized Church could really content them. Rebuffs, deprivations, imprisonment only accentuated their zeal. They were confident of the outcome. Udall spoke for all his brethren when he confidently predicted that the result of the whole controversy would be the triumph of that "gouernment of the Churche, by the rules of that Discipline which Christe himselfe hath prescribed in his worde, which I doe perswade myselfe to see before it bee long." [1]

The first shock of this onslaught dazed and bewildered the captains of the Church. Such men as Jewel or Sandys had no particular fondness for trappings and ceremony, but they considered it pedantry to concern themselves with such matters in the face of the life-and-death war with Rome. They themselves had, in all good faith, been the first to justify themselves by an appeal to Scripture. Jewel declared that they had searched out of the Bible "one sure form of religion," that they had "returned again unto the primitive church of the ancient fathers and apostles." [2] Now they suddenly

1. Udall, in *A Parte of a Register*, p. 352.
2. Jewel, "Apology of the Church of England" (1564), *Works*, III, 106.

found their own ranks strangely sundered; within the camp a vigorous faction was accusing them of never having searched out the holy Bible at all, and of being therefore not much better off than the Pope himself. Naturally the bishops were at first puzzled. But at least one man, the master of Trinity College, Cambridge, had seen enough of the "rash young heads" at close range to know what was in them; and as soon as the Puritans came into the open with their *Admonition* John Whitgift was prepared for them. His controversy with Cartwright rallied the scattered wits of the Establishment, and the lines of defense he erected in this voluminous combat warfare were, in the main, dutifully repaired and strengthened by the subsequent flood of publication.

Whitgift and the churchmen flatly denied that the Scripture contained any such concrete polity as the Puritans pretended. That, they insisted, was a thing which God had left men to determine for themselves, permitting it to be variable "according to circumstances of time and place." [1] He had commanded that a ministry should be, but he was equally pleased if the office were executed in a white garment or a black,[2] and in either case the decision of the Church upon an indifferent matter should be "borne withall for order and obedience sake." [3] Salvation was in no way dependent upon the ceremonies, discipline, or government of the Church.[4] Puritans were deluded by two baneful notions:

1. Francis Mason, *The Avthority of the Church*, p. 34.
2. *Ibid.*, p. 7.
3. Quoted from "a bishop," *A Parte of a Register*, p. 30.
4. Whitgift, *Works*, i, 181.

they thought that the Church must "have the same kind of government that was in the apostles' time . . . and no other," and that men might not "in any wise . . . retain in the Church anything that hath been abused under the Pope."[1] But Whitgift dared boldly to affirm that everything necessary to salvation was "as purely and perfectly taught, and by public authority established, in this Church of England at this day" as ever "in any church sithence the apostles' time, or now be in any reformed church in the world."[2]

If this reasoning was correct, then the Puritans were making a fuss over nothing; they were fetching out of the Bible things that were not in it, and theirs were then the corruptions, theirs the false teachings. False, wrote Bancroft, was exactly what Presbyterianism was,

that most counterfeyt and falsly patched vp government . . . a meere humane device devised by shiftinge and sleight, attayned by tiranny and bloud, and mainteyned with vntollerable pride and with most straunge boldnes in expoundinge the scriptures and falsifyinge of all antiquitye.[3]

For many centuries men who behaved in this fashion had been branded with one of two crimes: heresy or schism. Puritans professed theological orthodoxy, but if they thus cleared themselves of heresy, they could not avoid the charge of schism. "He is *schismatical*, which consentinge with the Churche in all articles of salvation and of substance, yet nevertheless varieth therefrom in orders and ceremonies, and for the same contendeth in the Church."[4] A schismatic, therefore, was an im-

1. *Ibid.*, p. 6.　　　　　　　2. *Ibid.*, p. 3.
3. Burrage, *Early English Dissenters*, II, 131.
4. Strype, *Life and Acts of John Whitgift*, I, 272-277.

pugner of unity, and to the sixteenth century was not only an enemy to the Church but to the State. He was something very close to a traitor, for as Laud assured Parliament, whosoever aimed to overthrow the ecclesiastical government "will not spare, if ever they get power, to have a pluck at the throne of David." [1]

When the prelates took this stand they were not making a fetish of uniformity *per se*. It was a day when men acted under what they believed to be the immediate direction of God's Word, and when all truth but their own was so much deception and work of Satan. As Hooker justly expressed it, once the minds of men are persuaded "that it is the will of God to have those things done which they fancy" there will be no limit to what they will attempt, "for which cause it behoveth wisdom to fear the sequels thereof, even beyond all apparent cause of fear." [2] In this respect the defenders of the Establishment qualified as wise; they never lost a chance to point ominously towards Anabaptism, the ever present bogey-man of the Reformation. "Let their petitions haue successe," Covell shrieked, "and in that one Act, let *Religion*, the Prince, peace, and all vtterly perish." [3] While the churchmen were altogether sure such miserable prospects would come to pass if the disciplinarians had their way, they were only the more inspired to take advantage of every weapon at hand, and to make it clear to the government that its interest and theirs were one and the same.

1. Laud, "Sermon to Parliament" (1626), *Works*, I, 83.
2. *Laws of Ecclesiastical Polity*, Preface, chap. viii, par. 12.
3. Covell, *A Modest and reasonable examination* (1604), p. 12.

The political argument was, indeed, the trump card in the prelates' hands. The principles of absolute subjection to superiors, of civil supremacy over the Church, of religious uniformity, which we have seen were fundamental to every Reformation creed, were far from being questioned by the Puritans themselves. Yet did not these very principles clearly condemn the Puritan cause as at best a thinly disguised rebellion? As long as the disputed question was merely whether or no the Bible prescribed a specific church polity, it was an academic affair. But it could not rest there; Puritans were bound, by the very nature of their case, to press for the actual substitution of their discipline for that which the Queen had set up. If they had been able to convince their opponents, the bishops would, by their own theory, have been compelled to listen, for the Church of England, as a Protestant organization, claimed to be founded on the Bible. An English magistrate, Whitgift was the first to admit, could "do nothing against the word of God." [1] But the Anglicans believed that no proof had been offered for further limitation upon the Queen's authority beyond what she and her Church had already admitted. Therefore in the government's eyes Puritans were guilty of seditious purposes. If, Whitgift said, it is not proper for individual men to decide external matters, if that "is proper to them only to whom God hath committed the government of his Church," then whosoever disobeys the laws of the Church "disobeyeth both God and the prince." [2] The age could not separate these allegiances; the single act necessarily entailed a double

1. Whitgift, *Works*, I, 22. 2. *Ibid.*, II, 50.

offense. "You cannot be the Queenes friend that thus looke for innouations in the state." [1]

The bishops' counter attack upon the Puritans' political loyalty did not find these expert disputants entirely unprepared. This was not the first time that religious innovators had had their own political tenets quoted against themselves. Protestant theory could afford extravagant precepts of non-resistance as long as civil powers coöperated with the reform. But if the princes opposed it, then Christians had been forced to remember that they should give unto Caesar the things that are Caesar's, but unto God what is God's. If a magistrate did wrong simply to themselves, they had no recourse: for Christians must bear with injustice as with the chastising hand of the deity lifted against them, if for no other reason than that they were naturally depraved and deserved punishment. But if the magistrate did wrong to God, if he commanded what was clearly contrary to the Word, then it was quite another matter. This appeal from the impious exactions of an earthly ruler to the clear prescriptions of the Bible was a necessary gesture of the whole Reformation movement; otherwise the initial revolution would never have taken place. Luther had little occasion to face the issue squarely, and justifiable resistance in his teaching never got beyond the passive stage. But in Zwingli the answer was a clarion call to action. The citizen was still in theory subject to the earthly powers God had placed over him, with the sole exception that when the magistrate trod upon sacred precincts the subject possessed "das Wider-

1. *A Parte of a Register*, p. 352.

standsrecht gegen die Obrigkeit." Calvin's position was essentially, though not so flagrantly, the same. After twelve hundred pages culminating in a defense of absolutism, the *Institutes* introduced in the last paragraph of the last chapter one exception to all that had gone before, which, we are told, "is entitled to our first attention." Our obedience to our governors must not

seduce us from obedience to him, to whose will the desires of all kings ought to be subject, to whose decrees all their commands ought to yield, to whose majesty all their sceptres ought to submit. . . . If they command anything against him, it ought not to have the least attention; nor, in this case, ought we to pay any regard to all that dignity attached to magistrates; to which no injury is done when it is subjected to the unrivalled and supreme power of God.[1]

The situation has been, I think, accurately characterized by a remark of G. P. Gooch: "We shall only read him aright if we figure to ourselves the proclamation of the duty of submission by a herald in the marketplace, and the whispering of the right of resistance in the by-lanes of the city." [2] Wherever this issue had been raised, the same dubious answer had ever been forthcoming. English Protestants as a whole had faced the problem under the reign of Catholic Mary, and the churchmen themselves had then thought it through to a similar conclusion. "If the ministers of the civill power command thee to dishonour God," Bishop Ponet had written, "thou oughtest not to do it, but to leave it undone: for it is evill," [3] and on that basis he had gone so far as to declare that the subject might lawfully de-

1. *Institutes*, bk. IV, chap. xx, par. 32.
2. *English Democratic Ideas in the Sixteenth Century*, p. 6.
3. *A Short Treatise of Politicke Power* (first edition, 1556; reprinted, 1639), p. 25.

pose or even kill an evil governor.[1] The Puritans, being sincerely patriotic and professing the same faith as their ruler, resisted Ponet's radical deduction; yet when the bishops threw the issue up to them and called upon them to obey the monarch in the name of the very loyalty they pretended, they could do nothing but utilize his argument. They could only remind the authorities that there was one consideration which was bound to have their first attention, and as the dispute grew more heated they were often compelled to raise their voices above a whisper, until in January, 1649, they spoke in unmistakable tones, and Bishop Ponet's teaching found its full enunciation.

The essence of the Puritan contention was that even the minutiae of ecclesiastical practice had been prescribed ages ago by Christ himself, and they were to remain forever unchanged by any man. The prince could and should rule over the Church, but he must respect the fundamental laws of its constitution. The prelates misled him if they told him that in these sacred and unalterable matters his will was law. In this respect, though only in this respect, his authority was not supreme. So far as the form of its government was concerned, the Church was sufficient unto itself. In the final analysis the ecclesiastical régime depended,

not vppon the authority of Princes, but vppon the ordinaunce of God, who hath most mercifully and wisely so established the same, that as with the comfortable ayde of Christian Magistrates, it may singulerlie flourish & prosper, so without it, it may continue, and against the aduersaries thereof preuail.[2]

1. *Ibid.*, p. 49.
2. *A Briefe and plaine declaration* (1584), p. 9.

The sovereign might wish God had ordained otherwise than he had, but there was nothing he could do about it. If he actually were a Christian, he would voluntarily accept this restraint. By so doing he would not diminish his office; his authority would still be the greatest on earth, even though he should acknowledge "it is not infinite, but it is limited by the word of God." [1] If, however, a deluded prince forgot that which God required of him, if he disregarded the immutable decrees, then the trouble was of his own seeking. If the government made it necessary for Puritans to choose between God and man, it could not blame them if they obeyed the higher authority. Hence the Puritans were ever certain that they were neither rebels nor schismatics, in the true sense, when they rejected the hierarchy: "The Magistrate must not be resisted, and yet that which is against the conscience, may without disloyaltie be refused." [2] No laws, however severe, and no cruelty, not even death, "can discharge the saints and servants of the Lord from going forward in that which is good." [3] If we do not ceaselessly defend the pure form of church government, if we do not denounce the prelates' usurpation, "we shall shewe our selues rather bastards, then naturall children." [4] The bishops might call them schismatics and scapegraces, but Puritans knew that in the eyes of God they were His only legitimate offspring, and could not forever be kept from their inheritance.

Limitation of the magistrate, however, was all very

1. Cartwright, quoted in Whitgift, *Works*, III, 295.
2. *A True, Modest, and just Defence* (1618), p. 6.
3. Cartwright, *op. cit.*, I, 13-14.
4. John Dayrell, *A Treatise of the Church* (1617), sig. A2 verso.

well as long as it remained theoretical. Trouble began
with the attempt to realize it. The Puritan assumption
was that the Bible gave explicit instructions, but even
the most confident admitted that it had some difficult
passages and that many particular cases had to be determined rather by inference than by specific provision.
Besides, man in his depravity was apt to distort even
the plainest text. Therefore the prince must leave the
delimitation of his authority to be determined, not by
himself or his courts, but by the godly ministers, the
professional experts in the rule by which all men should
walk. The ministers, naturally, would be just, impar-
tial, and righteous, so far as any men could be. They
ordered these things better, a Puritan might have said,
in Scotland:

where the ministerie of the kirk is once lawfully constitute, and
they that are placed doe their office faithfully, all godly Princes and
Magistrates ought to heare, and obey their voice, and reverence the
Majestie of the Son of God speaking in them.[1]

Of course, the Puritans conceded, one might object
"that for Princes to subscribe to the determination of
priestes . . . is no supremacie but a subiection"; and
they might well suppose so, for precisely that objection
was made, more times than we care to count. But the
ready reply was always on tap: "We answer, it is no
subiection vnto men, but to God & his worde, to doe
nothing in these matters, but by the faithfull aduise of
them, that know his will, & are bounde to teach it vnto
all men." [2]

1. *Seconde Booke of Discipline* (edition of 1621), chap. x, par. 9.
2. *A Briefe and plaine declaration* (1584), p. 142.

At this juncture we at last begin to perceive what was the real issue between the two parties. They both agreed, as we have seen, on the fundamental philosophy of civil supremacy, but they diverged when they came to make applications. "Of the title of the princes supremacie, if it be truely vnderstood, we moue no countrouersie." But the correct understanding was precisely the question: "herein resteth all the doubt, howe this is truely to be vnderstoode." [1] The Puritans did not interpret it to mean supremacy absolute and unrestricted; they qualified it, or rather read a qualification into it. The prince was to establish the Church by his authority, but that Church was to be specifically the one which "He hath appointed," and once established it was ever after to be "preserved in the same simplicity and sincerity undefiled." [2] Puritans could and did take the oath of supremacy whenever required, because it simply bound them to support the forcible establishment of the Church in uniformity throughout the kingdom, and that object they considered laudable. But they had a very concrete idea of what kind of church the oath ought to intend, and this interpretation their opponents could not accept. From the Anglican standpoint there was an element of equivocation in the Puritans' vows, but to the Puritans themselves all was open and aboveboard. In the final analysis the difference can be reduced to a matter of definition. And to the Puritans the proper definition of the Church was so obvious that even he who ran could not miss it if only he would run with a Bible in his hand.

1. *Ibid.*, p. 138.   2. Travers, *A full and plaine declaration*, p. 103.

Otherwise the Puritans had no objections to the government's policy. Presbyterianism involved no contribution to the development of liberty or toleration; on the contrary it was if anything more repressive, for it would have added to the almost purely political force of the Acts of Supremacy and Uniformity the blazing sanctions of the divine command. It intended only the substitution of the Genevan régime for that which prevailed, but it expected no other alterations: "We beseche her majestie to have the hearing of this matter of Gods, and to take the defence of it upon her, and to fortifie it by law, that it may be received by common order through out her dominions." [1] If only the sovereign would wait for the pronouncements of a synod, she then could proceed to her heart's content to order those opinions taught and to command "silence vnto those, who after playne & fonde refutation of their errours, notwithstanding gaynsaye the trueth." [2] Church and State, each thus resting upon its proper foundations, would be no less united than before, but rather, by virtue of their common dedication to the same holy end, would function even more efficiently in coöperation. "If anie shall offende against these lawes, whether he be Preacher or hearer, besides the Ecclesisatical censure, which he should not escape, he is also to bee punished in body by the Ciuill Magistrate." [3]

Because they professed complete adherence to the

1. "Second Admonition" (1572), in Frere and Douglas, *Puritan Manifestoes*, p. 130.
2. *A Defence of the godlie Ministers* (1587), sig. E1 verso.
3. *Ibid.*, sig. D3 verso.

orthodox political philosophy, the reformers took great care to avoid employing arguments or methods which might just as well be used against themselves on the inevitable day when they came into power. They wanted it clearly understood that they would countenance no opposition but that of their own making. The change they envisaged was to be, not an "alteration, but the perfection of the estates of the Church";[1] it was to emanate, not from a band of revolutionaries, but from the only legitimate author of the law, the sovereign in Parliament. The reform in polity should be accomplished "by the authoritie of our Christian King, with the consent of his Parliament,"[2] just as the reform in doctrine had been effected by Henry VIII. Puritans were above all economically and socially respectable; theirs was not an idle boast when they declared they abhorred democracy. In fact, they continually predicted that if the hierarchy were removed, the established order of society would not be affected; it would rather be reinforced.[3] The reformed régime would make for a surer triumph of law and order, because the monarch would not only continue to exercise full police powers, but would exact the complete subjection required by Reformation theory to godly magistrates. There would no longer be the shadow of a doubt that the throne of England was a Christian institution. As the *Admonition* put it at the beginning of the controversy, the Puritans ardently in-

1. *A Briefe and plaine declaration* (1584), sig. 4 recto.
2. William Stoughton, *An Assertion For true and Christian Church-policie* (1604), p. 28.
3. *Ibid.*, p. 22.

tended "that Christ being restored into his kyngdome, to rule in the same by the scepter of his worde . . . the Prince may be better obeyed." [1]

This fund of argument was among what Richard Hooker called the "certain general inducements" Puritans were using "to make saleable your cause in gross," [2] but in spite of much expert salesmanship, the government refused to be "sold." Elizabeth preferred to work behind the scenes, but a letter she wrote to James of Scotland in 1590 shows she knew what she was about. Presbyterians, she said, "wold have no kings but a presbitrye, and take our place while they inioy our privilege, with a shade of Godes word. . . . Suppose you, my deare brother, that I can tollerat such scandalz of my sincere government?" [3] James supposed nothing of the sort. He knew, if anything, more about the sect than his cousin, for had not Andrew Melville tweaked him by the sleeve and called him "God's silly vassal" to his royal face? He spoke from bitter experience when he told the Hampton Court Conference that a presbytery "as well agreeth with a Monarchy, as God, and the Diuell." [4] During his rule it became impossible for Puritans any longer to pretend that the supremacy could be converted intact to the uses of a Presbyterianized nation; James made it quite evident that his supremacy was inextricably identified with the specific organization of the Church. His brilliant aphorism at the Conference

1. Frere and Douglas, *Puritan Manifestoes*, p. 18.
2. *Laws of Ecclesiastical Polity*, Preface, chap. iii, par. 5.
3. *Letters of Queen Elizabeth and King James VI of Scotland* (Camden Society, 1849), p. 63.
4. Barlow, *The Svmme and Svbstance of the Conference* (1604), p. 79.

clinched the matter: "If once you were out, and they in place, I knowe what would become of my *Supremacie*. *No Bishop, no King*." [1] By him the Crown became publicly committed to a denial of the Puritan argument for scriptural discipline, and henceforth a change in the ecclesiastical régime would necessarily entail a political revolution. From the beginning of the controversy Puritans had nervously foreseen the possibility of the avowed hostility of the Crown, and they had tried to stave it off by quibbling. Now, however, their liege lord was frankly in the enemy's camp, and what could they do about it?

The root of the difficulty, as Professor Allen has brilliantly demonstrated,[2] lay in the peculiar character of the Establishment itself. The Elizabethan Settlement had incorporated almost exclusively one half of Reformation political theory. It had enshrined the ideal of unity, it had declared for the need of order in society. Therefore the Church was designed to retain the *status quo* and to be subjected to the ruler. By the time of James this had come to mean that no further reformation could be made in the direction of religious truth without disrupting the social order. In effect, the supremacy ultimately implied that the King, in the interest of society, could and must pass judgment upon all religious disputes, doctrinal as well as ecclesiastical. The power of the supremacy, Sutcliffe said, "doeth consist in making of lawes, and disanulling them; in com-

1. *Ibid.*, p. 82.
2. Allen, *The History of Political Thought in the Sixteenth Century*, pp. 168–175, 179.

manding, and not being subiect to the commandement of others; in appointing the principall officers or gouernours, and in supreme iudgement." [1] There was and there could be no effective limitation upon an indefinite power to issue "supreme iudgement." The churchmen betrayed this fact when they struck their hardest against the Puritan contention that the King was limited by a law higher than any of his own making, and especially at the proposal that this limitation should be imposed by the ministers themselves. Puritans might insist that their scheme of coöperating agencies, both ruled by the fundamental body of divine law, would maintain the social stability, but the King and his priests were convinced that the existence of coördinate authorities was impossible. "There cannot be two supreme iurisdictions in one state, the one not depending of another. For if the one command, the other forbid; whom should we obey, if both be equall?" [2]

Therefore James avowed his belief that the Church was sufficiently reformed, and by so doing took upon himself to settle a whole number of disputed religious points by royal fiat. This was conduct which Puritans could feel was proper only to the devil's advocate, but James and the clergy assumed his right to the power he exercised, and called upon the Puritans to obey in the name of that political loyalty which was an indispensable ingredient in the Puritan creed. The ceremonies and vestments, preached Francis Mason, do not have to be individually commanded in the Bible, for they are

1. Matthew Sutcliffe, *A Treatise of Ecclesiastical Discipline* (1591), p. 147.
2. *Ibid.*, p. 151.

enjoined "in euery place where God commands vs to
obey our Prince." [1] Puritans had tried to avoid the issue
by blaming the prelates alone, but they could do so no
more. "Know you whom you accuse?" asked Bishop
Hall, "Let me show you your adversary. It is King
James himself." [2] By 1630 the rift between the King
and his Puritan subjects was a yawning chasm, and the
Puritans were not colossal enough to straddle it; they
could not preach limitation of the King by the Bible
and still be accounted loyal citizens. "The Puritan
tenet," said Giles Widdowes, "is, that Kings must bee
subiect to the Puritan Presbyters. . . . Thus the oaths
of Supremacie, and allegiance are broken. This Puritan
is an Arch-traitor." [3]

Puritans had always attempted to reply to such an
accusation by declaring that they constituted the true
body of the Church and that the bishops were usurpers,
whom a loyal subject should labor to have evicted. As
long as the Church remained the ill-defined institution
of the Elizabethan Settlement, this claim could still,
though with difficulty, pass muster. But coincident
with the defeat of Spain there began to emerge within
the Church a new group of leaders, men who had been
reared in the Establishment and loved its ritual and its
government. They no longer accepted it as a mere
compromise between Catholicism and Calvinism, but
as a complete entity. Doctrinal uniformity was not
enough; they were determined to achieve unity in ad-

1. *The Avthority of the Chvrch*, p. 31.
2. "A Common Apology of the Church of England" (1610), *Works* (ed.
   Philip Wynter, Oxford, 1863), ix, 67.
3. *The Schismatical Puritan* (1631), sig. C2 recto.

ministration as well. The Church could not continue half Puritan and half Anglican, and it was now, they thought, high time that it became all one thing or the other. They pleaded their cause in a number of able pamphlets, of which Bancroft's and Sutcliffe's were typical and Hooker's incomparably the greatest.

The Stuarts were in complete sympathy with this rising determination to settle the Puritans' business. "If this bee all . . . they haue to say," James announced as he left Hampton Court, "I shall make them conforme themselues, or I will harrie them out of the land, or else do worse." [1] The clergy, headed by the vigorous Bancroft, responded eagerly to this encouragement, and in the first years of the new reign achieved what Professor Usher has termed the "reconstruction" of the Church. The miscellaneous laws and orders of the previous years were codified into the systematic *Canons* of 1604, with some new statements that were in actuality anti-Puritan legislation.[2] At the same time the Court of High Commission was brought to its greatest degree of efficiency, sending its pursuivants through every county with summonses to trembling divines.[3] In 1606 Henry Jacob truthfully lamented that there was no hope of "freedom" from Antichrist while the prelates ruled, "but a more direfull expectation of greater slaveries and servitude, then ever before, as may appear by the late *Canons*." [4]

But the *Canons* were not the sole cause of Puritan

1. Barlow, *op. cit.*, p. 83.
2. Cf. first twelve canons, Edward Cardwell, *Synodalia*, i, 249–253.
3. Usher, *op. cit.*, i, 91–110.
4. Henry Jacob, *A Christian and Modest offer*, p. 33.

despair. The reconstruction was expressed not only in legislation, but in a comprehensive restatement of the position of the Church, fortified by a number of broad confirmatory testimonies drawn from sources which seemed to the Puritans altogether irrelevant to the matter in hand. The new school of Anglicans frankly declared that the sacred Scripture was not the only law God had appointed for man to observe, nor had it ever been designed to be a complete guide for all activity. In the question of ecclesiastical polity they found abundant and authoritative directions in the collective wisdom of Christianity, the interpretations of the Councils and the Fathers, the traditions of the Church. Moreover, they put forward speculations from more secular realms — arguments from reason, nature, from the law of nations, or from the character and origin of public society. By enlarging the Puritan conception of law as only something "which superior authority imposeth" to comprehend the eternal decrees upon which God had erected the universe,[1] the learned apologists justified the Established Church upon a sort of cosmic basis. And as they resorted to these larger reflections they turned their backs upon the harsh bibliolatry of Puritanism. Through their influence Calvinism began to be unfashionable, or as a Church historian has put it, "the foreign Calvinistic teaching began to disappear before the larger Catholic doctrine of the love of God and the atoning work of Christ for all mankind."[2] In the Lambeth Articles of 1595 Whitgift still interpreted

---

1. *Laws of Ecclesiastical Polity*, bk. I, chap. iii, par. I.
2. William E. Collins, *The English Reformation and its Consequences*, p. 27.

the Church's theology in a thoroughly Calvinistic spirit, but the prelates at the Hampton Court Conference quashed the proposal to have the Lambeth statements incorporated into the Articles.[1] Presently the most prominent of the Church theologians were generally repudiating the rigorous doctrines of election and reprobation. Samuel Brooke wrote Laud in 1630 that he considered predestination the root of all Puritanism, and Puritanism "the root of all rebellion and disobedient intractablenesse, and schism and sauciness in the country."[2] Because of their opposition to this tenet the new school acquired from their Puritan foes the epithet "Arminian," although the two groups soon clashed on practically every other principle and practice. Every profession the school made was anathema to the Puritans, and when men of this persuasion became powerful enough in the Church to attempt forcing an elaborate sacerdotalism upon honest souls who for half a century had been striving against much milder rituals, when the Arminian bishops deliberately required the people to play games on Sunday and, from the Puritan standpoint, desecrate the Sabbath, when they refused to permit the Lord's Supper to be taken around a table, but insisted upon using altars and what the Puritans considered the paraphernalia of the Mass — when the Arminians did these things, they seemed to be systematically outraging every Puritan sensibility. Unless the Puritans could check this faction, their situation, diffi-

1. William Barlow, *op. cit.*, p. 38; Usher, *op. cit.*, I, 321–322.
2. Quoted in William Holden Hutton, *The English Church from the Accession of Charles I to the Death of Anne*, p. 34.

cult though it had been since the days of the *Admonition*, would become utterly hopeless.

At the beginning of Charles's reign the only satisfaction Puritans could derive from the aspect of affairs was that Laud and his ilk outraged more persons than themselves. It was about this time, Fuller tells us, that the word "Puritan" began to signify those who were defenders of matters which might be considered doctrinal in the English Church, or those who were simply "anti-Arminian in their judgments." [1] Clearly many old line supporters of the Establishment, who in pre-Laudian days had been hostile or indifferent to Puritanism, were shocked by the Popish aroma of the Arminian prelacy and became willing to join hands with the reformers, not so much because they wanted Presbyterianism, but because they did not want *jure divino* bishops. The Puritans, of course, encouraged such recruits. While they could cry down "those Hereticall and Grace-destroying Arminian nouelties, which haue of late inuaded, affronted, and almost shouldred out of doores, the ancient, established, and resolued Doctrines of our Church," [2] Puritans were assured of being the spokesmen for a larger proportion of public opinion than at any previous time. They could drive home their ancient claim that the bishops were only a usurping faction in the Church by playing upon the average Englishman's distrust of the "high church" party. Finally, the personal unpopularity of James, the immorality of his Court, and

1. Fuller, *Church History of Britain*, bk. x, sec. 6, par. 18.
2. Prynne, *The Church of Englands old Antithesis to New Arminianisme* (1629), sig. A2.

the recurrent suspicion that he and his son inclined toward Catholicism accounted for a swelling of the Puritan ranks which was not always a complete endorsement of the Puritan program.

The Arminian bishops, for all their claim to an apostolic succession, were a minority party; they were, therefore, in the face of mounting opposition compelled to look to the throne. "Defend thou me with the sword," concluded Montague in his *Apello Caesarem*, "and I will defend thee with the pen." [1] The speeches of the group carry the Reformation's apotheosis of the divine magistracy to the last degree; there was a feverish insistency about their phrases which suggests they were in constant apprehension lest they be not protected against their mortal foes. Laud's sermons to the Parliaments of 1625 to 1628 are a case in point, but the most notorious instances were the famous sermons of Sibthorpe and Mainwaring. These utterances aroused a hue and cry, though actually their theoretical content was Reformation platitude. They reiterated the familiar doctrine of the origin of kings: "This power is not merely human but superhuman and indeed no less than a power divine." Therefore, even if the King commanded flatly against the Word of God, we should remember that resistance to him was resistance to God, and so we should "endure with patience whatsoever penalty his pleasure should inflict upon them who in this case would desire rather to obey God than man." However, the sting in these gentlemen's renovation of the theory was their

1. Quoted in S. R. Gardiner, *History of England from the Accession of James I*, vi, 203.

decidedly specific application of it, for if resistance was not permissible even in the name of God's law, much less was it allowable for mere constitutional scruples. If the prince, said Sibthorpe, imposed an immoderate or unjust tax, the subject had no escape, "he is bound in conscience to submit"; if he resisted, corroborated Mainwaring, he was "resisting the ordinance of God and receiving to himself damnation." [1] The King, in other words, had a divine right to tonnage and poundage!

These quotations make comprehensible to us why in the course of James's reign the Puritan attack became in large part merged with the Parliamentary campaign against unlimited exercise of the King's prerogative. The Puritan agitation for limitation by a divine law in Church affairs found a counterpart in the struggles of the statesmen and common lawyers for an observance of the fundamental law in political and legal matters. The close identification of the unpopular Arminian faction with the fullest vaunting of royal pretensions made it a target for men like Eliot or Pym, men who were not particularly Puritanical to begin with. This combination of Puritans and Parliamentarians undoubtedly was, as Professor Usher declares,[2] fortuitous, since the discipline was always advanced as being self-evident, so that it should automatically be accepted by the ruler and imposed on his country. The polity was not originally designed to become a stalking horse for constitutional liberty. But its advocates had set out to get the appro-

1. Sibthorpe and Mainwaring, quoted in Prothero, *Select Statutes*, pp. 437–440.
2. *The Reconstruction of the Church*, II, 155.

bation of the government, and when the King repulsed them they had to capitalize what support they could find in Parliament. The Parliamentarians, on the other hand, became more and more forced by the tactics of the bishops into the position of pulling the Puritans' chestnuts out of the fire. The most conspicuous Arminian champions, Montague, Mainwaring, and Sibthorpe, were repeatedly attacked from the floor of the House. Even men who professed to reverence the order of bishops could not stomach some of the men who filled the offices, such men, for instance, as Bishop Neile, against whom a member from Huntingdonshire by the name of Oliver Cromwell delivered his maiden speech.

The King naturally could not stand by and see his best friends sacrificed. James had identified the cause of the Crown with that of the bishops, and Charles identified the bishops with the Arminian party. He persisted in regarding the Arminian tenets as the pristine teaching of the Church; in 1627 he commanded by proclamation that everybody accept the Thirty-Nine Articles without further discussion,[1] which might have been interpreted to suit either Pym or Montague, though, as Gardiner says, there was no doubt that "those who carried it into execution would interpret it in favor of Montague rather than of Pym."[2] When the opposition at last exhausted Charles's notoriously finite patience, he commanded that Parliament be dismissed. On March 2, 1629, with the Black Rod pounding at the door, the House of Commons, in the midst of historic

1. Cardwell, *Documentary Annals*, ii, 222.
2. Gardiner, *op. cit.*, vi, 123.

pandemonium, passed Eliot's resolution that "whoever shall bring in innovation of religion, or by favour or countenance seem to extend or introduce Popery or Arminianism, or other opinion disagreeing from the true and orthodox Church, shall be reputed a capital enemy to this Kingdom and Commonwealth." [1] Charles, convinced that Parliament's religious zeal was a "plausible theme to deprave our government," [2] a design "to erect an universal over-swaying power to themselves, which belongs only to us, and not to them," [3] put Eliot and Selden in the Tower and announced his determination to rule by himself thereafter. The constitutional struggle had most evidently failed. The cause of Puritanism was again at an impasse. Emanuel Downing, writing to John Winthrop on March 6, reported the melancholy events of the last week and concluded, piously but dubiously, "the good Lord torne all to a good yssue." [4]

With Parliament gone, the Puritans had shot their last bolt. They were now given over, without the possibility of mitigation, to that agonizing conflict between their political loyalty and their religious convictions which all their exertions had striven to avoid. The human and the divine law opposed each other in every particular. The words which Francis Mason had uttered at Cambridge in 1605 contained what, twenty-four years later, seemed to be the inescapable dilemma:

Then see, I beseech you, into what perplexities you cast your-selues. If you should conforme, you tell vs that you should sinne,

1. Gardiner, *The Constitutional Documents of the Puritan Revolution*, p. 82.
2. *Ibid.*, p. 92.
3. *Ibid.*, p. 95.
4. *Massachusetts Historical Society, Collections*, Series 4, VI, 36.

because it is against your conscience; and if you doe not conforme, wee must tell you that you sinne, because it is vniustifiable disobedience.[1]

The terrible thing about the dilemma was that the Puritans acknowledged the full force of both aspects. They believed in the supremacy; they had to believe in it, because it was the assumption of their age and because it was essential to their discipline. And so they swore fervent allegiance to a King who ingeniously tortured them, denied their basic conviction, assumed functions that belonged only to Christ, commanded their adherence to a Popish ceremonial, and deliberately enjoined the desecration of the Sabbath. On the other hand, the commands of Christ remained perfectly clear, and the Puritans were sure, as few men ever have been sure, "that wee seeke Gods glory, when wee followe Christe." [2] They could obey the King only at the cost of their eternal salvation. And they could not sidestep the issue; when the irrresistible force of the King's command clashed with the immovable object of scriptural decree, the Puritans had no chance to be anywhere but at the point of collision. Their whole cause would have been lost had they once broken the national uniformity; they could no more envisage themselves existing as a separate church alongside the Establishment than the prelates could have permitted it. Parliament never proposed any remedy but the compulsory maintenance of the proper uniformity, the condign punishment of those who "publish, either by word or writing, anything con-

1. Mason, *op. cit.*, p. 63.
2. *A Parte of a register* (1590), p. 15.

trary to orthodoxy." [1] Yet this very uniformity once more required the full doctrine of the civil supremacy. So Puritan reasoning went round in hopeless circles, and Winthrop in 1629 had good cause to be worried about the future of England.

The ultimate refinement in Puritan misery came from the reflection that if the King's eyes would only for one moment open to the truth, all would be well. Then he could enjoin uniformity, then he could be the supreme governor of the Church, — such a governor, of course, as was defined by the discipline, but none the less a forcible upholder of orthodoxy, — then political loyalty and religious allegiance would coincide. There would then be no further disturbances; there would exist the ideal society ruled directly by Christ's laws. All the shock of conflict had not diminished, but rather augmented, the appeal of this vision. The discipline was, as Hooker described it, set forth under that high commanding form as a thing "everlastingly required by the law of that Lord of lords, against whose statutes there is no exception to be taken." [2] Puritans could not arbitrate their cause. It was not that they refused to accept a higher judgment than their own; they honestly believed that their own judgment had not entered into the matter at all. They were only repeating the highest judgment ever recorded, and why the King would not listen to it was more than they ever could comprehend.

The Puritan dilemma, as long as it continued to be uttered in these terms, was insoluble. The medieval

1. Gardiner, *History of England*, VII, 66.
2. *Laws of Ecclesiastical Polity*, Preface, chap. ii, par. 2.

principle of uniformity could not be reconciled with the inveterate tendency of the Reformation to produce constant variety, unless one party could secure an absolute control over every corner of the realm; and England was too complex a society to give such an opportunity to any one faction. But with Laud in the saddle, determined to make a greater effort than had his predecessors, the disciplinarians could only expect to face that which the *Admonition* had originally foreseen when it had declared that rather than surrender they would lay their heads to the block, "and this shall be our peace, to have quiet consciences with our God." [1] Yet precisely at the moment when this dismal solution seemed to be the only one which ever would come out of England, a new enterprise was born, a way conceived of resolving the conflicting allegiances that had not yet been thought of, and that promised, with a greater degree of hardship, a greater possibility of success. Before we proceed to this latest proposal, however, we must still examine one other factor which profoundly influenced the decision and determined some of its most pronounced characteristics.

1. Frere and Douglas, *Puritan Manifestoes*, p. 36.

III

SEPARATIST CONGREGATIONALISM

WHEN Puritans asserted that the substitution of a Presbyterian polity for the episcopal hierarchy would not prove antagonistic to the aristocratic, centralized character of Tudor government, they spoke with some show of reason. Presbyterianism involved certain steps in the direction of what we might call democracy, as, for instance, the reduction of all ministers to a parity in rank, but it fully intended to counteract such tendencies by a system of control almost as centralized and autocratic as that of the prelates. The various parishes were to be governed through a pyramided series of ministerial conferences, each of which would have absolute power over the churches within its jurisdiction. The first sketches of the polity provided for the election of ministers by the people, but later ones, more directly under the influence of Scotland, required them to be nominated by one of these assemblies, and only approved by the congregations. The individual parish might appeal from the decision of a regional classis to a provincial synod, and from there to the national assembly, whose word, however, was final. The whole Church was to be truly a national one, including every person in the realm; in fact, everyone was to be forced into membership, to be compelled to have his children baptized, to attend services, and to pay tithes, precisely as in the Established Church.

Reformers everywhere in the sixteenth century had assumed that a national church should necessarily be all-inclusive. Yet they always had a knotty problem on their hands when they came to reconcile this notion with the doctrine of election. If eight out of every ten men, even in a reformed church, were destined to perdition, how could that church account them members at all? The answer, Calvin had explained, was that in reality there were two "churches," one composed only of the elect of all times and places, and the other of "the whole multitude, dispersed all over the world, who profess to worship one God and Jesus Christ." [1] The ideal, he admitted, would be to gather churches exclusively of the elect, so that the roll-call of the Church Militant might be made identical with that of the Church Triumphant; but, as Wyclif had long ago remarked,[2] it was almost impossible to tell for a certainty who was elect. Furthermore, the imperative demand for unity required that every person be subject to church censures. Calvin therefore concluded that, for the purposes of this world, if the congregation "possess and honour the ministry of the word, and the administration of the sacraments, they are, without all doubt, entitled to be considered as a Church. . . . In this manner, we preserve the unity of the universal Church." [3] Puritans and Anglicans, both aiming at exclusive sway in the kingdom, were in complete accord in this view. Those not elect, said Richard Field, may be in the Church, but they are not of it;

1. *Institutes*, bk. IV, chap. i, par. 7.
2. W. W. Capes, *The English Church in the Fourteenth and Fifteenth Centuries*, pp. 111 ff.
3. Calvin, *op. cit.*, par. 9.

they have fellowship in outward things, but they can have no part in effectual and saving grace. However, since unity must be preserved at all costs, every individual must be treated, while he lives, as a church member, and be subject to ecclesiastical as well as political rulers.[1]

This disposal of the matter, however, was far from satisfactory to many troubled spirits, among them a young Puritan of Norfolk by the name of Robert Browne. By the year 1581 he had come to the conclusion that a church of the elect existing within a church of the doomed was an anomalous arrangement, that there could be no true reformation on that basis. Whether or not he was influenced by continental Anabaptism remains a moot question, but there is no doubt he himself thought he had found his inspiration in the revealed Word. After six or seven years of imprisonments and persecutions Browne fell by the wayside and renounced his program, but other enthusiasts, though they repudiated his leadership and altered some details of his scheme, carried on what was essentially the same cause; and this cause must be noted as a constant factor in the subsequent religious history of England and New England.

The polity proposed by these persons differed in two important respects from Presbyterianism. It intended in the first place to interpret predestination literally. Only persons who could prove that they were "redeemed by Christ vnto holiness & happiness for euer"[2]

1. Richard Field, *Of the Church* (1606), pp. 16–18.
2. Williston Walker, *The Creeds and Platforms of Congregationalism*, p. 19.

could be church members, and they could not afford to admit into the fellowship any of the wicked and ungodly, for to do so would infect and corrupt all the rest. The faithful, therefore, should betake themselves apart "from the vnbeleeuers and heathen of the land" and form true churches, recognizing Christ alone as their direct head and ruler, and permitting themselves to be governed only by such officers and laws as He "in his last will and Testament hath therevnto ordeyened." [1] Sacraments should be administered only to received members and were profaned if used by or for the reprobate. Though it might be difficult to tell just who was an elected person, still if a man could give evidence of Christian character and make a confession of faith before the church, the congregation would have sufficient data by which to judge his "calling." A geographical parish, said Greenwood, could not make a church, but only "the profession which the people make." [2] Unless men uttered such public professions and were received by a particular congregation, they could not account themselves members of the visible Church. When a new organization was to be founded, the "visible saints" should come together, profess their faith, and take a covenant of allegiance to Christ as their king and prophet, and promise to be bound by His laws. This covenant and confession were worthless unless undertaken voluntarily. "To make a reformed church," said Robinson, "there must be first a reformed people." [3]

1. Henry Martyn Dexter, *Congregationalism of the Last Three Hundred Years*, p. 222.   2. *Ibid.*, p. 220.
3. John Robinson, *Works* (ed. Robert Ashton, Boston, 1851), II, 316.

Consequently no official could force a church to be gathered, constrain an individual to join, or compel "the church to receive any without assurance by public profession of their own faith; or to retain any, longer than they continue and walk orderly in the faith." [1] Calvin, the Establishment, and the Puritans had all been wrong when they said the marks of a true church were preaching of the Word and administration of the sacraments, for the Word could be preached and the sacraments administered to "assemblies of unbelievers." [2] The authentic touchstones of a true church were "faith" and "order"; only where God had called a company of His own together could "faith" be found, and "order" could exist only where they administered it. Though God alone knew whom He had chosen, still if the churches rigorously examined their candidates and kept a close watch over their members, they might be practically certain that those who took the church covenant had also been received into the covenant of grace with God Himself. The visible Church would thus become a genuine preparatory school for the invisible, and the covenanted brethren could make in it the acquaintance of their future neighbors in heaven.

Congregationalism differed from Presbyterianism in the second place by bringing the individual associations of Christians into direct relations with Christ. Every believer, being of the elect, was made, according to Browne, "a Kinge, a Priest, and a Prophet vnder Christ,

1. Benjamin Hanbury, *Historical Memorials Relating to the Independents and Congregationalists*, I, 52.
2. Robinson, *op. cit.*, III, 428.

to vpholde and further the kingdom of God." [1] Every group of such exalted personages was therefore self-sufficient, was an integral unit, independent of all external compulsion, and competent to manage its own affairs. No minister could have any authority whatsoever outside his own parish. Representatives of the churches might be assembled for consultation, there might be a lawful use of "Synods, Classes, Assemblies, or Councils, for mutual help & advise," but only so long as these gatherings did not challenge any authoritative jurisdiction over particular congregations.[2] The whole superstructure of Presbyterianism and Anglicanism, the hierarchy of ministerial assemblies and the hierarchy of lords bishops, were alike declared to be disallowed by the Bible. Christianity should, if properly reformed, consist of a myriad of little groups of the proved elect, all managing their own affairs in accordance with the rules delivered by Christ. And since those rules were held to be explicit and all-sufficient, and were to be administered only by God's chosen people, there would be complete unanimity. Ecclesiastical overseers were unnecessary.

Although this system of ecclesiastical regimen differed from that of the Puritans, the men who constructed it went upon much the same assumption: they thought it was unmistakably decreed in the Bible. Their polity was "exactly described, distinguished, limited . . . by most perfect and playne lawes in Gods word." [3] All Christians were bound to submit to it "and not to any

1. Walker, *op. cit.*, pp. 22–23.
2. Francis Johnson, *A Christian Plea* (1617), p. 251.
3. "Confession" of the London-Amsterdam Church (1596), Walker, *op. cit.*, p. 65.

other devised by man whatsoever." [1] Life, as John
Canne described it, was a sort of tight-rope act; it was as
though a man were always walking a narrow path between two great seas, and if he turned but a little aside,
he would irrevocably slip into destruction; "the like
may be said of God's pathe and institutions: if a man
keep not full in the way, do not everything according to
the pattern." [2] With this peril ever present to their
thoughts, the Congregationalists abandoned completely
every consideration but that of making the will of God
prevail in the fashion unalterably recorded in the revealed Word. "Unto all the power, learning, deceit,
rage, of the False Church, we oppose that little Book of
God's Word, which . . . as a heavy millstone shall press
her and all her children . . . down to hell. . . . By this
book, whoso is found in error or transgression, let them
have sentence accordingly." [3]

If, then, this Congregationalism was surely the sole
polity authorized by Christ, obviously the Church of
England was in an intolerable state. And immediately
Congregationalists had seen the Church in this light,
they were confronted with the same problem of divided
loyalties that the Puritans were facing. Like the latter
they too decided that they should obey God rather than
man. All Christians, said Browne, have a "freedome" to
consider what is lawful; "Therefore the Magistrates
commaundement must not be a rule vnto me . . . but as
I see it agree with the worde of God." [4] But a different

1. Henry Ainsworth and Francis Johnson, *An Apologie* (1604), p. 79.
2. John Canne, *A Necessity of Separation* (Hanserd Knolles Society, 1849),
p. 74.   3. Hanbury, *op. cit.*, 1, 40.
4. *Reformation without tarrying* (Old South Leaflets, No. 100), p. 8.

consequence hinged upon the determination in this case, for loyalty to God as the Congregationalists understood it required not merely verbal witness to His truth, but an immediate action. Puritans could choose to follow Christ and still remain within the Church, since they understood Him to mean that they should work merely for the remodeling of the existing national institution. In the gospel according to Robert Browne, however, "whosoeuer are not gathered from all false Churches, & from their false gouernment, can neither be the Church of God, nor preachers in the same." [1] Christians, therefore, must separate themselves not simply figuratively but physically:

> We may not eyther at allurement of parents, brethren, or most dear friends; or by the example or entisement of the multitude, or by the commandement of the Magistrate, doe these, or any of these evils: but following the word of God, to separate our selues. [2]

Hence, though with a full comprehension of what they were doing, these men did not hesitate to exercise their God-given "freedome." They set about a reformation "without tarrying for anie"; they came out of the Church which their sovereign had established and ordained to be uniform throughout the nation. They decreed that the injunctions of God should not wait upon occasions for their fulfillment. Since the majority of people would never be capable of beginning a reformation, the lead had to be taken by "the worthiest, Were they never so fewe." [3] These should not be deterred,

1. Browne, quoted in Dexter, *op. cit.*, p. 104.
2. Ainsworth, *The Commvnion of Saincts*, p. 104.
3. Browne, quoted in Dexter, *op. cit.*, p. 67.

"though al the Princes of the world should prohibit the same vpon paine of death."[1] So the Word was translated into action; although they were a pitiful "fewe," although the age believed that only one church at a time could exist within a kingdom, they set up their own churches and distinguished themselves from the Puritans, not only by flaunting a different discipline, but by enacting an actual secession.

Superficially considered, Separatism seems to have been in effect a denial of the prevailing assumption concerning national uniformity; and many writers have written upon this understanding, ascribing to the Separatists a liberalism and a tolerance utterly foreign to Elizabethan thinking.[2] If, however, we examine the writings of the men, we shall be compelled to recognize that though they may have strained the ideal of uniformity by their conduct, they did so only inadvertently, and that actually in their theory they no more questioned it than did their more cautious Puritan brethren. Like the latter, they did not seek to destroy the magistrate's control of the Church, but simply to delimit it by the Word of God. They held that the sovereign could not arbitrarily decide the regimen of the Church, but must "revyve and inquier oute the lawes of God which are commaunded in his word."[3] Since Christ had commanded that new churches were not to be formed by order of the magistrates, but by the vol-

1. Barrowe, in *ibid.*, p. 215.
2. Cf. Herbert L. Osgood, "Political ideas of the Puritans," *Political Science Quarterly*, VI (1896), 3: "By Browne's writings religious toleration was first effectively proclaimed in England."
3. Barrowe, in *Egerton Papers* (Camden Society, 1840), p. 169.

untary consociation of a body of Christians, the Separatists obeyed Him. They ruled the prince out of the internal affairs of particular churches, because no intermediary should come between God and His own. Civil magistrates were indeed "authorized of God" and were "to make and execute laws by public agreement," but over the churches they had "no authoritie at all, but onelie as anie other Christians, if so they be Christians." [1] They had no right "to compell religion, to plant churches by power, and to force a submission to Ecclesiastical gouernment by lawes & penalties," because an individual's participation in religious ordinances should be spontaneous expressions of the spirit.[2] Magistrates, if they were Christians, should profess their faith before a particular congregation, and be received into it if they could give satisfaction; once admitted, they could not figure in purely religious affairs any more than any other member, and they were, if necessary, even to submit to its spiritual censures, "openlie to humble them selues in vnfained repentaunce, when they haue openlie and greuouslie trespassed." For, as Browne succinctly put it, "all powers shall serue and obeye Christ." [3]

But beyond their categorical assertion of the duty of the ruler to abide by the Congregational system, the Separatists left his office precisely where Reformation theory had placed it. He was still "authorized of God"; [4] Queen Elizabeth, said Barrowe, was "the sacred or-

1. Browne, *Reformation without tarrying*, p. 13.
2. *Ibid.*, p. 13.
3. *Ibid.*, p. 15.   4. *Ibid.*, p. 2.

dinance of God, the supreme power he hath set over all causes & persons, whether ecclesiastical or civil." [1] Barrowe's congregation informed her that they "gladly obey, and never willingly break any of her godly laws." Their establishing a church without her consent was not actual disobedience, because they were willing to suffer what "the arm of injustice" should inflict upon them for having done "such things as Christ hath commanded us in his holy worship." They did not question that the government had a divine right to inflict punishment according to its own lights, and they always left "the reformation of the state to those that God hath set to govern that state." [2] Henry Ainsworth, writing after three Separatist leaders had been executed and most of the faithful banished to Holland, still remained in his views upon political subordination completely orthodox:

> We ought to be subject to all civill Magistrates high or low, & that of conscience; pay them . . . their duties for their common wealth; to bear their exactions, oppressions, persecutions, patiently, without rebellion or resistance; and euen pray for them that shall so misuse us.[3]

Since the Separatists accepted the institution of magistracy as expounded by general Reformation theory, they therefore confirmed the office in the obligation to maintain the true discipline. Their only point was that the discipline should be Congregationalism. Oddly though it may sound to us, they condemned "separation," understanding, however, separation from a true

1. Burrage, *Early English Dissenters*, II, 104.
2. Strype, *Annals of the Reformation*, IV, 131–136.
3. *The Communion of Saincts*, pp. 106–107.

church. "There is but one body, the church, and but one Lord, or head of that body, Christ: and whosoever separates from the body, the church, separates from the head, Christ." [1] Convinced that they alone were in "ye right way," the Separatists had no intention of tolerating other sects; the "Pilgrim" pastor, John Robinson, bewailed the very religious hospitality of the Dutch which made them willing to receive him and his people.[2] Because the profane multitude were excluded from church membership was no reason why they should not be forced to attend church services,[3] nor why civil magistrates should not "strike with their sword every one which . . . shal openly transgresse against the Lords commandements." [4] Browne himself recognized the danger in the centrifugal democracy of his polity and frankly trusted in the civil power to keep it in check: "If againe it be said, that while men might take & refuse their ministers as they list, all factions & heresies might grow I answere that the Ciuil Magistrate must restraine that licentiousness." [5] In fact it might be said that a passionate devotion to uniformity was the actual cause of the Separatists' departure; how, they asked, could the Puritans still remain in the Church and yet try to employ there different practices from what it prescribed, when everybody agreed "that the constitution, worship, ministrie, government, holy dayes of Church

1. Robinson, *op. cit.*, II, 259.
2. *Ibid.*, III, 418.
3. Browne, *An Answer to Master Cartwrights Letter*, p. 11; Barrowe and Greenwood in Hanbury, *Historical Memorials*, I, 25, 52; Robinson, *op. cit.*, I, 42; II, 314.
4. Dexter, *op. cit.*, p. 85.
5. *A New Year's Gift* (ed. Champlin Burrage), p. 30.

should be uniforme, and not variable in every coast"?[1]
The platform of the exiled church, published in Amsterdam in 1596, showed no indication that the congregation had come to doubt the very principles upon which the government had acted against them; they still held it the duty of princes "to suppress and root out by their authoritie all false ministeries, voluntarie Relligions and counterfeyt worship of God," and "to establish & mayntein by their lawes every part of Gods word, his pure Relligion and true ministrie ... yea, to enforce al their Subiects whether Ecclesiasticall or civile, to do their dutyes to God and men."[2]

The Reformation was full of incongruities, but this contrast between Separatist preaching and practice seems in a fair way to cap the climax. The sect wished to impose an incommodious system upon the Elizabethan State, and yet, at the same time, gave complete allegiance to the theory upon which the State proceeded against it. The only explanation can be that the Separatists, like the Puritans, were preaching a crusade, all the more furiously because they had much less hope of ever succeeding. Distinctions between State and Church were to be sharpened, but this was only to mean that the magistrates, when properly limited, would be genuine allies of the Church, accommodating the government to the true institution and enforcing conformity to it. Congregationalism, Robinson assures us, was far from intending that civil rulers might not use their "lawful power lawfully for the furtherance of

1. Ainsworth, quoted in John Paget, *An Arrow against the Separation of the Brownists* (1618), p. 5.   2. Walker, *op. cit.*, p. 71.

Christ's kingdom. . . . It is true they have no power against the laws, doctrines, and religion of Christ; but for the same, if their power be of God, they may use it lawfully, and against the contrary." [1] To the Separatists, Separation was a means to an end, a step toward the Congregationalizing of England.[2] Bishop Hall made precisely that point when he told the exiles, "Our land you could like well, if you might be lords alone." [3] Should their discipline have triumphed the Separatists were perfectly equipped to dictate the religious life of the nation. They never thought Christ had been so foolish as to intend dispensing with the assistance of the secular arm: "Unless the Magistrate doe vphold his honour against Sathan, it will fall to the ground, for ought men can see." [4]

Because the Separatists were few and inconspicuous they cannot be said to have figured prominently on the English political stage. Their principles have been dwelt upon here at perhaps undue length because they illustrate the tyranny which the ideals of uniformity and of civil maintenance of orthodoxy exercised over the mind of that age. However, the Separatists were important in the total situation, if not for themselves, at least for the reactions they evoked and the issues they raised. They represented something the Puritans

1. *Works*, III, 277.
2. Burrage, *op. cit.*, I, 104 ff.
3. "A common apology of the Church of England" (1610), *Works*, IX, 102.
4. Pierce, *John Penry*, p. 160. Cf. Robert William Dale, *History of English Congregationalism*, p. 170; Allen, *The History of Political Thought in the Sixteenth Century*, p. 229; Henry W. Clark, *History of English Nonconformity*, I, 200; Dexter, *op. cit.*, p. 282; Walker, *op. cit.*, p. 46.

denied, — a denial which further accentuated certain characteristics which were to play a large part in determining the ecclesiastical disposition of New England.

The Separatists quite logically regarded their own conduct as infinitely more consistent than the Puritans'. As long as the central issue was defined as the Puritans had defined it, that church discipline was given of God and that all else beyond what was so given was unlawful, then the Church of England was impossible. If the reading ministry, for instance, "be noe office nor callinge appointed by Christ, then is it an office of Antichrist . . . therefore we ought not to receiue or heare such a ministerie." [1] But Puritans refused to draw this conclusion. They were waiting for a legal reformation by the magistrate, because only by proceeding in that fashion could they remain politically respectable. According to Separatist reasoning, however, they were proving traitor to the real cause; they were betraying "not onlye themselves . . . but even Christ Jesus him self & his gospell into the hands of antichrist"; [2] they were admitting that after all polity did not depend exclusively upon God but waited upon the approbation of magistrates. "You colour all this with a cloake of tarying for further authority, & yet you say you are sent of God, & called of the Church, & yet you stay for further authority than these . . . offered you." [3] For it was from the Puritans themselves that

1. Browne, *An Answer to Master Cartwrights Letter*, pp. 125, 127.
2. Barrowe, "Four principall and waighty causes," *Congregational Historical Society Transactions* (1906), p. 292.
3. Harrison, "A treatise of the Church and Kingdome of Christ," in Albert Peel, *The Brownists in Norwich and Norfolk about 1580*, pp. 58, 41.

Separatists first learned to see the ungodly blemishes in the Church of England. "Thus haue we been taught by your selues, what *corruptions* there are in the Church"; yet when Separatists, acting upon these very teachings, fled from corruptions, the Puritans, their erstwhile masters, hung back and told them they were seduced. "Are not you then," Ainsworth pertinently asked, "the *seducers*?"[1] It can, I believe, be truthfully said that during the entire period the Separatists were attacking the Puritans with greater vehemence than they were the hierarchy. In Separatist eyes the Puritans were playing Judas to the bishops' Pilate, and their sin was incomparably "the greater and more fear full, whiles contrary to theyr knowledge they wittingly persist in disobedience against Jesus Christ."[2]

This sally upon the Puritan flank was enthusiastically applauded by the churchmen. As long as the Separatists were not personally too formidable, the hierarchy was almost delighted with them; they offered a golden opportunity to cry "I told you so." "The foolish Barrowist," Hooker announced, "deriveth his schism by way of conclusion, as to him it seemeth, directly and plainly out of your principles."[3] Since the Establishment had long been asserting that Puritan principles led inevitably to schism, it was only too happy to approve the Barrowist's logic. Bishop Burgess heartily declared that if he himself believed as did the Puritans, "I professe in Gods presence, I would pro-

1. *Counterpoyson*, pp. 3-4.
2. Johnson, *A Treatise of the Ministry*, p. 32.
3. *Laws of Ecclesiastical Polity*, Preface, chap. viii, par. 1.

claime separation from idolatrous worship, and Worshippers this day ere I sleepe; And not halte, as these men (by their own positions doe) betwixt *Idolatrie* and *Religion.*" [1]

The Separatist attack and the uses the hierarchy made of it put the Puritans in something of a quandary. That Separation did grow out of the Puritan movement seemed almost undeniable, but the Puritans were nothing if not excellent casuists and could, if given half a chance, argue their way out of anything. They now set themselves to prove that Separation was none of their doing. Once again they followed the footsteps of their master at Geneva. When a church was hopelessly corrupt, as Rome was, then Calvin had proclaimed that we must separate from it, because there could be no Christian unity in it; but where the essentials of a true church existed, ministry and sacraments, then such a society could not be rejected, "although it may be chargeable with many faults." [2] He who withdrew himself from an essentially true church was "a traitor and apostate from religion." [3] From the very first Cartwright had affirmed that the Church of England was a "true church," [4] and therefore he wanted its formal unity preserved:

We make no separation from the Church; we go about to separate all those things that offend in the Church, to the end that we, being knit to the sincere truth of the Gospel, might afterwards in the same bond be more nearly and closely joined together.[5]

1. Burgess, *An answer rejoined*, pp. 235–236.
2. *Institutes*, bk. IV, chap. i, par. 12.
3. *Ibid.*, par. 10.   4. Whitgift, *Works*, I, 93.
5. *Ibid.*, p. 102; cf. Pearson, *Thomas Cartwright*, p. 441.

As long as Puritans were committed wholly to the ideal of uniformity, as long as the coöperation of magistrates was the *sine qua non* of their system, as long as their ambition was the ultimate domination of a national institution, they had to pass as loyal sons of the Church. They might pick flaws, but they could not admit it had accumulated more corruptions than could be put up with if necessary. For Puritans to have granted the Separatist argument would have been not only for them to prove themselves hypocrites in the eyes of the government, but to undermine the sway they were preparing to establish on their day of triumph. Clearly the Separatists would as readily depart from a Presbyterian establishment as from an episcopal: "The reasons before noted, which warrant our separation from England, are a sufficient ground to keep us from you." [1] As soon, therefore, as Browne's schism was known at Antwerp, Cartwright pronounced him in error and had his works condemned by the congregation.[2] Innumerable Puritan pamphleteers hastened to deny the basic Congregational tenet that only the chosen should be church members, insisting that a true church must necessarily be made up of both elect and reprobate. It might, said Dayrell, even be so "ouerspread with wicked, that the righteous can hardly bee discerned, no more then the wheate that lieth hid vnder the chaffe." [3] If Puritans ever had accounted the Established Church "meerly and absolutely Antichristian," then Cartwright could

---

1. Ainsworth, as quoted in Paget, *An Arrow against the Separation of the Brownists* (1618), p. 5.
2. Pearson, *op. cit.*, p. 212.
3. Dayrell, *A Treatise of the Church* (1617), p. 31.

"see not how yt could be avoyded but that we must with ye Brownistes confesse that we have noe church at all in ye Land." [1] But they never granted such an assumption. So determined, indeed, were the Puritans to down the suggestion that they in any way fomented Separation, that they actively sought out opportunities to defend the very institution they were maligning, or, as the Separatist *Confession* of 1596 put it, "to dawbe vp that ruinous antichristian muddy wall, which themselves did once craftily vndermine." [2] They appeared, therefore, at one and the same time as critics and protagonists, and deliberately championed whatever in the Church they could still feel capable of being defended. Even the reckless Martin Marprelate made that matter plain: "For Martin . . . you must understand, doth account no Brownist to be a Puritan." [3]

To modern ways of thinking there may be very little difference between those who called everything about the Church corrupt, and those who called the Church itself corrupt. And indeed there can be no doubt that the Puritans often overstepped the limits of mere passive dissent. [4] As Fuller said about the business, "It is impossible to make a subordination in their practices, who have an opposition in their principles." [5] Yet that was precisely what the Puritans were seeking to do for a half century after Robert Browne preached Separation. But the point is that whatever the facts, Puritans re-

1. Pearson, *op. cit.*, p. 310.   2. Walker, *op. cit.*, p. 54.
3. *The Marprelate Tracts* (ed. Pierce), p. 252.
4. Cf. Roland G. Usher, *The Presbyterian Movement in the Reign of Queen Elizabeth*, passim.
5. Fuller, *Church History*, bk. IX, sec. v, par. 2.

fused to face them. They were not publicly Separatists, they could still make a show of submission to authority, and that show, they held, was sufficient to attest their political orthodoxy. We may, if we like, think them sophists, but that should not blind us to the issue. By twisting their way between episcopacy and Separation, the Puritans preserved intact the principles of uniformity and of civil and ecclesiastical coöperation, the principles which had come down to them from the Middle Ages and which were unquestionably presupposed in all social thinking of the time. The Separatists actually, as we have just seen, no more infringed upon these principles in their theory than did any other group, and would, if they could have had their way, have made them prevail as relentlessly in practice. By their separation they intended only to break the rule for the time being, in order that it might eventually be enforced in the proper form. But this was a hazard the Puritans could not take. Not only was there practically no hope of conquering that way, but even if they had staged a successful ecclesiastical revolution, there was no reason the same tactics could not be employed against them at a later date. And so, when Puritans faced the impasse to which it seemed Charles's dismissal of Parliament had brought them, there still was one other tremendous resolution in their creed which at the moment made their dilemma even more insoluble. And that was that at no time had they ever been, or would they ever become, Separatists from the Church of England, nor could anyone, in justice or reason, derive Separation out of their principles.

IV

NON–SEPARATIST CONGREGATIONALISM

FOR what we may apologetically term pedagogical purposes, we have hitherto considered Puritanism as practically synonymous with Presbyterianism. Although we have admitted that this is a stringent restriction of the term, we have seen that it does not altogether violate the facts, for the core of the Puritan movement was undoubtedly constituted by that group who wished the ecclesiastical system of Geneva and Scotland to prevail in England. It is, of course, demonstrable that many, perhaps the greater number, of reputed Puritans entertained but vague conceptions of the discipline. Moreover, the first English sketches of Presbyterianism, those of Cartwright, Travers, and Udall, were of a somewhat Utopian character, and many of the disciples seem to have accepted them without possessing any too concise notions of detailed provisions. Those who encouraged the movement chiefly as a means of protest against Stuart absolutism were even less aware of specific plans. When Hyde asked Fiennes in the summer of 1641 what government he and his party wished to substitute for the hierarchy, Fiennes answered "that there would be time enough to think of that";[1] and when Sir Philip Warwick asked Cromwell the same question, he blurted out, "I can tell you, Sirs, what I

1. *Life of Edward Earl of Clarendon* (Oxford, 1827), 1, 90–91.

would *not* have, tho' I cannot, what I *would*." [1] Richard
Baxter affirms that before the year 1641 he had "never
thought what Presbytery or Independency was, nor
ever spoke with a man who seemed to know it"; [2] and all
dissenting schemes looked so much alike to the authorities that Laud inscribed an intercepted document de-
scribing the Congregationalism of Massachusetts,
"Great newes out of New England touching the presbyterial government as it seems established there." [3] As
long as the reform remained primarily a negative movement, as long as the suppressing activities of the government held discussion down, and as long as many
individuals became allied with the movement out of
antagonism to the Court, the "Puritan party" remained amorphous.

However, in combating Separatists the Presbyterian
advocates took some steps toward clarifying their proposal. Not only were they compelled to condemn the
act of separation, but they had as well to refute the Congregational interpretation of the Bible. They denied
the existence of scriptural warrant for discrimination in
the admission of church members, and emphasized explicitly the legal power of the classes and synods. But
in an age when men habitually made a fetish of the
literal application of Scripture, and assiduously racked
their consciences to find more and more rigorous methods of subjecting themselves to Christ, one who entered
the polemical lists to combat a radical interpretation of

1. Sir Philip Warwick, *Memoirs of the Reign of King Charles I* (London,
   1701), p. 177.
2. Hanbury, *Historical Memorials*, II, 69.
3. *Cal. St. Pap., Colonial*, I, 194.

the Bible always ran the risk of finding that very radicalism attractive. Precisely this had happened in the case of Francis Johnson, who, as a Puritan, undertook to refute Congregationalism, was overpowered by the proof Barrowe offered, and turned Separatist himself.[1] Since historical Biblical scholarship was practically non-existent, a man's personal reaction to the cryptic utterances of the Word was bound to be his ultimate criterion of what they signified.

Thus, though Separatism as an organized movement was fairly well dispersed, still the discipline it proposed was at least plausibly construed from the Bible. During the reign of James we suddenly encounter a small group of men who were to all intents and purposes Puritans, who were insistently anti-Separatists, but who had, nevertheless, quietly accepted the Separatists' discipline. The genesis of their opinion is unfortunately not to be traced in the present state of our knowledge, but Henry Jacob seems to offer an indication of what happened. He began as a regular Puritan, and was among the dissenting ministers who endeavored to demonstrate their loyalty to the Church by nagging Separatist prisoners in the Clink; his correspondence with Francis Johnson, published in 1599 as *A defence of the Churches and Ministry of England*, was one of the host of Puritan condemnations of the Separatist way. In 1603 he was a moving spirit in the *Millenary Petition*, which he advanced in the interests of Presbyterianism; but in the following year, in his *Reasons taken out of Gods Word*, he

1. William Bradford, "Dialogue," Alexander Young, *Chronicles of the Pilgrim Fathers*, pp. 424–425.

suddenly emerged as an advocate of a clearly Congregational reformation. How much of his conversion he owed to Johnson cannot be determined, but the fact remains that he was converted.[1] The development of other men in the group is even more mysterious than that of Jacob, but their published works indisputably reveal that whatever their starting points, they came ultimately to the same termination.

In addition to Jacob the school produced at least four conspicuous spokesmen. There was Robert Parker (died 1617), who fled from the spiritual courts to Holland in 1607 and was for a time associated with Jacob at Leyden. William Bradshaw (died 1618) published the fullest account of the group's tenets in a series of able anonymous pamphlets, which historians have strangely overlooked. He was the centre of an important group of ministers in the vicinity of Stephenhill, Derbyshire. Paul Baynes (died 1617) was the preacher of the school. He was lecturer at St. Andrews, Cambridge, but was deprived for nonconformity, and led thereafter a peripatetic existence as the guest of Puritan patrons all over England. Greatest of the lot undoubtedly was Dr. William Ames (died 1633), about whom the others seem to have revolved. He was a student and friend of Baynes, was in communication with Bradshaw, and was associated with Jacob and Parker at Leyden in 1610. He was, moreover, a man of international importance, adviser to the Calvinist party at the Synod of Dort, for ten years professor of theology at the University of

---

1. *Dictionary of National Biography*; Burrage, *Early English Dissenters*, I, 281–286; II, 292–293.

Franeker, and the author of several widely circulated theological tomes.

The writings of these men, although showing some minor divergences, reveal their agreement upon the two essential features of the Congregational polity, i.e., restriction of church membership to the proved elect and the autonomy of particular congregations. Jacob defined a church, in 1605, as "a particular Congregation being a spirituall perfect Corporation of Believers, & having power in it selfe immediately from Christ to administer all Religious meanes of faith to the members thereof." [1] It was, he later put it more happily, "an entire and Independent body-politic." [2] It could be formed only by "a free mutuall consent of Believers joyning & covenanting to live as Members of a holy Society togeather in all religious & vertuous duties as Christ & his Apostles did institute & practise in the Gospell." [3] After 1604 he constantly attacked Presbyterianism: "I affirme that No Synod vnder ye Gospell hath power by Gods ordinance to prescribe & rule Ecclesiastically sundry whole Churches if they consent not." [4] In 1610 he presented one of his many petitions to James, which monarch at once perceived the rift in the Puritan ranks, for where Jacob had declared against synods, James immediately wrote in the margin, "But in this, your Skottish brethren are endewed with a contraire light." [5] Brad-

1. *Ibid.*, II, 157.
2. "A Declaration and Plainer Opening" (1612), Hanbury, *Historical Memorials*, I, 231.
3. Burrage, *op. cit.*, II, 157.
4. *Ibid.*, p. 165.
5. John Waddington, *Congregational History*, II, 176.

shaw declared, "We confine and bound all Ecclesiastical power within the limits onely of one particular Congregation, holding that the greatest Ecclesiastical power ought not to stretch beyond the same." [1] A church should consist only of "true beleevers, joyning together according to the order of the Gospell," [2] and it could not be subjected "to any other Superiour Ecclesiasticall Jurisdiction, then unto that which is within it selfe"; over it "there is noe superior Pastor but onely Jesus Christ." If a church is in error, officers of other churches have no power to censure or punish it, "but are onely to counsell or advise the same." [3] Bradshaw was as much opposed to the Presbyterians as to the bishops: "Thou maist herein observe," he said in the preface to his most important work, *English Puritanisme*, "what a terrible Popedome & Primacie these rigid Presbyterians desire. And with what painted bugbeares and Scare Crowes the Prelates goe about to fright the State of the Kingdome." [4] Baynes preached Congregationalism up and down England; John Robinson attributed to one of his sermons his own realization that mixed congregations were unlawful.[5] Baynes's most important work, *The Diocesans Trial*, issued posthumously in 1621, was an attack upon all ecclesiastical superstructures. "We affirme that no such head Church was ordained either virtually or actually, but that all Churches were singu-

1. "Protestation of the King's supremacie" (1605), *Several treatises of worship and ceremonies* (1660), pp. 91–92.
2. *English Puritanisme* (ed. 1640), p. 6.
3. *Ibid.*, pp. 7, 11.
4. *Ibid.*, p. 2.
5. Robinson, "A Manvmission to a Manvdiction" (1615), *Mass. Hist. Soc., Coll.*, Series 4, I, 190.

lar congregations, equall, independent each of other, in regard of subjection." [1] For a congregation to be subject "to a Presbyterie, as not having power of governing themselves within themselves," was to his way of thinking as bad as for it to be subject to a bishop. [2] When Parker sojourned with Jacob at Leyden he professed "the use of Synods was for counsell and advice onely, but had not authority to give definite sentence in the judging of causes"; he later, however, proved apostate to the cause and joined himself with John Paget, an exiled Puritan then ministering in Amsterdam to an English Presbyterian church. For this defection of Parker's Paget says that "some of Mr. Iacobs minds were offended with him," [3] but he had already done his important work, and John Cotton cited him along with Baynes and Ames as a protagonist of Congregationalism. [4] William Ames gave Bradshaw's *English Puritanisme* an international circulation by translating it into Latin in 1610, and he rescued Baynes's *Diocesans Trial* from oblivion. Paget says he often complained to Ames that Bradshaw's title implied a grave injustice to the majority of English Puritans, who held nothing like the tenets the book set forth, but Ames put him off by saying it "did not affirme those to be the opinions of all, but onely of the *Rigidest sort of those that are called Puritanes.*" [5] He wrote the preface to Baynes's book, "main-

---

1. *The Diocesans Trial* (1621), p. 13.
2. *Ibid.*, p. 21.
3. Paget, *A Defence of Church Government* (1641), p. 105.
4. John Cotton, *The Way of the Congregational Churches Cleared* (1648), pt. II, p. 23.
5. Paget, *op. cit.*, pp. 106, 200.

taining the divine constitution of a particular Church, in one Congregation," [1] and subtly disseminated the doctrine in his great works, his *Medulla Theologiae* and his *De Conscientia*.

It will be noticed that the principles of this school found their fullest expression in Holland. In England, where all Puritan energies were directed against the common foe, the hierarchy, differences between the two wings of the party did not become prominent; but when exiled Puritans gained an opportunity to attempt a positive reformation in the Low Countries, their divergences became apparent, and their verbal controversies of this date anticipate the historic rift of the Presbyterians and Independents in the 1640's. John Paget took up the defense of the Presbyterian cause, and what light early Congregationalists do not throw upon the cleavage themselves can be supplemented by his descriptions. He defined the polity of Jacob and Ames accurately as one "whereby Particular Congregations are made to be Independent, not standing under any other ecclesiastical authority out of themselves." [2] He had the acumen to see that this polity was essentially the same as that of the Separatists.[3] So conspicuous had become the split between the two factions of English Puritan exiles that when a friend of Ames, John Forbes, petitioned the Dutch Synod to permit the erection of an independent English classis, the Dutch officials refused because, they said, too many of the

1. *The Diocesans Trial*, sig. B1 recto.
2. Paget, "Answer to an unjust complaint" (1635), Hanbury, *Historical Memorials*, 1, 527.
3. Paget, *A Defence of Church Government* (1641), p. 30.

English ministers were either Brownists or "Brownistically affected in particular opinions," because they

condemne the Decisive & Iudging power of all Classes & Synods; & that they have only a power of Counsailing & advising, because every particular Congregation is a church; and that a Compleat church, and that it is Immediately given vnto every congregation from Christ to be a single & vncompounded policy.

These, the Synod declared, "are the very words of Mr. Iacob, & Parker, & Baines." [1]

There can be little doubt that these men were Congregationalists. But there can also be no doubt that though their discipline was the same as that of the Separatists, and though they were just as much opposed to Presbyterianism, they were not themselves Separatists. They would admit being the "rigidest sort of Puritans," but nothing more. Jacob, recognizing the similarity of his program with the polity of Separatists, could say that he did not regard them as "being so evil as commonly they are held to be," but as for himself, "I never was, nor am, separated from all public communion with the congregations of England." [2] "The Lord knoweth there is none in England more unwilling to runne vpon this rocke then I." [3] Even when in 1616 he set up a Congregational church in Southwark, the group protested that they "never intended separation from the Church of England." [4] At no time, Cotton says, was Parker "one of those whom you call Brown-

1. Burrage, *op. cit.*, II, 271; *Cal. St. Pap.*, *Domestic*, 1635, vol. CCLXXXVI. No. 94.
2. "A declaration and plainer opening" (1612), Hanbury, *op. cit.*, I, 230.
3. *Reasons taken out of God's Word*, p. 50.
4. Burrage, *op. cit.*, I, 172.

ists, or such like Separatists, but wrote against them." [1]
Ames consistently condemned the Separation in his
larger works, and he boasted to the bishops with, as we
shall see, some show of reason that he and his friends
had "soundly confuted" the Brownists. [2] In fact, one
of the greatest testimonies to the position of the school
was the influence it exerted upon John Robinson. In
1610, when Parker, Ames, and Jacob were in Leyden,
they conferred long and laboriously with the Pilgrim
pastor, [3] and they so much convinced him of the superior
wisdom of their Non-separating position that he did all
in his power to retrace his steps in their direction. Since
he had so vigorously spoken for the way of "rigid Separation" he could not entirely renounce it, but he did
come "more than halfe way of any just distance" [4] by
conceding that the Church of England possessed some
marks of a true church, and that therefore persons might
be saved though they remained in it, and that Separatists might lawfully hear its ministers. "I did," he
says, "through my vehement desire of peace, and weakness withal, remit and lose my former resolution: and
did, to speak as the truth is, forget some of my former
grounds." [5] Paget, ever on the lookout for Congregational inconsistencies, claimed at once that when Robinson made these concessions he lost his whole case; how,
he asked, could Robinson admit persons to his congregation without requiring them first to renounce their

1. Cotton, *The Way of the Congregational Churches Cleared*, pt. II, p. 12.
2. *A Reply to Dr. Morton's Generall Defence* (1622), p. 31.
3. William Bradford, "Dialogue," Alexander Young, *Chronicles of the Pilgrim Fathers*, p. 439; Cotton Mather, *Magnalia*, bk. I, chap. ii, par. 1.
4. Cotton, *op. cit.*, pt. I, pp. 7–8.   5. Robinson, *Works*, III, 103.

allegiance to the Church of England, "seeing that by your reasoning they are tyed in the cords of sin?" [1] The Separatists could not, however, come all the way back, but they saw the advantage of the less rigorous position and availed themselves of it as far as they could. When the congregation wished official permission for their migration to America they loyally protested that, as they held the doctrine of the Church was sound, they therefore could willingly acknowledge that "saving fayth" was begotten "in thousands in ye land (conformists & reformistes) as ye ar called," with both of whom they desired to maintain spiritual communion "as with our bretheren." [2]

When men in good Queen Bess's day had become convinced God wished them to be Congregationalists, in their straightforward fashion they could see no way to avoid separating from the Church of England. Yet here we are confronted with a group of Congregationalists, men skilled in the logic of the schools, who believed quite as sincerely in the same divinely appointed polity, and who yet refused to make the fatal deduction of Separation. We can easily appreciate their motive, for events had proved that in the way of Separation political madness lay. And yet by all the laws of logic, did not Congregationalism make Separation imperative, and was not such a furtive institution as Jacob's Southwark church a schismatical enterprise? How could these men justify the glaring inconsistencies of their position?

1. Paget, *An Arrow against the Separation of the Brownists* (1618), pp. 13, 31, 62.
2. Walker, *Creeds and Platforms*, p. 89; cf. Bradford, *Dialogue*, p. 457.

By the exercise of a superlative genius for casuistry, the school did make out a case, it did find ways to reconcile irreconcilables. Its solution may seem to us utterly fantastic, we may with difficulty believe that any men, much less sincerely religious men, ever told so thin a story and then so doggedly stuck to it; but to understand the operations of their minds we must realize what they conceived was at stake, what tremendous urgencies drove them to such desperate shifts. Separatists had flown in the face of the deepest political conviction of the sixteenth century, a conviction that was fortified not only by the prevailing philosophy of social cohesion and subordination, but by centuries of experience. They not merely attacked certain vested interests, but by rending the seamless garment of the Church they opened up a whole prospect of social demoralization. When, therefore, the "Jacobites," as Paget called them, confronted the problem of reformation, they were completely pervaded by the Puritan determination to keep themselves clear of Separation at all costs. Though they might strain their metaphysics to the breaking point, they were compelled by hook or by crook to reconcile their Congregational dissent with the inviolable preservation of the principle of uniformity. Their plea might be a cobweb of sophistry, their conduct might amount to virtual schism, but that did not matter if by their own rationalizations they could write for themselves a clean bill of political health.

The Separatist argument had been phrased in this fashion: a church could not be a true church wherein the elect communicated with the reprobate; in the Church of England the elect did so communicate; ergo, the Church of England was a false church. The Non-separating Congregationalists necessarily began with the same assumption; the only way, then, in which they could break the chain of this syllogism was by denying the minor premise, by asserting that the Church of England was a true one, or, to speak more accurately, by asserting that the churches of England were true churches. Manifestly they did not seem so, but Presbyterians had already hinted at a way in which the assertion might be risked, with their ingenious distinction between a true "substance" and a number of false but not mortal "accidents." Still, it had been a comparatively easy matter for Cartwright and the Presbyterians to read their plan into the Church of England, for they called at the utmost for a mere remodeling of the existing structure, and they confidently expected to rebuild upon the same foundations. But when Ames and Bradshaw set about to prove to an unsuspecting nation that the "substance" of the established parishes was, *au fond*, Congregational, they had very considerably to extend the list of "accidents." They had to condemn not only ceremonies and ritual, but the very idea of a centralized government and at least two thirds of the church membership. These items they did not intend to remodel but to dispense with entirely. They had to have the effrontery to allege that by these extensive nullifications they would be touching nothing vital, but only stripping superficial encumbrances from the true churches, that somehow, unbeknownst to the bishops and the government, a number of "saints" in each parish of the realm had for ages been unconsciously functioning in an essentially Congregational manner. It takes, to say the least, a large audacity to pretend when you are amputating limbs that you are only removing warts and moles, but these ecclesiastical surgeons were in all seriousness making precisely such an asseveration.

The Separatists, they said, had made a mistake, not in their conception of polity, but in their rash conclusion that the churches in England varied from the true pattern so far that it could no longer be discerned within them. The parish assemblies might be decayed, but they were not beyond repair. If one tried, he could still discover the kernel of truth in the husks of corruption. True, the laws did maintain many corrupt practices, "yet so long as we doe not actually communicate in those corruptions, but onely in the true parts of Gods worship, our communicating is never the worse for the said Laws of men." [1] At this point a puzzled John Robinson rose to object: were not all people in England forced to attend Communion, and was not a set form of prayer then used, and were not these things simply unlawful? Indeed, Ames blandly returned, they were, but they were matters which could be disregarded, "seeing there are many exercises of religion, wherein none are present by constraint, and where the service book doeth not so much as appeare." [2] As long as the Church of England left a remote possibility for the occasional existence of these voluntary services, it was paying tribute to the substratum of Congregationalism in its make-up,

1. William Bradshaw, *The Unreasonableness of the separation* (1640), p. 107.
2. Ames, *A Manuduction for Mr. Robinson* (1614), sig. Q4 recto.

and to that extent remained a true church. We should labor while we were in it to make its membership pure, but from a fundamentally true church "in which some wicked men are tollerated, we must not presently separate." [1]

But, the Separatist persisted, you teach that churches should properly be founded upon a covenant; have the parish assemblies sworn to any? No, they had not done so formally and publicly, but that did not hinder their having done practically the same thing. Whenever "good Christians" assembled to worship God, and did so voluntarily, were they not moved by a visible desire to serve Christ in Christian fellowship? So, then, they could be said to have "the essentiall & integrall forme of a visible church . . . howsoever they are defective in the puritie of their combination, & in the complete free exercising of their power." [2] They may never have expressly ratified a covenant, but in some rare spiritual sense it had to be predicated:

There wants not that reall and substantiall comming together, (or agreeing in Covenant, though more implicate then were meete) and that substantiall profession of Faith, which (thanks be to God) hath preserved the essence of visible Churches in *England* unto this day.[3]

If the good Christians of a parish came to service voluntarily, they could then disregard the unregenerate who were constrained to be present, and assume that they alone were assembling to covenant with God. By the

1. Ames, *Conscience*, p. 62.
2. Ames, *A Second Manvdiction for Mr. Robinson* (1615), p. 34.
3. Robert Parker, quoted in Richard Mather, *An Apologie of the Chvrches in New England* (1643), p. 36.

difference of their motive they became as much separated from the unregenerate "as is of absolute necessitie
to the being of a true church." [1] Separation from such a
congregation was, therefore, an inconsiderate and schismatical act.

The prize bit of circumlocution in this reasoning was
evoked by the question of the ministry. In Congregational theory pastors ought to be chosen by the people;
in Anglican practice they were nominated by a patron
and installed by a bishop. Could these two principles be
reconciled, so that pastors might be Congregationalists
and still retain their offices? Nothing, it seemed, was
simpler. If an Anglican clergyman based his calling
upon an episcopal ordination, believing he had acquired
the indelible character of a minister quite apart from his
belonging to a particular flock, he was doing something
"unlawful and sinful." [2] But in actuality, once a man
was ordained he was assigned to a particular parish.
What, pray tell, was then to hinder the godly of the
parish from accepting him as their pastor and considering their acceptance as the "substance" of his calling?
The other business could be regarded as negligible
abracadabra. A patron's nomination could not create a
valid summons, "yet the after consent of the people, by
acceptance and submission, may make it good"; [3] a
man could not become pastor of a parish because a
bishop invested him, but he could because "a believing
Congregation . . . consenteth to have him." [4]

1. Ames, *op. cit.*, p. 31.
2. Jacob, *A Confession and Protestation* (1616), p. 20.
3. John Davenport, *An Apologeticall Reply* (1636), p. 46.
4. Jacob, *op. cit.*, p. 19.

The true ratification and warrant of our Ministers calling which is by Gods word, standeth in this, & only in this, that our Visible Churches do consent and accept them whom they receave for such. . . . And this their consent, I acknowledge, giveth them (before God) their Ministry, though conioyned with many, great, & publique corruptions otherwayes.[1]

The candidate could go through the rite of ordination by the bishop with mental reservations; he need not thereby "implie an acknowledgement of his lawfull authoritie from whome it is sought." [2] As long as it remained possible for a divine to pick his diffident way through the morass of Anglican corruptions, and with the aid of a few pardonable pretences to hold himself comparatively uncontaminated by them, he could continue to be in reality a Congregational pastor, however externally he appeared to be a priest in the Establishment. Therefore his parishioners should not separate from him.

When Ames labored to make this abstruse point clear to John Robinson, the latter not unnaturally remonstrated that such an attractive "plot of ministry" was framed in Ames's study, and that as a matter of sober fact the Church of England allowed "no such calling as is chiefly grounded upon the people's choice; but only that which is grounded upon the bishop's ordination." [3] "But what the Church of England alloweth," Ames retorted, "maketh nothing to the question." If by any stretch of imagination it could be conceived that a minister *might* attribute his real calling to the congre-

1. Jacob, *Reasons taken out of Gods Word*, p. 50.
2. Bradshaw, *op. cit.*, p. 88.
3. Robinson, "A Manvmission to a Manvdiction," *Mass. Hist. Soc., Coll.*, Series 4, I, 170, 173.

gation, then the Church of England had not waxed utterly corrupt. "For a minister to lay the chief ground of his calling upon the peoples choice, so that he haue withall those formallities required, I knowe no law in England that doeth forbid or disallow it." [1] Suppose, Ames asked, a man should procure a license from a bishop and a patron, yet should assume his charge professedly upon the people's choice; suppose, indeed, that in order to get his license he had to perform some things which he knew were not lawful, yet suppose that all the while he continued to hold his faith "in the maine things of the ghospell"; might not, under these circumstances, "some faults of his entrance bee circumstantiall personal actions by which his calling is not abolished?" [2] The people would not receive him as "a branch of the prelacie . . . but on other & better groundes"; [3] conscious of these nice distinctions, they would communicate with him without sharing in the corrupt aspect of his office. Thus it followed, as the night the day, that the ministers of England, though ordained by the prelates, were none the less ministers of Christ in the full Congregational sense — if they chose to consider themselves so. "We utterly deny," Ames proclaimed, "that the calling of our ministers doth essentially depend upon the bishops calling." [4] For that reason he could maintain consistently that "though the prelacie were plucked vp by the rootes, yet the parochial ministerie might stand still, in all the substantiall parts of it." [5]

1. Ames, *op. cit.*, p. 10.
2. Ames, *A Manvdiction*, sig. Q1 verso, Q2 recto.   3. *Ibid.*, sig. Q2 recto.
4. *A Fresh Suit Against Human Ceremonies* (1633), pt. II, p. 207.
5. *A Manvdiction*, sig. Q3 recto.

For the time being, however, the prelacy was not plucked up, and at first sight it might seem impossible to declare that any system in which they existed was in reality a Congregational one. But Ames and Bradshaw were quite prepared to dispose of that objection. The prelacy was not at all an integral part of the real English church system. It was the result of an unfortunate combination of two offices, and it needed only to be resolved into separate incarnations for the whole problem to disappear. In a political respect the prelates were "generall visitors and overseers of Churches," appointed by the magistrate; they were "commissioners under the King to see that the Pastors doe their duties," [1] and such officers were entirely legitimate. But it so chanced that the men who were given this civil jurisdiction were at the same time ministers; originally bishops had been simple pastors upon whom the King had called to serve as his "commissioners"; they had used the power thus wrongfully acquired to usurp authority over other churches and to perpetuate the hierarchy. "In substance," nevertheless, they remained ministers of particular churches. It was now simply necessary for them to surrender their civil power to the proper civil authorities and they would all, bishops and archbishops, revert to a parity with all other ministers. "It is possible for them notwithstanding to be members in theire estate, of a true visible Church, and be bound . . . to one particular congregation, for the speciall ministry and government thereof." [2] They

1. Bradshaw, *op. cit.*, pp. 77, 49.
2. Ames, *A Second Manvdiction*, p. 22.

were pastoral stars which had wandered from their orbits, and they only needed to be restored to their pristine courses for order to reign once more in the ecclesiastical universe. Ames was sure that the largest part of the "faithfull congregations of England" would willingly be rid of the bishops,[1] thus attesting that they were stirred by obscure recollections of their pristine Congregationalism, that they were not "spirituall parts of a diocesan spiritual church . . . though civilly combined into a diocesan government."[2] They were, once again, true churches in substance and were not to be separated from.

Puritan Congregationalists put themselves through the labyrinthine process of this reasoning in the fond hope that even while demonstrating their loyalty to the scriptural discipline, they might salvage their allegiance to the principle of compulsory uniformity, that they would, in fact, conclusively prove the discipline and the principle to be indissolubly knit together. Thanks to their deft strategems they were always prepared to protest that they were not Separatists, even at the very moments when they were erecting independent churches in England or gathering them on foreign shores. They were trying to show that men who wished simply to realize potentialities already inherent in the Church were far different from men who wished to destroy it and begin anew. Those who never questioned that they should be coerced into conformity, even when a temporarily misguided monarch was coercing them in the wrong

1. *Ibid.*, p. 90.
2. *Ibid.*, p. 90.

direction, might reasonably be considered loyal Englishmen. They subjected themselves to their governors "to doe to vs whatsoeuer they please," and if they refused subscription to some ceremonies there was "neither contempt nor scandall" in their refusal.[1] They denied that any *ecclesiastical* authority had a right to expel ministers from particular churches; but just so soon as the King himself authorized the expulsion, though it remained intrinsically an unjust act, still, as it was the act of a *magistrate*, they did not rebel. They were, indeed, obliged to withhold their subscription, but they willingly undertook to suffer consequences. Though they refused, they were therein "neither Schismaticks, Seditious persons, enemyes to the Kings Supremacie, nor any way undutiful to King or State."[2] The peculiar twist of their philosophy enabled them to look upon these depravations with equanimity, even while they continued to declare that the act had not affected the essential character of the true churches. An English congregation might rest assured that though a magistrate took away their minister, "unjustly, & against the will of the Church . . . yet doth not the Church in that regard cease to be a church." God commands the church in such a case to obey. If the magistrate had "matter against us (whither just or unjust it skilleth not)," and forbade us to continue in our pastoral offices, "I see not by what warrant in Gods word we should thinke ourselves bound notwithstand-

1. Parker, *A Scholasticall Discovrse Against Symbolizing with Antichrist* (1607), pt. II, p. 33.
2. Jacob, *A Christian and Modest offer*, p. 3.

ing to exercise our ministry still." Nor had the church, however much she loved her pastor, any right

> to deprive her selfe of the protection of the Magistrate, by leaving her publick standing, to follow her ministery in private and the dark; refusing the benefit of all other publick ministerie, which with the leave and liking of the Magistrate, he may enjoy.[1]

Although the churches of England might suffer by the rough dealing of the monarch, yet like the true churches they were, they suffered in silence and humility, knowing that unless he led them back into Popery he could not undermine their essential constitution, and that however inconsiderate or even tyrannical he might seem to be, he was still the ordinance of God.

So, after this long excursion into dialectics, the Non-separating Congregationalists could safely reiterate the conventional political philosophy as their profound conviction. The magistrate's power to them was, of course, "the greatest of humane powers," "the institution of God." [2] Subjects owed the traditional obedience to their rulers, should submit to them and pray for them even when they were tyrannical or heathen.[3] Though a civil office was abused, "yet that doeth not make all subjection to it vnlawfull," [4] because "contempt of authority, and the offence thereby given to others, is by itselfe a sinne against the Law of God." [5] An excommunicated monarch retained all his civil powers unimpaired.[6] And since the churches of England were, after

1. Bradshaw, *The Unreasonableness of the separation*, pp. 90–91.
2. Ames, *Conscience*, bk. v, p. 164.   3. *Ibid.*, bk. v, p. 166.
4. Ames, *A Manuduction*, sig. Q3 recto.
5. Ames, *Conscience*, bk. I, p. 167.
6. Bradshaw, *English Puritanisme*, p. 24.

all, true churches, they were "such as the Princes of the earth are bound by God's Laws to maintaine and protect by their autority." [1] Bradshaw explicitly asserted that the supremacy granted by statute to Queen Elizabeth was "due in full and ample manner (without any limitation or qualification) to the King." [2] Whatever he perceived in the churches contrary to the Word of God, he, upon his own initiative, ought "to procure and force the redress thereof, yea, though it be without the consent and against the will of the Ecclesiastical Governers themselves." [3] The forcible suppression of heresy was his most sacred duty:

If therefore Heretikes be manifestly knowne and publikely hurtfull, they are to be restrained of the Magistrate by publike power. And if they be manifestly blasphemous, and pertenacious, and stubborne in those blasphemies, may suffer capitall punishment.[4]

Finally, the protagonists of the polity rehearsed the usual Puritan arguments that they meant no threat to society. Congregationalism, they pleaded, would not level the classes, or obstruct the monarchy, "which they acknowledge to be the best kind of civill Government for this Kingdome." [5] Jacob even promised that the Church rule for which he was soliciting would prove more compatible with the King's imperial sceptre than that of the prelates,[6] and he predicted it would settle "more vnitie and peace in truth a hundred times."

1. Bradshaw, *The Unreasonableness of the separation*, p. 31.
2. Bradshaw, "A protestation of the king's supremacie" (1605), *Several treatises* (1660), p. 87.
3. *Ibid.*, p. 88.
4. Ames, *Conscience*, bk. IV, p. 12.
5. *English Puritanisme*, p. 10.
6. Jacob, *To the right High and mightie Prince, Iames*, p. 8.

If only "our Magistrates would shew vs their favor and aide (which our adversaries enioy) this that I say would quickly & universally bee evident." [1]

The rub, the constantly more galling rub, was that the adversaries did enjoy "favor and aide." The King failed utterly to see the point of Congregationalism's ingenious schemes. When Jacob's petition of 1610 informed James that in his royal person was vested the power of overseeing churches, James commented on the margin, "Quhy, then, do ye not obey the Kinges lawes that are already maide, quhome ye grawnte to be your supreme magistrate?" [2] The elaborate casuistry of Non-separation convinced no one; though Robinson yielded some ground to Ames's persuasion, he still recognized that much of the latter's *Manvdiction* was an "exercise of wit." [3] A subtle distinction between the Church's "substance" and "accidents" had little meaning to the churchmen: "it cannot bee shewed," pronounced Burgess, "because it is a *non ens*, a fiction. . . . The New-nothing of all the faithful Congregations collectiuely considered, is but a meere mistie and inexplicable speech made for a covert." [4] The gulf between the prelates and the Puritans could not be bridged by split hairs; the opposition was too irreconcilable, such a one "as there is betwixt the light which commeth down from heaven, & that thick mist which ariseth from the

---

1. Jacob, *An Attestation of many Learned, Godly and famous Divines* (1613), p. 177.
2. Waddington, *Congregational History*, II, 175.
3. "A Manvmission to a Manvdiction," *Mass. Hist. Soc., Coll.*, Series 4, I, 192.
4. *An answer rejoined*, Preface, p. 61.

lowest pit." [1] Accumulated suffering no more convinced this brand of dissenters than it did the others that there might be a flaw in their program: "the more they haue sustayned for it, the more (by the mercy of God) they see the glorious evidence of it." [2] In spite of their extravagant adherence to the royal supremacy, the Congregationalists were preaching that the King was limited by the Word of God, by that which contained "all parts of the true Religion, both for Substance and Ceremony, and a perfect direction in all Ecclesiastical matters whatsoever." [3] But the King and the Church had already decided otherwise, and they were growing only more determined that Puritans should buckle under. All reformers were being forced to make increasingly clear choices between God and man. Congregationalists and Presbyterians could preach interminably that no reform should be sought but at the hands of the magistrate, yet when the magistrate obviously failed them, the best instructions they could give their flocks were that "every man is to look to himself, that he communicate not with the evils of the times, induring what it shall please the State to inflict." [4] But even seventeenth century Puritans could not continue indefinitely to labor and suffer in vain. They kept hovering closer to the brink of rebellion, and Jacob ominously warned that if the prelates persisted in imposing the tenets of Arminianism, "& shall vrge them so hotely as they begin; both the Ministers &

1. Ames, Preface to *The Diocesans Trial*, sig. A3 verso.
2. Jacob, *A Christian and Modest offer*, p. 8.
3. Bradshaw, "A protestation of the king's supremacy," p. 90.
4. *Ibid.*, p. 94.

many of the people wilbe forced to leaue their ordinary standing in these Churches." [1]

As the Puritan predicament became more difficult and more hopeless, the Separatists seemed to see events proving their course wiser in the long run. They energetically renewed their cry that Separation had grown out of Puritan teaching, and they found in the crazy structure of Puritan Congregationalism an excellent case in point. Canne, in his able *Necessity of Separation*, quoted Bradshaw and Ames at length, and showed with smashing effectiveness that their polity unmistakably pointed to an ultimate schism. "I am sorry they laid such a snare, whereby to undo themselves." [2] Burgess told Ames, "Your Master Bradshawes very Arguments against conformitie are pretended by the Separatists, as grounds for their separation"; they themselves prove "their pedigree from you: and no man can deny it, who hath any forehead left." [3] Cotton tells us that in the reign of Charles Separatists were more favored by the authorities than Puritans,[4] and Roger Williams explains that we are not to marvel thereat: "It is a principle in nature to preferre a professed enemy, before a pretended friend." The bishops knew that the Separatists were enemies, and also that they were comparatively harmless,

whereas the Puritans profest subjection, and have submitted to the Bishops. . . . And yet (as the Bishops have well knowne) with no

1. Jacob, *op. cit.*, p. 39.
2. Canne, *A Necessity of Separation*, p. 67; cf. pp. 131, 242.
3. John Burgess, *An answer rejoined*, p. 236.
4. Cotton, "Letter to Roger Williams" (1643), *Publications of the Narragansett Club*, I, 309.

greater affection, then the Israelites bare their Egyptian cruel Task-masters.[1]

Along with all other Puritans the Congregationalists had identified themselves with the Parliamentary cause. With the dissolution of 1629 their last hope was gone, and they faced a situation which for them was even more intolerable than for other Puritans. Presbyterians might be able to afford to wait, but every moment was forcing the Congregationalists into Separation. "Was it not," remembered Thomas Shepard of Cambridge in Massachusetts,

was it not a time when humane Worship and inventions were growne to such an intolerable height, that the consciences of Gods saints and servants . . . could no longer bear them? was not the power of the tyrannicall Prelates so great, that like a strong Current carried all down streame before it? . . . Did not the hearts of men generally faile them?[2]

Must we have stayed in England, he asked, and studied "some distinctions to salve our Consciences in comply-ing with so manifold corruptions of Gods worship?" Adroit as the Congregational Non-separating subter-fuge had been, it could not be maintained for ever. And if it could not, what was the alternative? "Should wee forsake the publique Assemblies, and joyne together in private separated churches?" No, that would have been suicide: "how unsufferable it would then have been, the great offence that now is taken at it, is a full evidence."[3]

1. Roger Williams, "Mr. Cotton's Letter Lately Printed" (1644), *Publica-tions of the Narragansett Club*, 1, 382.
2. Thomas Shepard and John Allin, *A Defence of the Answer* (1648), p. 3.
3. *Ibid.*, p. 4.

It was, then, at this opportune hour, when all the tried intents had seemed to fail, that still another solution loomed over the troubled horizon. If a body of Puritans could be carried into a virgin wilderness, and be carried legally, so that the government they set up there might claim legitimate descent from the Crown, then the civil strife of the spiritual and political loyalties could be reconciled. In a new state erected in accordance with Puritan ideals, the refractory magistrate could be brought into line. At the same time, because those who emigrated would come from that section of Puritanism which had never separated, they could call any church they established part of the Church of England, and therefore, by grace of magistrates of their own creating, could enforce complete obedience to it. They could, in other words, figuratively but effectively transport both the English State and Church to Massachusetts and there reform them at will. Massachusetts would be a piece of England such as all England ought to be. Could God have expected us, Shepard once more queried, to remain helpless in England, futilely protesting and only finding a "way to have filled the Prisons . . . when a wide doore was set open of liberty otherwise?" [1] Through a remarkable concatenation of historical events, at that very moment a door of liberty

1. *Ibid.*, p. 4. The reasoning behind the great migration, which we have to reconstruct from such stray passages as we can cull from later works, can be supplemented by the thinking of the Pilgrim migration some ten years earlier. As we have seen, the Separatist problem, from the Separatist standpoint, was practically the same as the Puritan: it was an attempt to hitch the divine discipline and the civil maintenance of orthodoxy to the same cart. The removal to Holland did not solve the question, and Robinson's congregation undertook the voyage to America to work out a more perfect answer.

was indeed thrown open to those who were able to walk through it, and by the unwitting hand, ironically enough, of no less a person than King Charles himself.

Before they left, Robinson made them a speech, in which the central problem of seventeenth century dissent appears explicitly:

"Whereas you are to become a body politik, using amongst your selues ciuill government . . . let your wisdome and godlinesse appeare . . . in yeelding vnto them [magistrates] all due honour and obedience in their lawfull administrations; not beholding in them the ordinarinesse of their person, but God's ordinance for your good; nor being like vnto the foolish multitude, who more honour the gay coate, then either the virtuous mind of the man, or the glorious ordinance of God.

"But you know better things, and the image of the Lords power and authoritie which the Magistrate beareth, is honorable, in how meane persons soeuer. And this dutie you both may the more willingly, and ought the more conscionably to performe, because you are at least for the present to haue onely them for your ordinary gouernours, which your selues shall make choice of for that worke." — *Mourt's Relation*, 1622 (ed. Henry Martyn Dexter, 1865), p. xlvi.

The whole key to the Puritan and Separatist migrations is imbedded in this passage. In order that they might continue to behold in magistrates the ordinance of God, they had to escape from those who refused to live up to the part and to choose for themselves some that would. And above all the principle that the magistrate *was* the ordinance of God had to be preserved.

V

A WIDE DOOR OF LIBERTY

THE origins of the Massachusetts Bay Company are to be sought, as all histories assure us, in the Dorchester Adventurers, an organization founded in the year 1623, chiefly through the labors of John White, rector of Trinity Church at Dorchester in Wessex. The avowed purpose of this association was the maintenance of a permanent base for the fishing industry along the coast of New England. By 1627 the enterprise had practically failed and would altogether have collapsed had not, so the story goes, the patriarch of Dorchester persuaded Roger Conant and a few trusting souls to carry on the plantation at Cape Anne until he and those adventurers who "still continued their desire to set forwards the Plantation of a *Colony* there"[1] could rout out reinforcements. The West Country having contributed lavishly and lost, White sought further support in the one place where investors abounded; conferring, as he puts it, "casually with some *Gentlemen* of *London*,"[2] he aroused so much interest in the scheme that "it grew to be more vulgar," and a number of merchants appeared ready to take a chance on it.[3] By the influence of these Londoners and the compliance of certain prominent (and

1. John White, *The Planters Plea* (1630), p. 75.
2. *Ibid.*   3. *Ibid.*, pp. 75–76.

Puritanical) gentlemen, who lent "the names of honest and religious men" to the affair,[1] a patent was secured from the Council of New England transforming the old Dorchester Company into "the Governor and Deputy of the New England Company for a Plantation in Mattachusetts Bay." [2] John Endecott was sent by this organization to take over the plantation which Conant had been nursing along. Endecott returned optimistic reports, which were the cause of "more *Aduenturers* joyning with the first *Vndertakers*," [3] wherefore he learned in a letter of the next February that the Company was "much inlarged sence yor departure out of England." [4] The affair was now, White says, being agitated "in sundry parts of the *Kingdome*," and not only other Londoners became interested, but a number of wealthy men from the Eastern counties.[5] Some of these had come in before [6] the New England Company was itself transformed into the Massachusetts Bay Company by a royal charter issued on March 4; others invested afterwards, until by the summer of 1629 the London and East Coast additions entirely outvoted the few remaining Western shareholders.

It is impossible to say with certainty that before the month of July, when Governor Craddock made his motion for transporting the charter, any recruits to the

1. "Records of the Council for New England" (ed. Charles Deane), *Proceedings of the American Antiquarian Society*, April, 1867, p. 76.
2. *Records of the Governor and Company of Massachusetts Bay* (ed. W. B. Shurtleff), I, 397 (mentioned hereafter as *Massachusetts Records*).
3. *The Planters Plea*, p. 76.
4. *Massachusetts Records*, I, 383.
5. *The Planters Plea*, p. 77.
6. *Massachusetts Records*, I, 28.

Company deliberately intended to use it as a bridge to America, but it seems probable the Easterners expected great things of it. Thomas Dudley, in his letter of 1631, wrote that "about the year 1627" a number of friends in Lincolnshire "fell into discourse about New England, and the planting of the Gospel there"; after communicating, he declared, with other friends in London and the West, "we" procured a patent in 1629 and sent out Endecott.[1] Obviously Dudley's memory was playing him false in this statement, for Endecott had been sent out before the East Anglia element had joined; but the fact that he took unto his own faction the credit for having conceived of "the planting of the Gospel" in New England indicates that early in the Easterners' association they had become ready to direct the Company toward something more than a purely commercial end. At any rate it was certainly by the timely support of the newcomers, Easterners like Winthrop, Dudley, Pynchon, Johnson, and one or two Londoners, Saltonstall and Increase Nowell, that Craddock's motion was carried and the great migration precipitated.

Thus, though there are a host of baffling mysteries in the triple transformation of the Dorchester Adventurers, one fact at least seems clear: when John White sought capital in London and the East, he got more than he bargained for. White was a Puritan of the Presbyterian variety, and his original supporters had been of the same stripe.[2] A subsidiary incentive to their underwriting the venture had undoubtedly been a desire to have

1. Young, Chronicles of Massachusetts, p. 309.
2. Frances Rose-Troup, John White, p. 103.

the Gospel preached in America, and White had specifically argued that a plantation would offer, among other
things, employment for one or two Puritan ministers.
But it is altogether improbable that he ever dreamed of
founding a great Puritan refuge; in 1635 he himself deposed that the purpose of the Dorchester Adventurers
had been simply to fish and to trade with the Indians.[1]
Even if he had entertained notions of a Biblical commonwealth, since he was a Presbyterian and remained
conspicuously so to the end of his life, the last thing he
would ever have desired to behold in New England, next
to an episcopal hierarchy, was a Congregational state.
Although he kept up his connection with the enterprise,
it is evident that after the reins had been seized by the
bumptious Easterners the Company's ecclesiastical
complexion was radically transformed. Thereafter the
ministers whom it attracted were, almost to a man,
either confirmed Congregationalists or on the highroad
to becoming so. In fact, I think it may safely be held
that the New England divines constituted a sort of
second generation to the Ames-Bradshaw group, that
they lisped their elementary notions of church polity at
the feet of those masters, and that they went to Massachusetts fully prepared to realize there the teachings of
Non-separating Congregationalism.

This thesis, which has hitherto received no recogni-
tion from the historians of New England, is more than
confirmed by certain events in Holland in the years 1628
to 1635. Several of the important members of the group,
unwilling to accept exile in the wilderness except as a

1. *Mass. Hist. Soc., Proc.*, XLIII, 494.

last resource, attempted at first to find a refuge in the Low Countries, in the hope that they could remain close at hand until circumstances in England should become more favorable. Burroughs, Nye, Goodwin, and the others of the famous five Independent members of the later Westminster Assembly did succeed in eking out their existence in Holland until the Long Parliament met; but the other men failed, and only then turned in despair to New England. The reasons for their failure have never been made clear, yet it is essential that they be understood before the true history of New England can be known.

In the British Museum exists a volume of manuscript letters received during these years by the British ambassador at The Hague, Sir William Boswell. From these crabbed pages emerges the story of a strange episode in the history of English diplomacy. Boswell assumed his duties in 1628, and apparently a goodly portion of his instructions from Whitehall dealt with the task of making Holland a less hospitable refuge for fleeing Separatists and Puritans. Laud's endeavors to secure unity at home were handicapped if every Puritan could find a convenient refuge just across the Channel. Boswell put all the pressure he could upon the Estates, and employed numerous spies to keep him informed of what every exile in every locality was up to. It is their letters that now repose in the Museum. But of course Boswell found it difficult, not to say impossible, to make the Dutch refuse a welcome to English divines who came to them dedicated to precisely the same Presbyterianism for which they themselves had fought and bled. How-

ever, Boswell could do the next best thing: he could stir
up the Dutch against those Englishmen who did not
agree with them. And in this task he at once received
the enthusiastic aid of English Presbyterian exiles, who
were only too anxious to demonstrate their loyalty and
to show that they sympathized in principle with this
official attempt to maintain uniformity. Religion, no
less than politics, makes strange bedfellows. Thus we
are confronted with the amusing spectacle of the agent
of Laud working hand in glove with a Puritan minister
like Paget, whom Laud and his party had driven from
England to the embraces of a Dutch classis. The objects
of this unnatural alliance could be only the Separatists
or else those unfortunate Puritans who at home could
not conform to the prelacy nor in Holland comport with
the presbyters. As we have already seen, the Dutch
Synod pronounced against the opinions of Jacob, Bradshaw, and Ames, and it was quite prepared, with a little
prodding from its English members, to make life uncomfortable for the younger disciples of Congregationalism.

Of this younger group the most prominent on the
English stage was undoubtedly Thomas Hooker. He
was a student of one of Ames's masters, Alexander
Richardson,[1] and by 1626 was a recognized Puritan
leader in the county of Essex. Stephen Collins, vicar of
Braintree and confidant of Laud, affirmed that he had
seen the people of the shire idolize many ministers, but
that Hooker surpassed them all both for abilities as a
preacher and for the number of his followers; even if he

1. Cotton Mather, *Magnalia*, I, 336.

were silenced, "his genius will still haunte all the pulpits
in ye country, where any of his scholars may be admitted
to preach." [1] When the authorities began to deal with
him, his case excited more "noise" in the vicinity than
"the great question of tonnage and Poundage." [2] At
that rate Hooker knew what to expect if he should
appear before the High Commission, and he chose the
better part of valor by fleeing to Holland, where he was
entertained as a possible colleague for John Paget by the
elders of the English church at Amsterdam. Paget, who
had already come to blows with Ames, Bradshaw, and
Jacob, quickly recognized in Hooker another of the
same stripe. He forced the candidate to submit to cross-
examination, secured from him a complete confession of
his Congregational creed, and carried the matter to the
Classis, "who made it an Act that a man holding those
opinions could not be chosen pastor within the power of
the Classis & that so the Elders should desist." [3] Hooker
finally was forced to move on to Delft, where he succeeded Hugh Peter as assistant to Dr. Ames's friend
Forbes.

By word and action Hooker declared himself in this
contingency. To several of Paget's questions he simply
replied, "In all of them I concurre with the iudgment of
Doctor Ames . . . his Cases of Conscience . . . of Mr.
Parker the 3 booke of Ecclesiasticall Policie . . . of Mr.
Baynes his Diocesans Tryall," and, he added ironically
enough, "Wherein how farre they differ from you I

1. *Cal. St. Pap., Dom., 1628–29*, vol. CXLIII, No. 113.
2. *Ibid.*, vol. CXLIV, No. 36; cf. vol. CLI, No. 45.
3. Additional Manuscripts 6394 (*Boswell Papers*, vol. I), fol. 146, in the British Museum.

doubt not but yow fully knowe." [1] Paget indeed knew. To the question of whether children of parents not in the Church should be baptized Hooker gave an unequivocal no, though he tried to be politic by adding that he was willing, nevertheless, to leave the Dutch churches to their own practice. His dictum on classes and synods was more than enough to justify the hostility of the authorities; he roundly declared that "particular Congregations had power from Christ to call a Minister, and so did by that their power choose and call their Ministers, fully & compleatly before there was a Classis." This power he said was derived "from the direct ordinance and appoyntment of Christ which power they may not give away, being a legacy left them by the Lord Jesus, as Doctor Ames disputes and détermines in his 4th booke of Cases of Conscience page 165." Once again he tried to be as politic as his conscience would permit, and granted that a congregation might consult a classis if they so wished, but that "they may lawfully and without sinne choose, without or against the Approbation of the Classis, if they sawe good reason." [2] Furthermore, Hooker proved that he did not intend these to be idle words, for when the Classis agreed with Paget that the elders should turn away a man of these opinions Hooker "taught them . . . that they might go on," and the Classis had to make a hasty appeal to the Synod to keep the Amsterdam elders from acting upon Hooker's heretical doctrine. [3]

1. *Ibid.*, fol. 69–70.
2. *Ibid.*, fol. 69–70.
3. *Cal. St. Pap., Dom., 1633–34*, vol. ccxxxvii, No. 48; Hanbury, *Historical Memorials*, I, 532.

Like all the other Non-separating Congregationalists, Hooker betrayed a disposition toward friendly relations with his fellow Congregationalists, the Separatists, even while disclaiming Separation himself. When Paget called him to account on this score Hooker once more revealed his allegiance to the Congregational idea by replying that while Separation was a sin, it was not unlawful to receive into a church a former Separatist who had not renounced his schism, "vnlesse wee will say that such a man (being in his iudgment & life otherwise altogether vnblameable) in Judicious Charitie is not a visible Christian." But if the Separatist may "in the iudgment of reasonable Charitie . . . be counted a member of Christ and so a saint by the same Charitie he may be counted fit to be a member of a Congregation." [1] Here clearly spoke a confirmed Congregationalist, who was yet resolved that at all costs Congregationalism should not be also Separation, and by such statements Paget took Hooker's measure. He opposed him for the same reasons he had opposed "Mr. Parker, Dr. Ames, Mr. Forbes, Mr. Peters, etc." Hooker, he said, was one of those who professed to abhor schism but, from a Presbyterian standpoint, were not so averse to schismatics as they might have been:

Not Mr. Hooker, while he maintained that such of the Brownists as persisted in the Schism or Separation from the Church of England might lawfully be received of us for Members of our Church: while he would not disallow such of our Church as went to hear the Brownists in their schismatical assembly: while he maintained that Private men might preach and expound the Scriptures at set times and places where the members of sundry families met together . . .

---

1. Add. MS. 6394, fol. 67.

while he maintained that Churches combined together in the Classis, might choose a Minister either without or against the consent of the Classis under which they stood.[1]

Hooker's pretended reverence for synods, as long as they were confined to mere consultation and giving of advice, was, Paget could readily perceive, "no more than that which Mr. Jacob and his company did give to Classes and Synods, 'for counsel and advice.' Yea, the Brownists themselves do give as much." [2]

Hooker, however, remained unshaken by such criticism, for, thanks to Ames, he was confident of his position. According to his reckoning his followers had given public satisfaction that they were not Separatists "by our Constant renouncing of their Course of the one side, and by our free and open profession of our intents, on the other side." [3] He identified himself further with Ames by serving as the latter's colleague at Rotterdam in 1633, and by writing the preface for his last work, *A Fresh Suit against human ceremonies*,[4] wherein he spoke also of Bradshaw as one "whome we are not ashamed to owne." [5] He seems to have been familiar with Jacob's writings, for he jotted down one of Jacob's definitions of a church in a manuscript notebook and obviously paraphrased the passage in his own work of 1648, the famous *Survey*.[6]

1. Hanbury, *op. cit.*, pp. 540–541.
2. *Ibid.*, p. 542.
3. Add. MS. 6394, fol. 67.
4. *Magnalia*, 1, 248; notation of Thomas Prince, flyleaf of the copy of *A Fresh Suit* in the Prince Collection, Boston Public Library.
5. *A Fresh Suit*, sig. F2 recto.
6. Notation of Josiah H. Benton, manuscript copy of Jacob's *A Confession and Protestation*, Boston Public Library.

If Hooker was a Congregationalist, his friend Hugh
Peter was quite as much so. This worthy attributed his
conversion to "the Love and Labours of Mr. *Thomas
Hooker*," [1] and also sat under the ministry of John
Davenport in London. For several years he was apparently assistant to Forbes at Delft, being ordained there
by the latter "with Imposition of hands . . . who was
before ordained in England." [2] When Hooker came to
Holland it was "upon Peters his commondations of
him" that Paget's church sent Hooker his call, [3] whereby
Peter incurred the wrath of the Presbyterian. After
Hooker was repulsed, Peter moved to Rotterdam while
Hooker succeeded him with Forbes. He took his new
charge resolutely in hand and resorted to some rather
heroic measures to make the church Congregational. He
refused to accept his call by the vote of the vulgar; he
permitted only those who swore to a specific covenant to
have a voice in his election or to participate in the Communion service, wherefore about two-thirds of the former congregation found themselves shut out. "What
authority he hath to do these things," one of the excluded complained, "I know not." [4] Hooker was for a
time his colleague there, as well as the "Learned *Ame-
sius*," who, Peter says, "breathed his last breath into
my bosome." Ames had come to Rotterdam "because

---

1. *A Dying Fathers Last Legacy to an Onely Child* (1669), p. 99.
2. Add. MS. 6394, fol. 172.
3. *Ibid.*, fol. 146.
4. Quoted by Rose-Troup, *John White*, p. 223; one of Boswell's agents
   promptly secured a copy of this covenant, Add. MS. 6394, fol. 161. Cf.
   Burrage, *Early English Dissenters*, I, 300–303; *Cal. St. Pap., Dom. 1633–
   34*, vol. CCLII, No. 32; *ibid., 1635*, vol. CCLXXXVI, No. 94; Rathband,
   Briefe Narration, pp. 17–19; Baillie, *Dissuasive*, p. 75.

of my Churches Independency," and he "charged me often, even to his death, so to look to it, and if there were a way of publik worship in the world, that God would owne, it was that." [1]

The third of these figures, John Davenport, began his career as a conforming minister of St. Stephen's in Coleman Street, London, where he achieved considerable reputation as a preacher. By 1628 he had reached the conviction that Anglican ceremonial was wrong, "which was not wraught at once, but by degrees, nor suddenly, but slowly, nor upon slight, but weighty considerations, nor without much labour, day and night." [2] He did not become wholly converted, evidently, to Congregationalism until he exchanged notes on church polity in 1632 with John Lathrop, Jacob's successor at Southwark; [3] he was confirmed in this resolution by a conference he held the next year with Cotton and Hooker just previous to their departure for America, at which Goodwin and Nye, subsequently two great leaders of English Independency, were also present. [4] Soon thereafter Daven-

1. *Last Report of the English Wars* (1646), p. 14. A thorough-going study of the life and thought of Hugh Peter during this period will be found in a forthcoming dissertation by Mr. Raymond P. Stearns at Harvard University; at the present writing his evidence seems to more than substantiate my briefly indicated thesis.
2. Davenport, *An Apologeticall Reply*, pp. 107–108; cf. John Waddington, *Congregational History*, II, 302.
3. Burrage, *op. cit.*, II, 298.
4. Cotton, *The Way of the Congregational Churches Cleared*, pp. 24–25; "Davenport-Paget Controversy" (ed. Worthington C. Ford), *Mass. Hist. Soc., Proc.*, XLIII, 57; *Magnalia*, I, 264, 323; Waddington, *Congregational History*, II, 288. Cf. Goffe's report to Boswell, June 7, 1633: "It is written unto me from England that Mr. Cotton of Boston hath convinced Mr. Damport & Mr. Nye two of the great preachers of the city that kneeling at the sacrament, etc — is plaine Idolatry, & yt for that

port fled to Holland. Paget's congregation, who must
have been a somewhat recalcitrant group, immediately
invited him to share the pulpit. Paget had his work to do
over again. One of Boswell's agents, Stephen Goffe,
reported that since "the miscarriage of Mr. Hooker"
Davenport and his friends were trying to be diplomatic;
they were making "Love to the Dutch ministers," but
Goffe easily perceived their intent: "So he may scape
the examining & be taken on upon their words; & if so
(if his owne friends speake truth) Mr. Hooker under
another name wil beguile them." [1]   Both Goffe and
Paget appealed to the classis, which was at once aroused,
for Davenport was already preaching Congregationalism. He announced that he would not baptize children
whose parents were not within a church covenant by
"externall profession."

> The seale of the covenant belongs only to those in the covenant,
> — nor can a man be judged to be in the covenant, without faith, nor
> to have faith unlesse he be called, nor to be called, unlesse he be
> taken off, from the world, and joyned to the congregation of the
> faithful.[2]

"As he was Mr. Hookers convert," commented Goffe,
"so you may see him walke." [3] The presbyters could permit nothing of this sort, and demanded that Davenport
"conforme to the orders and customs of the Dutch

---

reason Mr. Damport hath absented himself every sacramental day wch is
once a month since Christmas, & Mr. Cotton is going for New England."
(Add. MS. 6394, fol. 144.)
1. Add. MS. 6394, fol. 176.
2. "Davenport-Paget Controversy," p. 52, *Mass. Hist. Soc., Proc.*, vol.
XLIII; *Magnalia*, I, 324.
3. Add. MS. 6394, fol. 170.

Church." [1] When he refused they ordered him silenced.[2]
By that time there came hastening over from Rotterdam that doughty Congregationalist and Hookerite,
Hugh Peter, with Forbes and Batchellor in tow, "who
have (as they phraise it) strengthened him." The
strengthening seems to have taken the form of putting
the issue between Congregationalism and Presbyterianism trenchantly before the more recent convert: "And
they spake it in praise of Mr. Peters courage & zeale
that he should offen use the speech to Mr. Davenport,
Take heed, Mr. D. what you do, for you were as good
yeald to the English Bps as to the Dutch Classis."[3] Thus
reinforced, Davenport stuck to his Congregational guns.
He retorted with a categorical denial of a classis' right to
exercise the power of silencing a minister who had been
called by a specific congregation. Coercive synods, he
declared, had been "the cause of many mischiefs in the
Church, for thereby the writings and decrees of men are
made infallible and equall with the word of God, which
is intolerable." [4] He insisted that a church was entitled
to choose whatever minister it pleased without the consent of a classis; [5] many of Paget's congregation agreed
with him and seceded from the church in protest.[6]

A lengthy controversy ensued, in the course of which
Davenport attested the sources of his belief by quoting
Ames, Baynes, and Hooker to support his opinion against

1. "Davenport-Paget Controversy," p. 54.
2. Report of Sir William Boswell, April, 1634, *ibid.*, pp. 45–46.
3. Add. MS. 6394, fol. 198.
4. "Davenport-Paget Controversy," p. 51.
5. Davenport, *An Apologeticall Reply*, p. 220.
6. Cf. Burrage, *op. cit.*, i, 306–309; ii, 278–286.

promiscuous baptism,[1] and Ames, Parker, Baynes, and
Jacob for his stand against the classis.[2] He specifically
declared that he was writing not only in his own defense, but in defense as well of Parker, Ames, Forbes,
Hooker, Weld, and Peter.[3] Like all those worthies he
was not a Separatist; he told Sir William Boswell that he
was still "his Maiesties Loyall & faythfull subiect in
simplicity and trueth," and that he witnessed "against
haeresyes, and schysme and against all sectaryes, as
Familists, Anabaptists & Brownists."[4] To assert "the
lawfullness of admitting onely their infants to baptisme,
who are members of a true church," did not in the least,
he said, argue "such separation from true churches (for
defects and corruptions which are found in them) to be a
bounden duety."[5] He defended both himself and
Hooker[6] from the charge of schism by quoting their
common master, William Ames,[7] and by invoking the
casuistry of Non-separation. He had not left England
"out of any Schysmaticall propension to *forsake* the
Church *assemblies* of England, as if I thought there were
no true Churches of Christ in the land."[8] However
much the churches of England were defective, "yet to
dischurch them wholly, & to separate from them, as no
Churches of Christ, or to deny baptisme to the infants
of their knowne members is not warranted by any rule

1. "Davenport-Paget Controversy," p. 55; Davenport, *An Apologeticall
   Reply*, pp. 145, 160.
2. *Ibid.*, pp. 224, 227, 235, 238–243.
3. *Ibid.*, sig. C1 verso.
4. Burrage, *op. cit.*, 11, 283–284.
5. *An Apologeticall Reply*, p. 281.
6. *Ibid.*, pp. 256–248.
7. *Ibid.*, p. 281.   8. *Ibid.*, p. 107.

in Scripture." [1] Like Hooker and Peter, he also held that
Separatists could be admitted to his church,[2] whereupon
Paget felt perfectly justified in bracketing Davenport
with Hooker as one whose professed enmity to schism
was insincere. How, he asked, could Davenport be
opposed to Brownism,

> while he gathered unto himself a great and solemn assembly apart,
> by preaching unto them at set times in a private house without
> allowance of the Church: while he approved the Act of our Elders in
> admitting him to preach as an Assistant without the consent of the
> Classis . . . while he maintained the power of every Particular
> Church to be chief in its own particular matters? [3]

These, according to Paget, were precisely "such opinions and practices" as Ainsworth and Robinson held,
and no minister who promulgated them could be safely
called to "any of these Reformed Churches," for the
reformed churches of Holland were Presbyterian, and
Davenport clearly was not that kind of Puritan.[4]

One other of the prominent New England leaders, John
Cotton, did not go to Holland, but before he left England he betrayed his adherence to the party of Ames
almost as completely as did those upon whom Boswell's
spies made their reports. He had been an intimate friend
of Baynes, through whom he met his first wife.[5] He says,
of course, that he descried the polity in the Bible, but
admits also:

> Besides, I had then learned of Mr. *Parker*, and Mr. *Baynes* (and
> soon after of Dr. Ames), that the Ministers of Christ, and the Keyes

---

1. *Ibid.*, pp. 281–282.
2. *Ibid.*, p. 60; Hanbury, *Historical Memorials*, 1, 532.
3. *Ibid.*, p. 541.   4. *Ibid.*, pp. 541, 545.   5. *Magnalia*, 1, 258.

of the Government of his Church are given to each particular Congregationall Church respectively: And therefore neither Ministers
nor Congregations subject to the Ecclesiasticall jurisdiction of
Cathedrall Churches, no, nor of Classical Assemblies neither, but by
voluntary consociation.

This teaching caused him, he continues, "to breath after
greater liberty and purity not onely of Gods Worship,
but of Church estate"; therefore, thoroughly in keeping
with the reasoning we have already noted as characteristic of the school, he gathered "some scores of godly persons in *Boston* in *Lincoln-shire*" and they "entered into
a Covenant with the Lord, and one with another, to
follow after the Lord in the purity of his Worship."
This, he admits, was a defective arrangement, "yet it
was more than the Old Non-conformity." [1] This statement attests that prior to his ever setting foot in New
England he was aware of the divergence between the
two wings of the Puritan party, and that he himself had
deserted the old line Presbyterianism. Goffe apparently
understood this fact better than subsequent historians,
for in writing to Sir William Boswell of a certain Genevan preacher who in Holland had defended the Church
of England he declared, "And by that thesis he gott the
ill will of all that tribe: Mr. Cotton of Boston sent him a
lettre about it, blaming his medling, & Dr. Ames another." [2] Goffe knew well enough that Cotton and Ames
were of the same "tribe." And it would seem that
Thomas Hooker knew it as well, for when he decided to
move to New England his first choice for a colleague

1. *The Way of the Congregational Churches Cleared*, pt. 1, p. 20.
2. Add. MS. 6394, fol. 134.

there was Cotton.[1] Cotton declined the honor, and
Hooker took Samuel Stone instead; but all three of the
ministers found passage on the same ship, where they
demonstrated their full Congregationalism by refraining
from baptizing the son born to Mrs. Cotton on the
voyage, "1. because they had no settled congregation
there; 2. because a minister hath no power to give the
seals but in his own congregation."[2]

Concerning many of the first generation of New
England divines we have but little positive evidence for
their ecclesiastical affiliations at the time of their migration. But a few stray facts reveal a sufficient number of
connections on the part of some of the most important
of them with leaders of the Non-separating school of
Congregationalism to warrant our inferring that they
were either members of the group or at least on cordial
terms with it. Shepard, Norton, and Stone were disciples
of Hooker, and any of the three was satisfactory enough
to be accepted by him as his colleague after Cotton refused the offer.[3] Stone was a school-fellow and friend of
Shepard;[4] Shepard thought so much of Hooker and
Cotton that when they left England he "saw the Lord
departing."[5] For a time Shepard resided with Weld in
Essex, and they both evidently attended Hooker's sermons.[6] Davenport cited Weld along with Ames, Hooker,
and Peter as a man he was defending from Paget's

1. Cotton Mather, *Magnalia*, I, 340, 434.
2. John Winthrop, *Journal* (ed. J. K. Hosmer), I, 107.
3. *Magnalia*, I, 434.
4. Shepard, "Memoirs," Young, *Chronicles of Massachusetts*, pp. 506, 518.
5. *Ibid.*, p. 529.
6. *Ibid.*, pp. 512, 514; Waddington, *Congregational History*, II, 297.

attack.[1] John Eliot's connection with Hooker is well
known, for he was an usher in Hooker's school at Little
Baddow in 1630.[2] Nathaniel Rogers must be listed
among the young men through whom Stephen Collins
expected Hooker's genius to haunt the pulpits of Essex;
Rogers also was in correspondence with Cotton in 1631.[3]
John Lathrop, Jacob's successor at Southwark, migrated
to Massachusetts in 1634, though he presently settled at
Scituate within Plymouth boundaries.[4] Richard Mather
had become a Congregationalist by 1633, which, his
biographer tells us, "came to pass by his much reading
of the holy Scriptures, and his being very conversant in
the Writings of *Cartwright*, *Parker*, *Baynes*, and *Ames*";
his decision to remove two years later was strongly influenced by a letter from Hooker.[5] Nathaniel Ward we
know was in correspondence with Cotton at least by the
end of 1631.[6] Ezekiel Rogers, who brought a Yorkshire
company to Massachusetts in 1638, was already convinced that the chief defect in the Church of England
was "their receiving (nay, compelling) all to partake of
the seals."[7] John Phillips of Wrentham, who arrived at
the same time and served as minister at Dedham, was
married to a sister of Ames, and had been by him en-

---

1. Davenport, *An Apologeticall Reply*, sig. C1 verso.
2. *Magnalia*, I, 335.
3. *Ibid.*, pp. 416, 420. Rogers was the son of a famous Puritan preacher,
   John Rogers of Dedham, whose treatise on justification was quoted by
   Hooker in his controversy with Paget (Add. MS. 6394, fol. 71).
4. Winthrop, *Journal*, I, 134, 136.
5. *Life and Death of . . . Mr. Richard Mather*, p. 136; *Magnalia*, I, 448–449;
   K. B. Murdock, *Increase Mather*, pp. 16–17.
6. Alexander Young, *Chronicles of Massachusetts*, p. 113, n. 5.
7. Winthrop, *Journal*, I, 282.

couraged to adopt the Congregational way.[1] Nathaniel
Eaton, first teacher at Harvard, was a student of Ames
at Franeker.[2] Little enough at best is known of John
Harvard, but among the books he bequeathed to the
college library were five titles by Ames, as well as two by
Baynes, and one by Bradshaw.[3] To all these men, and
doubtless to many others who reached the colony after
the foundations of its church way were laid, an assertion
of Cotton's seems to apply: when the New England
ministers crossed the ocean, he says, they fully intended
to join the American churches, which plainly argued that

we did not upon our coming hither, goe contrary to our former
judgment, and fall into a liking of this way. For then we would
never have taken so long and hazardous a voyage to joyn to
Churches, whose way was contrary to our judgments all the while
of our abode in *England*.[4]

What Cotton declares of himself must evidently be pos-
tulated of many others: "I knew their Religion before I
came into *New England* . . . and I came with a purpose
to joyn with their churches." [5]

As a matter of fact, of only five ministers among all
those who crossed in the first twenty years of the

1. *Ibid.*, II, 83; Julius H. Tuttle, *Pub. Col. Soc. of Mass.*, XVII, 210–211.
2. *Ibid.*, p. 210; F. B. Dexter, *Mass. Hist. Soc., Proc.*, Series I, XVII, 344.
3. Alfred C. Potter, *Pub. Col. Soc. of Mass.*, XXI, 190–230.
4. *The Way of the Congregational Churches Cleared*, pt. I, p. 20.
5. *Ibid.*, p. 25; Cotton was not speaking amiss, even though he wrote this
   some fourteen years after his arrival; at the time Winthrop had written to
   Sir Simonds D'Ewes (September 26, 1633) that the church estate in New
   England was "suche as the Lords holy & wise servants . . . doe approve
   of, & accordingly doe joyne wth us in the same Course. I meane especially Mr. Cotton & Mr. Hooker, who lately arrived heere" (*Pub. Col.
   Soc. of Mass.*, VII, 70).

colony's existence can it be declared they were out and out Presbyterians. The church that settled Dorchester, Massachusetts, was gathered under the supervision of John White, who preached at the ordination of the two ministers, Maverick and Wareham; [1] these men reflected White's position after their arrival by holding "that the invisible church may consist of a mixed people, — godly, and openly ungodly." [2] Maverick soon died, and Wareham evidently was converted, for by the time he moved to Connecticut he was an ardent follower of Thomas Hooker. Thomas Parker, the son of Robert Parker, came with his cousin James Noyes, and the two settled at Newbury; [3] although Parker had been a student of Ames, yet he followed rather in his father's later than earlier steps, and remained obstinately Presbyterian to the end of his days. The last of this sort was Peter Hobart, pastor of Hingham, of whom we shall have occasion to speak hereafter.

Into the activities of the Company itself during the crowded months before the migration we are permitted only a few tantalizing glimpses, and these not extensive enough to justify a positive declaration of the ecclesiastical sentiments entertained by the secular leaders. But most assuredly these men were busy at the time discussing what form the churches of the New World should assume: "how many serious consultations with one another, and with faithfull Ministers, and other eminent servants of Christ . . . is not unknowne to some." [4] At

1. Roger Clap, "Memoirs," Young, *Chronicles of Massachusetts*, p. 347.
2. Bradford, "Letter Book," *Mass. Hist. Soc., Coll.*, Series 1, III, 74.
3. *Magnalia*, 1, 480, 484.
4. Shepard and Allin, *A Defence of the Answer*, p. 6.

least some participants in these consultations must have
cherished rather definite intentions, for on the day after
one of them, Arthur Tyndal wrote Winthrop that upon
second thought he had become willing " to liue under the
Hierarchie of your church & civill gouernment, proposed
& concluded among yourselues." [1] The best indication
we have of what sort of ministers Winthrop and his
friends were seeking for the "Hierarchie" of their
church is afforded by a letter Johnson indited to the
governor on December 17, 1629:

> Touching Mr. Hooker, we are not yet resolved what to doe, saue
> only to write to him, or go to him, to see whether hee entends to
> go or write, that wee may doe accordingly. Dr. Ames would haue
> the like respect, as Mr. Cotton well remembers us off. . . . Touching
> Mr. Peters your caution is good, but I hope wee shall give you con-
> tent, that his place will not be unsupplyed, nor his coming over
> offensive nor dangerous.[2]

The four ministers here mentioned were Congregationalists, and that they should be grouped together is im-
mensely significant, particularly when one remembers
how many Presbyterian Puritans were available had
Johnson been interested in them. However, as far as
Hugh Peter is concerned, Johnson's letter is not the first
sign of his connection with the Company. Probably
through the influence of John White, whom he called
"my dear firm Friend," [3] Peter became one of the patentees of the New England Company in May, 1628.[4]
He signed the corporation's instructions to Endecott in

1. Robert C. Winthrop, *Life and Letters of John Winthrop*, II, 413.
2. *Mass. Hist. Soc.*, *Coll.*, Series 4, VI, 31.
3. Hugh Peter, *A Dying Fathers Legacy* (1660), p. 101.
4. J. B. Felt, *Annals of Salem*, p. 508.

that month,[1] and was present at least at two meetings in
May of the next year.[2] He finally went to Massachusetts, he says, because "many of my Acquaintance going for *New-England*, had engaged me to come to them
when they sent." [3] Peter's devotion to the Congregational polity was well known at this time, and his affilia-
tion with the Company may very possibly have been
the entering wedge of the Congregationalists' control.
Hooker remained in close contact with the Company
from the time of Johnson's letter; his sister travelled
with the great migration in 1630,[4] and a number of his
Essex parishioners went over in 1632 to await his coming, being at once known as "Mr. Hooker's company." [5]
Cotton figured as official valedictorian by preaching the
farewell sermon to the fleet at Hampton in 1630; [6] he
himself says one of the reasons he ultimately decided to
follow was that many from Boston in Lincolnshire had
preceded him.[7] Davenport, like Peter, was a patentee
in 1628, though his name did not appear in the list for
politic reasons; [8] he was present at many meetings after
the royal charter had been secured, including the one of
August 29 when the decision to transport the patent was
reached.[9] On November 25, 1629, in order that the ses-

1. Thomas Hutchinson, *History of Massachusetts Bay* (1765), i, 9.
2. *Massachusetts Records*, i, 39, 40.
3. *A Dying Fathers Legacy*, p. 101.
4. Dudley, "Letter to Countess of Lincoln," Young, *Chronicles of Massa-*
   chusetts, p. 314.
5. Winthrop, *Journal*, i, 90.
6. Bradford, "Letter Book," *Mass. Hist. Soc., Coll.*, Series i, iii, 75.
7. Young, *op. cit.*, p. 440.
8. *Magnalia*, i, 325; Franklin B. Dexter, *Papers of the New Haven Historical*
   Society, ii, 218.
9. *Massachusetts Records*, i, 37, 47, 54, 57, 61, 67.

sions of the Company might be opened with prayer, two ministers were admitted to the freedom of the Company; one of these was Philip Nye, subsequently the great Independent leader; another name recommended at the time was "Mr. Nathaniel Ward, of Standon." [1] In these crucial hours the Company was evidently keeping an eye upon the young men who were in the same camp with Hooker, Peter, and Ames, for we find Humfrey writing on December 18, 1630, that lecturers and ministers were daily being "put by" and that "Mr. Weld of Essex is now upon the stage & expects his doome. I think he will be easilie for us." [2]

The supreme proof, however, of the Company's connection with Ames's ecclesiastical clique is its relations with that great man himself. On December 29, 1629, possibly in reply to the very letter which Johnson said he was sending to him at the suggestion of Cotton, Ames wrote to Winthrop, "with his associats for New England." He was then praying daily "for the good successe of the busines yow have undertaken," and he declared he so longed "to bee with yow" that he intended to follow "upon the news of your safe arrivall, with good hope of prosperitie." Evidently he had been asked for advice upon certain matters of which he was qualified to speak, since he added,

Concerning the directions yow mention, I have nothing to write: as being ignorant of special difficulties: and supposing the general

1. *Ibid.*, p. 63.
2. *Mass. Hist. Soc., Coll.*, Series 4, VI, 11; on November 4, 1629, John Maidstone wrote to Winthrop praising George Phillips; Winthrop must have approved the man, for he paid his passage (*Mass. Hist. Soc., Coll.*, Series

care of safetie, libertie, unitie, with puritie, to bee in all your mindes & desires.[1]

Such a guarded statement was the wise move of a wise man in a day when Puritan letters were subject to search, but "libertie, unitie, with puritie" could mean to Ames only one thing, — free, uniform, and pure Congregationalism. There can hardly be any doubt in view of this letter that the faction which stampeded the Massachusetts Bay Company into becoming the Commonwealth of Massachusetts met his approval because it was hospitable to the ecclesiastical polity he had so conspicuously championed. Ames never abandoned his intention of joining the colony. Humfrey wrote to both Johnson and Winthrop in December of the next year that Ames retained "his first affection to you & the worke," [2] and he sent to Winthrop a copy of Ames's *De Conscientia* among some books "that are lately come out." [3] So widely known was Ames's inclination that a friend in the Bermudas, hearing "there is a supposition that you intend to come for New England, and Mr. Peeters, as many reverent Divines are gone from England before you," wrote to him attempting to divert his course to the southern plantation.[4] Ames died in 1633, and his family ultimately crossed over in 1637, bringing his books with the intention of making them "the first furniture" of the college library.[5]

5, I, 190; *Massachusetts Records*, I, 131). Phillips was already a radical Congregationalist (cf. *infra*, p. 134).

1. *Mass. Hist. Soc., Coll.*, Series 4, VI, 576.
2. *Ibid.*, pp. 11, 16.   3. *Ibid.*, p. 4.
4. George Lyman Kittredge, *Pub. Col. Soc. of Mass.*, XIII, 61.
5. Julius H. Tuttle, *Pub. Col. Soc. of Mass.*, XIV, 63–66; *Magnalia*, I, 236; *Mass. Hist. Soc., Coll.*, Series 4, I, 100.

Hitherto the stumbling block to our interpretation of Massachusetts ecclesiastical origins has been the rooted conviction that the Bay towns contracted their church polity by a species of contagion from the Separatists of Plymouth. This theory has persisted in spite of the fact that it does not explain how the marked Anti-separatist current seen in the Company's official manifestoes of 1630, *The Humble Request* and *The Planters Plea*, got turned awry, and hostile critics have sniffed hypocrisy or even deliberate fraud. Robert C. Winthrop was sure that could a hiatus among his ancestor's papers be supplied, there would be discovered an explanation for the governor's religious conduct, which otherwise seemed to remain a blot on the 'scutcheon of the family consistency.[1] Commentators invariably have puzzled over what seems to have been a vast discrepancy between English profession and New England practice; the most recent to take up the cry is Mrs. Frances Rose-Troup, in a case of special pleading for John White, wherein she intimates that by accepting "Separatist" forms of worship from Plymouth, John Endecott virtually betrayed his trust.[2]

The assumption behind all these perplexities is that Congregationalism and Separatism are synonymous terms. I believe, however, we have sufficiently demonstrated that there is reason to suppose the influential element among the emigrating Puritans could very easily have been Congregational and at the same time most emphatically not Separatist. Furthermore, we

1. Arthur B. Ellis, *History of the First Church in Boston*, p. xxix.
2. Rose-Troup, *John White*, pp. 145, 179, 180.

must remember that when the Plymouth congregation left John Robinson, he had yielded to the arguments of Jacob and Ames and had abandoned "rigid Separation" for what has been termed a "Semi-separatist" position; also we know that Non-separating Congregationalists were always meeting their Separatist brethren on friendly terms, communicating with them freely as long as it remained understood they themselves were not thereby approving the act of Separation. With these antecedents in mind, we might be prepared to forecast that neither Plymouth nor Massachusetts would have to persuade the other to become Congregationalist, and that their relations would be rather a matter of putting their heads together over a common program they had approached from slightly different but important angles. In their parleyings the word of Plymouth would carry weight with the younger colony because the Plymouth church would have had some twenty years' practical experience with the system, whereas the people of the Bay would possess at best the blueprints of Bradshaw. If the churches of the Bay then sought the advice of Plymouth about details it would be because they were already disposed to erect a Congregational régime, and because they would have proceeded along essentially the same line had there been no Plymouth at all.

Such a version seems to me substantiated by what happened. The Salem settlers became afflicted with scurvy in the spring of 1629, and Bradford charitably despatched Dr. Fuller, a deacon of the Plymouth church, to render medical service and spiritual consolation. Endecott replied in a letter of thanks, which Bradford quotes in his *History* because it "shows the beginning of their acquaintance, and closinge in the truth and ways of God." Fuller probably talked polity as much as he did pills, but surely he found a ready audience. Endecott himself was a friend of Hugh Peter, whom he had asked the Company to secure as minister for the post.[1] This fact speaks volumes on Endecott's opinion, since in 1628 he could not have had Peter at Salem without having Congregationalism there also. He was, consequently, speaking more literally than has generally been supposed when he told Bradford that Fuller had satisfied him "touching your judgment of the out ward forms of Gods worship; it is (as far as I can yet gather) no other then is warranted by the evidence of Truth, and the same which I have professed and maintained ever since the Lord in mercie revealed him selfe unto me." Endecott could not have spoken this way had he just been converted from Presbyterian Puritanism to Congregational Separatism; his whole tone is that of a man who has received corroboration for his own belief from unexpected quarters, because Fuller's description of Plymouth polity, he added, was "far from the common reporte that hath been spread of you touching that perticular." Hence he concluded that "God's people are all marked with one and the same mark," that among them "there can be no discorde," and that Plymouth and Salem ought to be great friends.[2]

There is every reason to believe the ministers of Salem

1. *Massachusetts Records*, I, 385.
2. Bradford, "Letter Book," *Mass. Hist. Soc., Coll.*, Series I, III, 64–66; Bradford, *History* (ed. W. C. Ford), II, 90.

were of the same mind. When Skelton and Higginson took passage in April, 1629, the Company told Endecott they had "declared themselues to vs to bee of one judgment, & to bee fully agreed on the manner how to exercise their ministry." [1] They were given *carte blanche* to do what they wished: "For the mannor of the exercising their ministrie, & teaching both or owne people and the Indians, wee leave that to themselues, hoping they will make Gods word the rule of their actions." [2] If the Company did not know what to expect of these men under such circumstances, it was unaccountably stupid. Higginson was one of Thomas Hooker's "scholars," and had already shown his Congregational leanings in his English ministry by attempting to debar ignorant and scandalous persons from the Lord's Supper. [3] He was recommended to the Company by Increase Nowell on March 23, 1629, [4] and at the time he was notified of his opportunity was hourly expecting pursuivants from the High Commission. He was also well known to Arthur Hildersham, whose recommendation the Company instructed Humfrey to secure before he engaged Higginson. This Hildersham was a prominent Puritan, a conspicuous enemy of Separation; he was not himself a Congregationalist, but seems to have been friendly with those who were, for Cotton wrote prefaces to two of his works. Less is known about Skelton, but the Company wrote they were informed that Endecott himself had "formerly received much good by his ministry." [5] If he was satis-

---

1. *Massachusetts Records*, I, 394.   2. *Ibid.*, p. 387.
3. *Magnalia*, I, 356–357.
4. *Massachusetts Records*, I, 37.   5. *Ibid.*, p. 386.

factory to Endecott, the friend of Peter, the probabili-
ties are he was a Congregationalist, which is a conclusion
Cotton later substantiated when he wrote, "Sure I am,
Mr *Skelton* . . . was studious of that way, before he left
Holland in *Lincolnshire.*" [1]

Therefore it seems to have been quite in keeping with
the predilections of Endecott and the ministers that on
July 20, 1629, the Salem church was founded and the
ministers ordained along Congregational lines. Skelton
and Higginson acknowledged a twofold calling, one
from within and the other "an outward calling, which
was from the people, when a company of believers are
joyned togither in covenante, to walk togither in all the
ways of God and every member (being men) are to have
a free voyce in the choyce of their officers." They were
then ordained by the laying on of hands.[2] It is utterly
inconceivable that so completely Congregational a ceremony could have been enacted by these people merely
because Deacon Fuller bent a headstrong man like
Endecott, or suddenly converted two able ministers like
Skelton and Higginson to a Separatist way of thinking,
and it is nothing short of absurd to conclude that all
later churches in Massachusetts followed the lead of
Salem like so many sheep. Sixty years of ecclesiastical
disputation lay in the background of these men, and by
this time they knew what they wanted. Fuller may have
furnished helpful suggestions, but the mainspring of the
action had been wound up by other hands in England.

If the ministers at Salem had really stolen a march

1. Cotton, *The Way of the Congregational Churches Cleared*, pt. 1, p. 16.
2. Bradford, "Letter Book," *Mass. Hist. Soc., Coll.*, Series 4, III, 67.

upon the Company, if the establishment of a Congregational church had been distasteful to the reigning element in the corporation, the whole proceeding could
have been disallowed by the proper authorities; and if
the authorities did not do so, it was not from lack of opportunity. Among the men who came out with Endecott were two brothers by the name of Browne. They
were not very radical Puritans and were shocked at the
ecclesiastical revolution enacted in Salem. Gathering a
few like-minded settlers apart, they read the Prayer
Book. Endecott arraigned them, and after the ministers
had denied their charge of having turned Separatist,
shipped them back home, saying "New England was no
place for such as they." [1] Naturally, they raised trouble
in England and very decidedly embarrassed the Company; the way it met the occasion, however, is eloquent.
The Brownes were recompensed for what they had ad-
ventured,[2] and letters which are in a fair way to being
masterpieces of a sort were immediately sent to the
ministers and to Endecott. First the ministers were
properly scolded and told to repent their miscarriage, or
"at least to take notice that wee vtterly disallowe any
such passages, and must and will take order for the
redress therof, as shall become vs." But upon what
grounds? Because Congregationalism was schismatical?
Not at all. In the next sentence the letter revealed the
pole-star by which at the moment the Company plotted
its course, and the ministers hardly had to read between
the lines to perceive just where their offence had lain:

1. *Massachusetts Records*, I, 51–64, 69, 407.
2. *Ibid.*, pp. 60, 69.

But hoping, as wee said, of yor vnblameableness heerin, wee desire only that this may testify to yow & others that wee are tender of the least aspersion which, either directly or obliquely, may bee cast vpon the state heere, to whome wee owe soe much duty, and from whom wee haue received soe much fauor.[1]

The letter to Endecott never even suggested a condemnation of the principle on which he had acted, but emphasized merely the question of his tact:

We may haue leave to think that it is possible some vndigested councells haue too sodainely bin put in execution, which may haue ill construction with the state heere, and make vs obnoxious to any adversary. Lett it, therefore, seeme good vnto yow to bee very sparing of introduceing any lawes or commands which may render yorselfe or vs distastefull to the state heere, to which (as wee ought) wee must and will haue an obsequious eye.[2]

Those about to depart from England knew well enough when they wrote this in what direction their advance guard had turned; and their only concern was that the English government should not get wind of it until they too could escape with their precious charter.

When the main body finally did get away, and settled in the Bay, then Plymouth seems to have figured in about the same rôle as at Salem. The Dorchester society, we have already noted, was composed of followers of John White and was not yet of a Congregational temper; Deacon Fuller, who visited Charlestown in June, 1630, argued with Wareham, "till I was weary," without being able to convince him that promiscuous admission to church membership was unlawful — an example, certainly, of how little Fuller would have succeeded the year before if Endecott and the Salem minis-

1. *Ibid.*, pp. 407–408.   2. *Ibid.*, p. 408.

ters had been disciples of White rather than of Peter and
Hooker. The two other ministers of the Bay, however,
could meet with Fuller's approval. John Wilson was a
student of Baynes and a friend of Ames; he had already
twice been silenced in England.[1] Phillips of Watertown
was, as Cotton Mather says, "better acquainted with
the true *church discipline* than most of the ministers that
came with him into the country";[2] he told Fuller, "if
they will have him stand minister by that calling which
he received from the prelates in England, he will leave
them," which meant simply that he would acknowledge
only the same kind of calling that Skelton and Higginson invoked. Fuller declared that among the immigrants
there were some enemies to Plymouth, but also "many
friends," among whom he accounted Winthrop, since
that gentleman told him they should probably need
some advice and might send for Bradford. Fuller learned
from Coddington that "Mr. Cotton's charge at Hampton was that they should take advice of them at Plymouth, and should do nothing to offend them." By this
time the deacon found Endecott "a second Burrow."[3]
At the moment of the colonists' arrival an inclination
toward Congregationalism clearly existed among some
of them, which needed only a little guidance to be translated into action. The prod came from Salem, whither
Winthrop wrote for advice; Fuller, Winslow, and Aller-
ton were then up from Plymouth, and the Salem ministers conferred with them. All agreed that Winthrop and
his group should form a church, but at first should admit

1. *Magnalia*, I, 303, 304, 310.   2. *Ibid.*, p. 377.
3. Bradford, "Letter Book," *Mass. Hist. Soc., Coll.*, Series I, III, 74–75.

only a few whose sentiments were well known. Salem
and Plymouth both set apart a day to beseech the Lord's
blessing.[1] Upon July 30 the Charlestown church was
formed, the first membership consisting of only Winthrop, Dudley, Johnson, and Wilson.[2] On the same day
the church at Watertown under George Phillips was
gathered in a similar Congregational fashion.

That Massachusetts deliberately copied its order from
Plymouth was first charged against the colony some
fourteen years later by the Presbyterian chieftains,
Rathband, Baillie, and Edwards, who then wished to
discredit English Independency.[3] Cotton replied by ad-
vancing substantially the interpretation we have out-
lined and which, upon the basis of such evidence as we
possess, seems the only one permissible. Although it is
true, he said, that Massachusetts and Plymouth did set
up "the same modell of Churches, one like to another,"
yet that "it was after Mr. *Robinson's* pattern, is spoken
gratis: for I beleeve most of them knew not what it was,
if any at all." [4] The Bible, he declared, had been the
source of the colonists' objection to "the burden of
Episcopacy and Conformity," and the second commandment the reason for their having laid aside the
Book of Common Prayer; as for their other doctrines,

The particular visible Church of a Congregation to be the first
subject of the power of the Keyes, we received by the light of the
Word from Mr. *Parker*, Mr. *Baynes* and Dr. *Ames*: from whom also,

1. *Ibid.*, p. 75.
2. *Ibid.*, p. 76; Walker, *Creeds and Platforms*, pp. 105, 108.
3. Rathband, *A Briefe Narration*, p. 1; Baillie, *Dissuasive*, p. 54; Edwards,
Antapologia, pp. 42–43.
4. *The Way of the Congregational Churches Cleared*, pt. 1, p. 17.

(from two of them at least) we received light out of the Word, for the matter of the visible Church to be visible Saints and the Form of it, to be a mutuall Covenant, whether an explicite or implicite Profession of Faith, and subjection to the Gospel of Christ in the society of the Church, or Presbytery thereof.

Since these tenets had been handed down by men who were not Brownists, their consanguinity "with any the like found amongst the Separatists, will not demonstrate the Separatists to be our Fathers." [1]

This contention seems secured beyond dispute when Plymouth itself agrees. Bradford specifically approved Cotton's version of the story and declared there "was no agreement by any solemn or common consultation" between the two colonies, although they both, moved by the same spirit of truth, did happen to erect similar polities.[2] Winslow, in his *Hypocrisie Unmasked*, in 1646, reiterated the same plea; the "chiefe" of the great migration, it is true, "advised with us," and we "accordingly shewed them the Primitive practice for our warrant. . . . So that here also thou maist see they set not the Church at *Plimouth* before them for example, but the Primitive Churches were and are their and our mutuall patternes and examples." [3]

A final and I think conclusive indication of the true sources for Massachusetts Congregationalism lies in a fact with which, so far as I can discover, commentators have never adequately grappled: although the good wits of Plymouth and the Bay did, as Hubbard put it,

1. *Ibid.*, p. 13.
2. Bradford, "Dialogue," Young, *Chronicles of the Pilgrim Fathers*, p. 426.
3. *Hypocrisie Unmasked* (1646), ed. Howard Millar Chapin, The Club for Colonial Reprints (Providence, 1916), p. 92.

"strangely jump very near together," [1] Massachusetts nevertheless consistently maintained it was not and never had been Separatist. From the beginning the enterprise had remained officially loyal on that score. The Dorchester Company, being the brain-child of John White, naturally was hostile to schismatics and welcomed Lyford and Conant to Cape Anne when they left Plymouth, disgusted with the way of Separation. [2] The new elements in the Company took power from White's hands and dedicated the adventure to a Congregational ideal, but they retained the original public allegiance to the Church of England. As Land's End faded from view, Francis Higginson is reputed to have cried out "Farewell," not as Separatists were wont to say farewell to "Babylon," but as a churchman to the Church of God in England:

We do not go to New-England as separatists from the Church of England; though we cannot but separate from the corruptions in it: but we go to practise the positive part of Church reformation, and propagate the gospel in America. [3]

When the brothers Browne accused the Salem ministers of becoming Separatists, Higginson and Skelton replied they were "neither Separatists nor Anabaptists," that they had not separated from the Church of God in England but from its corruptions, and that since they

had suffered much for their non-conformity in their native land . . . being in a place they might have their liberty, they neither could nor

1. William Hubbard, *General History of New England* (1680), *Mass. Hist. Soc., Coll.*, Series 2, v, 117.
2. *Ibid.*, p. 106.　　　3. *Magnalia*, 1, 362.

would use them; inasmuch as they judged the imposition of these things to be a sinful violation of the worship of God.[1]

In 1629 the Company blindly engaged another minister, one Ralph Smith, and then discovered he was a Separatist; the line between the two kinds of Congregationalists was sometimes hard to discover, but the fact that the corporation did, if somewhat too late, realize the distinction in this case proves at once both its own position and that of Skelton and Higginson. Smith was required to forswear exercising a ministry unless by Endecott's permission,[2] and Craddock wrote in haste to explain how Smith had been shipped "before wee vnderstood of his difference of judgment in some things from or ministers." Craddock instinctively assumed the tone of a guardian of an established order confronting an incendiary, a tone strangely similar to that in which the bishops habitually spoke:

Hence it is feared there may growe some distraction amongst yow. . . . We haue therfore thought fitt to giue yow this order, that vnless hee wilbe conformable to or gouernment, yow suffer him not to remaine within the limitts of or graunt.[3]

When the *Arbella* was riding in the harbor at Cowes, Winthrop and the leaders of the migration signed a brief address to "the rest of their Brethren in and of the Church of England," which shortly thereafter, while they were yet on the high seas, was published as *The Humble Request*. The authorship of this pamphlet, a moot question among antiquarians, is not a material

1. *Ibid.*, p. 73.
2. Hutchinson, *History of Massachusetts Bay* (1765), I, 10.
3. *Massachusetts Records*, I, 390.

question, for all the leaders subscribed it, and none of them need have strained their consciences in doing so, since it said nothing beyond what Jacob and Bradshaw had already profusely uttered:

We . . . esteem it our honor to call the Church of England . . . our dear mother . . . ever acknowledging that such hope and part as we have obtained in the common salvation, we have received in her bosom and sucked it from her breasts. We leave it not, therefore, as loathing that milk wherewith we were nourished there; but blessing God for the parantage and education, as members of the same body, shall always rejoice in her good.[1]

Behind such an assertion it is not difficult to trace the familiar casuistry of Non-separation, but there was a gusto in this statement that arose from its being employed in the prospect of a new effectiveness. While Puritans remained in England, the more they utilized the plea, the more they found it throwing their actions into unpleasant contrast with their professions; but when they employed it from across the ocean, where even the sharp eye of Laud could not scan their doings too closely, then they saw in their shift an almost invulnerable defense. Behind this bulwark the churches could become completely Congregationalized, even to the point where they would no longer be distinguishable from Separatist organizations, and yet as long as there had been no formal Separation, as long as the churches could claim to be simply purified and transported English parishes, the principle of uniformity had not been infringed. Massachusetts was not schismatical.

If the pose was to be effective at all, it had to be stated clearly from the very beginning, all the more because at

1. Young, *Chronicles of Massachusetts*, p. 296.

the time certain critics had evidently realized the truth. There were "suspicious and scandalous reports" being raised, which "by casting the vndertakers into the jealousie of State" threatened "to shut them out of those advantages which otherwise they doe and might expect from the Countenance of Authoritie." [1] These rumors had to be quashed, in order, as Coddington said, "to satisfie the Godly minded of our Removal out of England." [2] The difficult task devolved upon John White. He published *The Planters Plea* soon after the fleet sailed, and the point of this ingenious work is utterly lost today unless the reader comprehends how very urgent it was at that particular moment that the adventure be cleared of all taint of Separation. White was aware of reports being circulated that the migration had been made up of "men of ill affected minds" who secretly "harboured faction and separation from the Church" under the cloak of religion. *The Humble Request* and the record of the men ought to be sufficient evidence that they had never been factious nor had ever separated from the assemblies or ministry of the Church.

I perswade my selfe there is no one Separatist knowne unto the Governours, or if there be any, that it is as farre from their purpose as it is from their safety, to continue him amongst them.

But there were other whisperings which hinted that though these men were not Separatists,

yet they dislike our discipline and ceremonies, and so they will prove themselves semi-separatists at least, and that is their intention in removing from us, that they may free themselves from our government.

---

1. *The Planters Plea*, p. 77.   2. *Mass. Hist. Soc., Proc.*, XLIII, 503.

To this, as it seems to us rather accurate, suspicion, White's reply is extremely significant. "I conceive," he said, "we doe and ought to put a great difference betweene Separation and Non-conformity." Thus he invoked the already historic distinction whereby he could exonerate mere dissent by loudly condemning Separatism as something "we cannot beare." But when he came, as he could not avoid coming, to the question of what the Non-conformist practice in New England would be, the poor man plainly hedged, for he well enough knew what Winthrop and his friends had in mind. You might say, he granted, that the emigrants were wearied of church ceremonies "and goe over with an intention to cast them off"; "intentions are secret, who can discover them; but what have they done to manifest such an intention?" He was sure there could be no extensive conspiracy among the mass, for they had come from too diverse sources, and Winthrop should answer for the leaders, "a publike person," who had always been "euery way regular and conformable in the whole course of his practise." The emigrants were, it was true, taking only Non-conforming ministers with them, but they could get no others. And after all, even granting they intended a few innovations,

there is great oddes betweene peaceable men, who out of tendernesse of heart forbeare the use of some ceremonies of the Church . . . and men of fiery and turbulent spirits, that walke in a crosse way out of distemper of minde.

Have not those men who know themselves unable to conform and therefore withdraw themselves rather than disrupt the peace of their beloved Church — have they not such dispositions as should "be cherished with great tendernesse?" It was indeed probable that many would insist upon a few departures, and others might admit the innovations "for the maintaining of peace and unitie"; furthermore, "wants and necessities cannot but cause many changes." But that the men were far "from projecting the erecting of this Colony for a Nursery of *Schismatickes*" appeared from the history of the Company and of the charter, which White recounted, concluding that such evidence was enough to bring God's vengeance upon those who followed "that base and unchristian course of traducing innocent persons, under those odious names of Separatists and enemies to the Church and State." [1]

It was, surely, a flimsy and transparent "plea," but it was the only line circumstances left open to a people who were at one and the same time convinced of the absolute truth of a dissenting program and of the absolute necessity for orthodox uniformity. It was the old attempt to maintain a subordination in principle where there was an opposition in practice, and at best it was bound to rest on an illogical foundation. Puritans were simply wearied out with sixty years of fruitless controversy, and with Laud in power they completely despaired of the prospect. Upon Non-separating Congregationalists the situation pressed the heaviest, for their subordination to the Established Church was supremely difficult to maintain. The wisest policy for them was to save appearances in the best way possible and get out. "And truly," said Hugh Peter, "my reason for my self and others to go,

1. *The Planters Plea*, pp. 59–78.

was meerly not to offend Authority in that difference of Judgment." [1] Thus it was, when "times were so bad in England that they could not worship God after the due manner prescribed in his most holy word, but they must be imprisoned, excommunicated," [2] when, as Gorges remembered, Parliament was dismissed, "whereby divers were so fearfull what would follow so unaccustomed an action," when "the principall of those liberall speakers being committed to the Tower . . . tooke all hope of Reformation of Church-Government from many not affecting Episcopal Jurisdiction," then it was that "some of the discreeter sort to avoid what they found themselves subject unto, made use of their friends to procure from the Councell for the affaires of *New-England* to settle a Colony within their Limits." [3]   The royal charter was obtained, Craddock wrote, "with great cost, fauor of personages of note, & much labor," [4] but it was worth all that, because

by which said lettres pattents wee are incorporated into a body pollitique, with ample power to gouerne & rule all his maiesties subiects that reside within the limitts of our plantation. [5]

A political government set up in the colony "by virtue of his Majesty's letters patent, and under his gracious protection" [6] was, from a legal standpoint, impeccable.

1. *A Dying Fathers Legacy* (1660), p. 101.
2. Roger Clap, "Memoirs," Young, *Chronicles of Massachusetts*, p. 356.
3. Sir Ferdinando Gorges, "Briefe Narration," J. P. Baxter, *Sir Ferdinando Gorges and his province of Maine*, II, 58–59; Gorges's memory has here confused the charter of 1628 with the royal charter of 1629, but his account of the motives rings true.
4. *Massachusetts Records*, I, 387.
5. *Ibid.*, p. 386.
6. Dudley, "Letter to Countess of Lincoln" (1631), Young, *op. cit.*, p. 331.

On the other hand, the Christians of the colony, departing from the churches of England, not as from false churches, but merely from "the corruptions found among them," were, Cotton insisted, excused by "Doctor *Ames* . . . (yea, and the Holy Ghost also) from aspersion of schism or any other sin, in so doing." [1] Thus whatever state and church the colony erected were legitimate offshoots of the State and Church of England, and within the jurisdiction of the grant could perform all the acts pertaining to a commonwealth and an established church, could coöperate to maintain orthodox uniformity, and could define heresy to suit themselves. This may have been sophistry, but Massachusetts was founded on it.

It is impossible to say how early the complete vision of this solution for the Puritan dilemma dawned upon those who ultimately carried it through. Endecott and Peter may have cherished hopes in 1628. Considerable light would be thrown upon the story could we unravel the baffling mystery of the charter itself. Contrary to the universal custom, this document entirely omitted to specify a particular residence for the corporation's headquarters. The evidence we possess seems to indicate that this hiatus was not accidental. Winthrop wrote in 1644 that heretofore it had been the manner for those who procured patents to keep the chief government resident in England, and "so this was intended & with much difficulty we gott it abscinded." [2] The docquet containing the application for a charter asked the privi-

---

1. *The Way of the Congregational Churches Cleared*, pt. I, p. 14.
2. R. C. Winthrop, *Life and Letters of John Winthrop*, II, 443.

lege of "electing governors and officers here in England," [1] and the strange failure of this restriction to be transcribed into the final draft appears, to say the least, providential. But however it was brought about, the fact that the Company was not bound to one locality provided a priceless opportunity to those who very badly needed it. From the day the Company made its decision, the tone of the leaders was unmistakable; they went to work with as little commotion as possible, feverishly intent upon getting their patent beyond reach of their enemies. On September 29 a committee was appointed "to take advice of learned councell" whether the removal might legally be made;[2] whether or not the committee turned in a report we do not know, but the Company's scruples were evidently satisfied. Otherwise they showed themselves no particular sticklers for form. The meeting of October 20 was called for the election of governor, and Winthrop was chosen several months before the annual election was due, which according to the charter should have been the last Wednesday of the Easter term; Craddock stepped out before his term was over without there being any provision for resignation. When the proper day came round, the Company was all thankfully on shipboard and forgot elections until the next year, so that Winthrop held office under an illegal ballot for a good eighteen months. These acts were infringements of the charter, but they were means to an

---

1. *Lowell Institute Lectures*, p. 381; Charles Deane, *Mass. Hist. Soc., Proc.*, Series 1, xi, 166 ff.; Mellen Chamberlain, *ibid.*, Series 2, viii, 110; Frances Rose-Troup, *The Massachusetts Bay Company and Its Predecessors*, pp. 76–78.
2. *Massachusetts Records*, i, 52.

end and they eloquently betray the determination of these Puritans to make the most of their one chance to escape.[1]

By hook or by crook, then, the Non-separating Puritans, the energetic and hard-pressed disciples of Ames and Bradshaw, extricated themselves from the toils of English ecclesiastical disputation and set out to achieve in Massachusetts what they had failed to accomplish in England. The implicit Congregationalism their masters had read into the English parishes was now to be made explicit. "That which the most in theire churches maintaine as truth in profession onely," Winthrop lectured passengers on the *Arbella*, "wee must bring into familiar and constant practice."[2] If they could not abolish the hierarchy, Puritans could remove it by putting between it and themselves a ditch so wide "they could not leap over with a lope-staff."[3] America to the Puritans spelled opportunity as distinctly as ever it has to later immigrants, for it meant the cessation of protest and the beginning of construction. "It is one thing for the church, or members of the church," Cotton declared, "loyally to submit unto any form of government, when it is above their calling to reform it, another thing to chuse a form of government and governors discrepant from the rule."[4] In New England there was no longer need "to strive against ceremonies, or to fight against

1. Osgood, *The American Colonies in the Sixteenth Century*, I, 145 ff.; Rose-Troup, *op. cit.*, pp. 78–80.
2. *Mass. Hist. Soc., Coll.*, Series 3, VII, 45.
3. Edward Johnson, *The Wonder Working Providences of Sion's Saviour in New England* (ed. W. F. Poole, Andover, 1867), p. 20.
4. Hutchinson, *History of Massachusetts Bay* (1764), I, 494.

shadows." [1] "What you may doe in England, where things are otherwise established," Winthrop wrote to Sir Simonds D'Ewes, "I will not dispute; but or case here is otherwise, being come to dearer light & more Libertye, which we trust by the good hand of or God with us, & the gratious indulgence of or Kinge, we may freely enjoye it." [2] That "gratious indulgence" was a neat touch, for when Charles and his great archbishop found out how nicely they had been duped they were not particularly "gratious" about it; but New Englanders had already closed that chapter in their lives. Confident that they had sidestepped the dilemma of English Puritanism by legitimate and respectable means, they had dedicated themselves wholeheartedly to the serious business of living "under a due form of government, both civil and ecclesiastical." [3]

1. Young, *Chronicles of Massachusetts*, p. 441.
2. *Pub. Col. Soc. Mass.*, VII, 71–72.
3. *Mass. Hist. Soc.*, *Coll.*, Series 3, VII, 45.

VI

THE NEW ENGLAND WAY

JOHN WINTHROP defined the supreme objective of the Massachusetts Colony as "a due form of government," in both State and Church. But for reasons not far to seek, the leaders realized that in church matters they must proceed cautiously. Their conceptions of polity had hitherto been largely theoretical; many exigencies had not been foreseen, and they preferred not to cross bridges until they came to them. Also, they had not forgotten the instructions they themselves had given Endecott, that "an obsequious eye" should be kept open upon the English government. The leaders were at liberty to realize their own likes and dislikes, but they readily perceived that there was no sense in flaunting their deeds before a notoriously unsympathetic monarch. The clergy, therefore, once they found themselves securely established in America, revealed a marked tendency to stave off as long as possible a formal codification of their Way. Richard Mather explained to a number of English Puritans that in Massachusetts written platforms were frowned upon because Christians should find truth directly in the Bible, and the imposing of man-made confessions "doth seem to abridge them of that liberty."[1] Winthrop spoke more to the point when he

1. *Church-Government and Church-Covenant Discussed*, p. 64.

objected to codifying the colony's laws in 1634 because thereby some principles would have to be declared which surely would run counter to English law; whereas, he said, if things were simply allowed to grow, "by practice and custom . . . as in our church discipline," there would be no formal repudiation of English precedents.[1] Consequently, when "these persecuted servants of Christ Jesus first set foot on these American shores," their first concern was to satisfy their long-starved appetites for sermons; realizing that their tongues were at last "untied from the Prelates Injunctions, they preach with all diligence to their auditors, doubling their hours to regain their lost time."[2] Behind the barrage of this pulpit oratory the discipline was unobtrusively set up and started on its career.

Step by step the principles which had been implicit in the ecclesiastical creed of the immigrants received an outward expression. Throughout the course of this development the issues which Puritanism had raised in the homeland continued to occupy men's minds. The New England settlers carried to virgin shores a set of complex problems, for which they had one definite solution, and dedicated themselves to proving that solution to be not merely feasible, but the only fashion in which the difficulties of society at large could ultimately be disentangled. A due form of government in Massachusetts was to be an object-lesson for the resolution of the religious dissension of an erring world.

1. Winthrop, *Journal*, I, 324.
2. "Good newes from New England" (1648), *Mass. Hist. Soc.*, *Coll.*, Series 4, I, 211.

The enterprise was a by-product of the Reformation, a spark shot out from a century of religious friction. From its inception the colony was consciously dedicated to achieving the uniformity to which all reformers had aspired. It was to prove that the Bible could be made a rule of life, that the essentials of religion could be derived from Scripture, and then reinforced by the enlightened dictation of godly magistrates. It was to show that these essentials included polity as well as dogma, and that the one legitimate polity was Congregationalism. Because it would harmonize true uniformity with the true Church, the colony must continue theoretically loyal to its sovereign and his Church; it must give no encouragement to Separation, in either England or New England. It was to convince the world that a government could admit the Puritan claim for delimitation of the civil supremacy by the Word of God without sacrificing a genuine control over the nation's Church, that the King of England could easily permit the churches of England to become Congregational without destroying their continuity or altering the fabric of society. It was, in short, to demonstrate conclusively that Congregationalism could and should be a competent state religion.

The mainstay of the Massachusetts system continued to be Non-separation. New England apologists devoted a larger proportion of their writings to the elucidation of this position than to any other theme, reproducing the arguments, and even sometimes the phraseology, of Ames and his school. "As for our selves, wee look not upon our departure to these parts to be a separation (rigidly taken) but a lawfull secession, or a heavenly

translation from corrupt to more pure churches." [1]
Corruptions in the English churches were still held to be,
at the worst, venial. "The Church may be Christs love,
yea, and a fragrant and pure flower in his sight and nos-
trils, and yet live amongst bryars and thornes:" [2] hence,

to make the *English* Churches, and their Ministries, and their Worship, and their Professors, either nullities, or Anti-christian, is a
witnesse not onely beyond the truth, but against the Truth of the
Lord Jesus, and his word of Truth. [3]

The parishes had gone astray out of ignorance, and
though they were to be commiserated, yet

in as much as the Articles of Religion, which they professe, containe
such wholesome doctrine, that whosoever beleeveth and walketh
according thereunto, in sinceritie, shall undoubtedly be saved, and
in as much as the corruptions are not persisted in with obstinacy,
therefore wee deny not but they have the truth of Churches remaining. [4]

The unimaginative Dudley once objected that the
Church of England held the wrong theological interpretation of Christ's descent into Hell, but Winthrop put
him aside, saying, "the faithfull in England (whom we
account the Churches) expound it as we do." [5] New
Englanders still remembered that English magistrates
forced men to be members of the Church, but "this doth
not hinder the voluntary subjection of others, who with
all their hearts desired it." [6] In fact, Thomas Hooker

1. Shepard and Allin, *A Defence of the Answer*, p. 28.
2. Cotton, *A Briefe Exposition of the whole Book of Canticles*, p. 62.
3. Cotton, "A Reply to Mr. Williams" (1647), *Pub. Narragansett Club*, II, 187.
4. Richard Mather, *An Apologie of the Chvrches in New England*, p. 41.
5. Winthrop, *Journal*, I, 105.
6. Richard Mather, *op. cit.*, p. 38.

actually argued that as long as the congregations of England voluntarily submitted to any ecclesiastical law, no matter how false, "they declare *that* by their *practices, which* others do hold forth by publike *profession.*"[1] The mythical covenant could still be posited as the unsuspected foundation of the parishes. "Congregations in England are truly Churches having an implicite covenant,"[2] and therefore "no voyce of Christ hath declared the Churches of *England* to be false Churches."[3]

To Puritans three thousand miles from Lambeth the Non-separating casuistry held out advantages that had been unsuspected in closer proximity. If, for instance, their migration actually was nothing more than a translation from good churches to better, the ministers had a logical explanation for accepting offices from their congregations, without necessarily renouncing their loyalty to England. If in the homeland their ordination had been defective, it had been, as Ames taught them, none the less true "in substance." We do not believe, Cotton explained, that ministers ever received a calling from bishops; "their vocation or calling is from Christ by the Election or at least acceptation of the Congregation."[4] The confirmation of a bishop or patron was "adventitious and accidental." Pirates capturing a ship might prevent a man from coming to his own goods, but they could not give him a true and proper right to that which he held by a former just title: "I need not apply it to the

1. Hooker, *Survey of the Summe of Church Discipline*, pt. 1, p. 48.
2. Shepard and Allin, *op. cit.*, p. 13.
3. Cotton, "A Reply to Mr. Williams," p. 150.
4. *Ibid.*, pp. 221–222.

case in hand, the Application is obvious."¹ When a minister left his church, even if it was a true church, he was, by Congregational theory, no longer a minister until reordained by the church to which he had removed. Consequently when Skelton and Higginson took up their office at Salem on the strength of an "inward call" from the Lord, and an "outward calling which was from the people," they understood no reference was necessary to their ministry in England, for they had automatically ceased to be ministers when they had left their congregations, or rather had been forced out by the prelatical "pirates." Phillips of Watertown, in 1630, meant the same thing when he said he would not stand by that calling he had received in England. At the formation of the Charlestown church the principle was more clearly enunciated. Wilson was ordained by the imposition of hands, "but with this protestation by all, that it was only as a sign of election and confirmation, not of any intent that Mr. Wilson should renounce his ministry he received in England."² In essence there was no difference between this and the Salem ceremony or the attitude of Phillips; the protest was added only as a political protocol. But not until 1637, at the formation of the Concord church, was the theory given its final touch. It was then decided that ministers who had been ordained in England were lawfully invested by the call of their congregations there — that is, in so far as the churches of England could be described congregationally, they were true churches and could give the substance of a

1. Cotton, *The grovnds and ends of the baptisme of the children of the faithfull*, p. 182.   2. Winthrop, *Journal*, 1, 52.

true call — "notwithstanding their acceptance of the call of the bishops (for which they humbled themselves, acknowledging it their sin) but being come hither, they accounted themselves no ministers, until they were called to another church." [1]   Any description of the ministers' removal, said Cotton, would be a "fraudulent expression" if it did not continually insist that the exiles had been "cast out from thence by the usurping power of the Prelacy, and dismissed (though against their wills) by our Congregations." [2]   New England represented the residue of truth inherent in the Church, a residue now freed from its English alloys. By removing, the Puritans did not separate, but merely began in America a reform which would some day be carried to completion at home.

When rumors of practices in New England spread abroad, some of them were not unnaturally interpreted to be those of the Separatists, and the conclusion to many onlookers seemed obvious. But such deductions Weld insisted were "against all common sense," for we "(professedly) in our writings, preachings, practises manifest the contrary, and testifie as oft as occasion serves, the great dislike of their rigid Separation." [3] Williams, with his customary eye for realities — and his habitual lack of tact — bluntly declared that the people of Massachusetts walked "betwixt Christe and Antichriste . . . in practising separation here, and not repenting of our preaching and printing against it in our

1. *Ibid.*, I, 213.
2. Cotton, "A Reply to Mr. Williams," p. 219.
3. Weld, *An Answer to W. R.*, p. 8.

own country," but Cotton said that this was a willful misrepresentation of the path they had hewn out of the wilderness, for instead they were walking "with an even foote between two extreames; so that we neither defile our selves with the remnant of pollutions in other Churches, nor doo we for the remnant of pollutions renounce the Churches themselves." [1]

Navigation between the Scylla of Separation and the Charybdis of corruption was a hazardous undertaking, but the Massachusetts divines were convinced it could be done. They refused to see in Congregationalism any necessary connection with schism, and Cotton was properly incensed that Williams should attempt to prove Separation "out of the Principles and grounds of those holy Saints of God, whom he misnameth Puritans." [2] Richard Mather triumphantly adduced "Master *Parker* and Doctor *Ames*," both of whom "plead for Church-Covenant, and yet neither of them were Brownists, but bare witnesse against that riged Separation." [3] Do not believe, Davenport pleaded, that "we here justified the wayes of rigid separation, which sometimes amongst you we have formerly born witnesse against." [4] "Be it so," chimed in John Norton, "that we are in the utmost parts of the Earth; we have onely changed our Climate, not our mindes." [5] Indeed, so widely known were the intentions of the New England immigrants in 1631 that a Separatist author bewailed the numbers of his persua-

1. Cotton, "A Letter to Roger Williams," *Pub. Narragansett Club*, i, 308.
2. Cotton, "A Reply to Mr. Williams," p. 198.
3. Richard Mather, *An Apologie of the Churches*, p. 41.
4. Davenport, *An Answer of the Elders*, p. 53.
5. John Norton, *A Copy of the Letter Returned . . . to Mr. John Dury*, p. 1.

sion who were backsliding, "going a great compasse to new England to communicat with the Church of England." [1]

The advantages of the Non-separating position were abundantly demonstrated in 1637 when several Presbyterian Puritans wrote from England complaining that reports of Separation in Massachusetts were encouraging Brownists. John Davenport replied in the name of his colleagues, acknowledging that there had been some matters they had misunderstood at home, and had there accepted as "indifferent and lawful"; but "when we came to weigh them in the ballance of the Sanctuarie, we could not find sufficient warrant in the Word to receive them, and establish them here." [2] In other words, the isolation of Massachusetts permitted Congregationalists to work out projects they had never been able to realize in England, but in so doing they did not play false, they did not abandon their membership in the Church. One of the brethren's questions, for instance, concerned the lawfulness of a set liturgy. In New England ritual had become one of those "shadows" against which it was no longer necessary to strive. The elders had never been called upon to face the issue, because all prayers read out of a book had tacitly been dropped overboard the moment the ships had got under way:

As for our judgement concerning the practise of others, who use this Liturgie in our native Countrey; we have been alwayes unwilling to expresse our minds there against, unless we had been necessarily

1. Burrage, *Early English Dissenters*, I, 177.
2. Davenport, *An Answer of the Elders*, pp. 51–52.

called thereunto . . . contenting ourselves with . . . these Liberties, which wee, by the mercy of God, doe here enjoy.[1]

Thus by remaining consistently Non-separatist, Massachusetts deliberately evaded facing its irreconcilable opposition to the Church of England, while it spread its pretense to legitimacy before the world as a conclusive rebuttal to all accusations of disloyalty. The actualities might be what they would; three thousand miles of ocean protected the colony from any abuse more serious than verbal, which the Massachusetts divines were eminently capable of resenting.[2]

This very Non-separatist position was perhaps the nub of the colony's famous quarrels with Roger Williams and Anne Hutchinson. Williams, from the moment of his arrival, was an authentic Separatist, and refused an offer from the Boston church, "because I durst not offi-

1. *Ibid.*, p. 60.
2. As so often happens with an issue carried to a frontier, this platform continued to be preached in Massachusetts long after the world had ceased to be overmuch concerned with schism and dissent. In its petrified form the tenet of Non-separation can be found in the *Magnalia*:
    "If it now puzzle the reader to reconcile these passages [from *The Humble Request*] with the principles declared, the practices followed, and the persecutions undergone by these American Reformers, let him know that there was more than one distinction, whereof these excellent persons were not ignorant. First they were able to distinguish between the Church of England as it contained the whole body of the faithful . . . and the Church of England, as it was confined unto a certain constitution by canons. . . . Again, they were able to distinguish between the Church of England, as it kept the true doctrine of the Protestant religion . . . and the Church of England as limiting that name unto a certain faction, who, together with a discipline very much unscriptural, vigorously prosecuted the tripartite plot of Arminianism and conciliation with Rome, in the church, and unbounded prerogative in the state. . . . The planters of New England were truer sons to the Church of England, than that part of the church which . . . banished them into this jurisdiction." (Bk. 1, chap. v.)

ciate to an unseparated people, as, upon examination
and conference, I found them to be." [1] When the Salem
congregation wished to choose him for their teacher, the
Court wrote to Endecott in surprise that he should
approve a Separatist.[2] There was no law on the books at
that time to justify this interference with a church's
"liberty" of electing officers,[3] but the Non-separating
policy had to be maintained. Williams eventually gave
other causes for offense, but his Separatism "provoked
the Lord to moove the Court to proceed" against him.[4]
The government's action was in part an advertisement
of its religious position, and Cotton could proudly point
to Williams's banishment as a sign that New England
had not renounced the churches of England.[5] In 1636 an
anonymous correspondent sent Winthrop a letter of
complaint, and in an extensive list of the colony's mis-
deeds could find but one bright spot: "Your disclay-
ming of Mr. Williams' opinions & your dealing with
him soe as we heare you did, took off much preiudice
from you with vs." [6]

English reactions were once more an important factor
in determining the government's policy toward the Antinomians. Reports of the crisis spread rapidly, encouraged by those who were convinced that the colony was
in reality schismatical and were only too eager to behold
it go the way of all Separation. Stansby wrote in April,

1. Williams, "Letters," *Pub. Narragansett Club*, VI, 356.
2. Winthrop, *Journal*, I, 61.
3. Osgood, *The American Colonies in the Seventeenth Century*, I, 266.
4. Cotton, "A Reply to Mr. Williams," p. 75.
5. Cotton, *A Copy of a Letter* (1641), sig. A2.
6. *Mass. Hist. Soc., Coll.*, Series 4, VI, 445.

1637, "I am sory much for your diuisions, we heare great speche of them, & I ame sure that they dant many wise, faythfull Christians & men of ability from comeing. . . ." [1] By distinguishing between two kinds of ministers, Anne Hutchinson offered grounds for a new Separation, wherefore the Court took particular pains to list this aspect of her heresy as one of the reasons for her sentence:

> The servants of God, who are come over into New England, do not think themselves more spirituall then others of their brethren whom they have left behind, nor that they can or doe hold forth the Lord Jesus Christ in their ministry more truly then he was held forth in England.[2]

As soon as Mrs. Hutchinson and Wheelwright had been banished, an account of the proceedings was "sent into England to be published there." [3] In order to maintain its case before the world, Massachusetts had to exterminate Antinomianism, and do so quickly and effectively.

Behind the bulwark of Non-separation Massachusetts theologians brought the Congregational system into working order. They proceeded upon the fundamental assumption of the whole Puritan agitation, that the Bible was a complete practical guide. Their favorite textbook, Ames's *Medulla*, informed them that Scripture was "not a partiall, but a perfect rule of Faith, and manners," that nothing in the Church depended in any way upon mere human tradition.[4] Means of worship, Bradshaw had written, "ought evidently to be pre-

1. *Ibid.*, Series 4, VII, 12.
2. *Antinomianism in Massachusetts Bay* (ed. Charles Francis Adams, Prince Society), p. 178.   3. Winthrop, *Journal*, I, 241.
4. Ames, *The Marrow of Sacred Divinity*, p. 150.

scribed by the word of God, or els ought not to be done." [1] Furthermore, the assumption ran, Scripture was self-evident; it needed no light from other sources, and every verse admitted of but one interpretation. At first, when details of the polity had not yet been worked out, the church covenants cautiously bound the members merely to walk in the ways of the Gospel and "in all sincere Conformity to His holy Ordinaunces." [2] All developments of the next eighteen years were assumed, nevertheless, to have been implied in those covenants, and additions or improvements were continually found justified by holy ordinances:

> The partes of Church-Government are all of them exactly described in the word of God being parts or means of Instituted worship according to the second Commandement. . . . Soe that it is not left in the power of men, officers, Churches, or any state in the world, to add, diminish, or alter any thing in the least measure therein. [3]

With the completed fabric of their government thus authorized in every particular, Cotton declared that New Englanders had never discovered such an exception "as might give us just ground to scruple it"; [4] and though he modestly declined the imputation of perfection he still was certain the New England Way was the nearest thing possible to what would be set up "if the Lord Jesus were here himselfe in person." [5]

To such a conception of church polity any idea of toleration was necessarily foreign. There would be no occa-

1. Bradshaw, *English Puritanisme*, p. 4.
2. Covenant of Charlestown-Boston Church, July 30, 1630, Walker, *Creeds and Platforms*, p. 131.
3. "Cambridge Platform" (1648), chap. i, par. 3, Walker, *op. cit.*
4. Cotton, *Of the Holiness of Church-Members*, p. 30.
5. Cotton, "A Reply to Mr. Williams," p. 237.

sion for our insisting upon this point were it not for the innumerable comments upon the "bigotry" of Massachusetts Puritans. We have seen that for over half a century the Puritan party had been heroically striving for an absolute uniformity. The Massachusetts Bay Company had exhibited its sentiments before leaving England by instructing Endecott to maintain religious conformity even in the frontier outpost of Salem:

> Because it is often found that some busie persons (led more by their will then any good warrant out of Gods word) take opportunitie of moving needless questions to stirr vp strife, and by that meanes to begett a question, and bring men to declare some different judgment (most commonly in things indifferent) from which small beginnings great mischiefs haue followed, wee pray yow and the rest of the councell, that if any such disputes shall happen among yow, that yow suppress them, and bee carefull to maintaine peace and vnitie.[1]

When the ministers had at last erected the consecrated system, for them to admit contradiction would have been to confess they had not reformed according to the Word of God. "A strong motive" to the colonization, declared the historian Edward Johnson, had been "the great enmity betweene that one truth as it is in Jesus" and any other doctrine whatsoever; truth could not stand with falsehood "in one Common-wealth long together, as sixteene hundred yeares experience will testifie."[2] Therefore, since the New England Way was derived "from that patterne of wholesome words written in the Scriptures, Gods good spirit opening our eyes to see it,"[3] New Englanders were compelled to pronounce

1. *Massachusetts Records*, I, 394.
2. Johnson, *The Wonder Working Providences*, p. 12.
3. Weld, *An Answer to W. R.*, p. 11.

all their foes so many heretics. When English Puritans asked if a body of Presbyterians might be allowed to practise their way in Massachusetts, Richard Mather, speaking for all the elders, replied that if "the Discipline appointed by Jesus Christ for his Churches is not arbitrary," but is one and the same for all churches, and if that polity "which we here practice, be (as we are perswaded of it) the same which Christ hath appointed, and therefore unalterable," then "we see not how another can be lawfull; and therefore if a company of people shall come hither, and here set up and practise another, we pray you thinke not much, if we cannot promise to approve of them." [1]

But the colony's determination to maintain uniformity was more than a theological matter. Separatist communities in Holland had horrified the Protestant world by their squabbles, and one of their most ardent leaders had sadly confessed that "the Saincts are subject, (if they be not wary, and haue their wits exercised to discerne good and evill) to be caried about with divers and strange doctrines; to fall into errors, heresies, & idolatries." [2] The Massachusetts experiment would have been shattered had the centrifugal forces of Protestantism broken loose. How, Cotton rhetorically queried, could dissenters be tolerated in a commonwealth "if their worship and Consciences incite them to Civill offences?" [3] The Reformation knew of no instance where the existence of divergent opinions in one com-

---

1. *Church-Government and Church-Covenant Discussed*, p. 83.
2. Ainsworth, *The Commvnion of Saincts*, p. 329.
3. Cotton, *The Bloudy Tenent Washed*, p. 50.

munity had not led to "Civill offences." To tolerate
many religions in a state, declared a committee of ministers in 1635, would not only provoke God and destroy
the peace of the churches, "but also dissolve the continuity of the State." [1] And the experience of the colony
with the Hutchinson faction only confirmed that im-
pression.

To the leaders of the colony the Antinomian heresy
was simply a challenge to live up to their professions.
The heresy itself was an old, old story. As Hugh Peter
thundered at young Harry Vane, the policies of the dissenters were those which "both in the Low Countries
and here" had ever been the "principal causes of new
opinions." [2] At the beginning of the fracas Wilson made
a sad speech before the General Court on "the inevitable danger of separation, if these differences and aliena-
tions among brethren were not speedily remedied," [3] and
the Court itself ordered the opposition disarmed because
they feared that the Antinomians "as others in Germany, in former times, may, vpon some revelation,
make some suddaine irruption vpon those that differ
from them in iudgment." [4] Anne Hutchinson condemned herself when she publicly acknowledged that
she believed her directions came to her "by an immediate revelation"; she thus set herself down as a clear instance of a recognized heresy which Protestantism had
agreed in condemning for over a century. "It is the

1. Quoted in Williams, *The Bloudy Tenent of Persecution*, ed. Samuel L.
   Caldwell, *Pub. Narragansett Club*, iii, 278.
2. Winthrop, *Journal*, i, 204.
3. *Ibid.*, p. 204.
4. *Massachusetts Records*, i, 211.

most desperate enthusiasm in the world, for nothing but a word comes to her mind, and then an application is made which is nothing to the purpose and this is her revelations." [1]   Any orthodox Protestant community would have looked upon her as Massachusetts did, and have disposed of her in pure self-defense.

All the colony's preconceptions were substantiated by the social upheaval the business seemed to threaten. Mistress Hutchinson, the Court declared,

hath manifested that . . . she walked by such a rule as cannot stand with the peace of any State; for such bottomlesse revelations . . . if they be allowed in one thing, must be admitted a rule in all things: for they being above reason and Scripture, they are not subject to controll.[2]

That this was not a baseless apprehension had been shown when the men of Boston refused at a critical moment to go to the Pequod war because their chaplain, John Wilson, was under a "covenant of works." It is no wonder Winthrop answered Anne's charge that the ministers alone were persecuting her by declaring, "It is not their cause, but the cause of the whole country," [3] or that he justified the government's measures before the Boston congregation, because "those brethren were so divided from the rest of the country in their judgment and practice, as it could not stand with the public peace, that they should continue amongst us." [4]

The resemblance of this tempest in a teapot to the greater storms of Europe seemed to become unmistak-

1. *Antinomianism in Massachusetts Bay*, pp. 269, 275.
2. *Ibid.*, p. 177.
3. *Ibid.*, p. 256.
4. Winthrop, *Journal*, I, 257.

able when the emotional reactions on both sides outran
the doctrinal disagreements. Cotton and Shepard defined their differences with Wheelwright so narrowly that
"except men of good understanding, and such as knew
the bottom of the tenets of those of the other party, few
could see where the difference was." [1] During the controversy "it began to be as common here to distinguish
between men, by being under a covenant of grace or a
covenant of works, as in other countries between Protestants and papists." [2] Exactly the same results as had
followed "in other countries" were reproduced in minia-
ture in Massachusetts: "Upon these public occasions,
other opinions brake out publicly in the church of
Boston . . . and others spread more secretly." [3] When,
therefore, the orthodox party arose in their might and
banished the Hutchinson crowd, they not only exiled a
transcendental dame, but, according to their lights,
saved the Reformation. They preserved in at least one
corner of the world a discipline derived out of the Word,
and they proved it altogether capable of serving as a
basis for national uniformity.

The theory upon which the New England churches
dealt with dissenters resulted logically from their regard
for the Bible. So obvious were the teachings of Scripture averred to be that anyone who did not embrace
them, particularly after a godly minister had consulted
with him, must, *ipso facto*, be perverse. Once more
Ames was the master:

Such an one is to be accounted stubborn, as when the truth is not
onely manifestly revealed in Scripture, but is also sufficiently pro-

1. *Ibid.*, p. 217.   2. *Ibid.*, p. 209.   3. *Ibid.*, p. 206.

pounded, and manifested unto him, yet doth so adhere to his errour, that he either opposeth himselfe to the plaine Scripture, and will not through the naughtinesse of his mind perceive the sence of it, for he is obstinate which is not ready to captivate all his understanding and reason unto Scripture.[1]

This machinery of conviction was transported intact to America. "We have meanes to preserve the Churches in unitie and verity," boasted Richard Mather: "First, the holy Scriptures, which are a perfect rule for Doctrine and practise.... Secondly, the Ministery appointed by Christ."[2] Cotton defined "persecution" as "the affliction of any for their Righteousnesse sake,"[3] and he held that it was unlawful to act against any "for conscience sake rightly informed."[4] But the fundamentals of religion were so clear that a man could not help perceiving them when they were pointed out to him. "After once or twice Admonition, the Heretick cannot but be convinced in his owne Conscience."[5] If, nevertheless, he persisted in his fault, then it was not out of conscience, "but against his Conscience . . . so that if such a man after such Admonition, shall still persist in the Error of his way, and be therefore punished, He is not persecuted for cause of Conscience, but for sinning against his Conscience."[6] This sort of persecution was not only justifiable, it was even merciful, for it took into consideration the "many scores or hundreds of the soules of such, as will be infected and destroyed by the

1. *Conscience with the Power and Cases therof*, bk. IV, p. 10.
2. *Church-Government and Church-Covenant Discussed*, p. 62.
3. "A Reply to Mr. Williams," p. 32.
4. Cotton, *The Controversie Concerning Liberty of Conscience*, p. 7.
5. Cotton, *The Bloudy Tenent Washed*, p. 29.
6. *Ibid.*, pp. 26–27.

toleration of the other." [1] Upon this theory heretics in Massachusetts were invariably cross-examined, shown the error of their ways, found "stubborn," and censured accordingly. Williams had not been afflicted for his righteousness, but for "that which is left of old *Adam*" in him.[2] The modern rejoinder would be that Cotton, the agent of affliction, also determined what constituted "old Adam," but Cotton considered such a retort irrelevant. The determination was not his but the Lord's. "As for *New England*," Shepard announced, "we never banished any for their consciences, but for sinning against conscience, after due meanes of conviction, or some other wickednesse which they had no conscience to plead for." [3]

These observations make quite comprehensible a fact which critics have often supposed a gross inconsistency in the conduct of the clergy. There was, after all, nothing amiss in the persecuted of England becoming the persecutors of New England. The Puritans should never have been repressed, not, however, because repression itself was wrong, but because Puritans, "though they consented not to the State-Government of the Church; yet neither did they tumultuously and seditiously resist it." [4] They had not separated, they had not taught that it was unlawful for magistrates to pursue "apostate seducers" with just revenge. Now that they at last were "sitting at Helme," what were the clergy teaching which

1. *Ibid.*, p. 35.
2. Cotton, "A Reply to Mr. Williams," pp. 27–28.
3. Shepard, *New Englands Lamentation for Old Englands present errors* (1645), p. 3.
4. Cotton, *The Bloudy Tenent Washed*, p. 137.

they had not themselves allowed when they "were under the Hatches"?

> What we measure out to others, wee should never thinke it hard measure to have the same returned to our selves in the like case, Onely this measure we desire of all hands to be kept . . . that the Righteous should not be as the wicked: nor that Truth, and Fidelity, should suffer as Heresie and Apostacy.[1]

If, Weld said, the New England Way were simply "our way" and not Christ's, then forcible measures "were our great sinne and (in part) the same with the Prelates of late"; but since the Way was manifestly divine, its conduct was none other than what "Christ himselfe would doe if in our places."[2]

During the weary years in which Puritans and Separatists had labored to convince the English nation that the divine will should prevail, they had been compelled to place a mighty emphasis upon the conception of a fundamental law. All would-be reformers had agreed that the Church should be required to show biblical authorization for every act. In the period of its incubation Congregationalism became thoroughly imbued with this legalistic character. Consequently churches in New England were assumed from the beginning to have not only a structure divinely ordained, but a government continually regulated by a written and unamendable constitution. Christ was the sole source of ecclesiastical legislation, and he had long ago published all the statutes Christians would ever find necessary. Churches possessed at best merely a "ministerial" or "stewardly"

---

1. *Ibid.*, p. 170.
2. Weld, *An Answer to W. R.*, p. 13.

power, given them by commission, permitting them "onely to publish and execute his Laws and Ordinances, and to see them observed."[1] Ministers, Ames had taught, could not "propound or doe any thing in the Church which they have not prescribed to them in the Scriptures."[2] It was not within the churches' power, said Cotton, to perform any act "of their own head, but to receive all as from the hand of Christ, and to dispense all according to the will of Christ revealed in his Word."[3] The Congregational structure was founded upon the principle that church policies were never to be determined by any human considerations, but by the basic law, "by rules from the word of Christ, whose will, (and not the will either of the Major, or Minor part of men) is the onely rule and Law for Churches."[4]

Into this philosophy of a fundamental ecclesiastical constitution Congregationalism introduced a peculiarly complicating element. The essence of a Congregational organization was the voluntary consociation of a fraternity. All the superstructure — sacraments, ministry, government — was to be created by that body after the covenant had been sworn; such things were "appurtenances and dependants of the true Visible Church," but a church was "the body, the foundation, or the subject whereon they depend, and where in they all consist, and by vertue of whose authoritie they all are & have their true being."[5] Obviously, therefore, the govern-

1. Cotton, *The Keyes of the Kingdom of Heaven*, p. 30.
2. *The Marrow of Sacred Divinity*, p. 154.
3. *The True Constitution of a particular visible Church*, p. 9.
4. Richard Mather, *Church-Government and Church-Covenant Discussed*, p. 60.   5. Jacob, *The Divine Beginning*, sig. D2.

ment of a church was not only bound to a basic scriptural constitution, but it was perpetually subject to the
will of the society from which it sprang. This doctrine,
no less than the other, was carried to New England.
Hooker, controverting Presbyterian attacks upon the
church covenant, took especial pains to point out that
"Mutuall covenanting and confoederation of the Saints
in the fellowship of the faith according to the order of
the Gospel, is that which gives constitution and being to
a visible Church." [1] In such a philosophy one thing at
least seemed certain, that the common members of the
church possessed a decided share in the government, a
share allowed by neither Anglicanism nor Presbyterianism. Cotton willingly admitted as much. The Apostle
Peter, he held, was given church power by Christ because he professed his faith in the name of the church:

How can it stand either with Faith or Reason, That a Church of
Believers professing the same Faith with *Peter*, shall receive no part
of Church-power at all, in respect of their profession of the Faith,
but only in respect of their Officers that preach the Faith? [2]

The question then remained in what this power of the
multitude consisted? What authority did the members
acquire by virtue of their being themselves the *raison
d'être* of the church? Clearly they had a power to select
their officers. It could be only by the voluntary subjection of those who had a choice of rulers that a person
chosen stood possessed of rule and authority over them.
Once appointed, the officers had to remain in some
fashion responsible to the congregation. They could not,

1. *Survey*, pt. 1, 46.
2. *The Way of the Congregational Churches Cleared*, pt. 11, p. 35.

for instance, excommunicate one of their own constitu-
ents without first proving to the whole number that he
held such and such an opinion and that this opinion was
"an errour by the word of God, and that it deserveth
such a Censure, before they doe proceed against him." [1]
If the ministers did not live up to the terms upon which
they were elected, if they did not abide by the laws of
Christ, then, Robinson had preached, the church, even
"the meanest member therof," was not bound to submit; the clergy were not to be obeyed "for the authority
of the commander, but for the reason of the commandment, which the ministers are also bound in duty to
manifest, and approve unto the consciences of them over
whom they are set." [2] Finally, if officers were elected by
the acclamation of the fraternity, then they were cen-
surable by it if they failed in their office. "The Congregation that chose them freely, hath as free power to
depose them, and to place others in their room." [3] This
theory was dutifully echoed in Massachusetts: the
ministers, said Richard Mather, could not do "any
thing in their places, which the word of Christ . . . commandeth not . . . nor ought the Church to consent unto
them, if they should." [4]

The inescapable conclusion seemed to be that since
the people by their covenant had created the organization, in the final analysis the people were to decide
whether any act of the society fell within the scope of
the covenant. To this extent Congregational philosophy

1. Bradshaw, *English Puritanisme*, p. 25.
2. Robinson, *Works*, III, 61.
3. Bradshaw, *Several Treatises*, p. 99.
4. *Church-Government and Church-Covenant Discvssed*, p. 58.

involved a step in the direction of what we today call democracy. But such praise as we might bestow upon seventeenth-century Congregationalists on the score of their democracy would assuredly be considered by them gratuitous. The age was no admirer of government by the people; Puritans had constantly demonstrated their abhorrence of it, and Congregationalists, whether Separatist or Non-separatist, had done their best to ward off the insidious aspersion of equalitarian leanings. They had found their rebuttal in a characteristic Reformation idea. When Calvin discussed the possible kinds of government, he distinguished monarchy, aristocracy, and democracy; and he concluded that a mixture of the last two or even of all three was the ideal form for this world. The notion had been glibly repeated throughout the sixteenth century. When, therefore, Congregationalists admitted a certain democracy into their polity, they hastened to explain that it was only one element in the total make-up. The people, they had to admit, were the source of the clergy's commission, but the process of government undoubtedly was not democratic, it was "mixed." As Ames phrased it:

> The forme of this polity is altogether monarchicall in respect of Christ, the head and King; but as touching the visible and vicarious administration, it is of a mixt nature, partly as it were aristocraticall, and partly as it were democraticall.[1]

Robinson and the Separatists advanced the same conception: "In respect of Him, the Head, it is a monarchy; in respect of the eldership, an aristocracy; in respect of

1. Ames, *The Marrow of Sacred Divinity*, p. 145.

the body, a popular state." [1] However radical the
Separatists were in some respects their social philosophy
was not unconventional. "So then for *popular government*," declared Ainsworth, "we hold it not, we approue
it not, for if the multitude gouern, then who shalbe
gouerned?" [2]

As long as Congregationalism remained the creed of
embattled minorities or of persecuted Separatists, these
rather generalized declarations did them yeoman's service; the one group were absorbed too much in demonstrating their political orthodoxy by not separating, and
the other too much in proving theirs even though they
had separated, for either of them to work out a specific
application of their "mixed" government. As far as
they went, their qualification of the polity's democratic
aspects simply meant stressing the powers of the elders,
both spiritual and lay. The whole church, congregation
and ministry alike, was bound by the absolute and arbitrary law of the Bible; but the elders were the students
and interpreters of the law, and in ordinary practice they
were to guide the congregation. Though a brotherhood
might choose to follow Christ, they needed to have
Christ expounded to them. Robert Browne had at first
intended matters of rule to be determined by the whole
body of saints, but his successors, more experienced in
the workings of the system, exalted the tutelary guidance of the elders as a necessary check upon an irre-
sponsible exercise of the congregation's liberty. [3] Robin-

1. Robinson, *Works*, II, 140.
2. Ainsworth, *Counterpoyson*, p. 103.
3. Dexter, *Congregationalism of the Last Three Hundred Years*, p. 222;
   Walker, *Creeds and Platforms*, p. 31; Burrage, *Early English Dissenters*,

son's exposition of the machinery of Congregational government reveals the extent to which the prophets were employing every device in their power to counteract its fundamental democratic principle:

Now lest any should take occasion to conceive, that we either exercise amongst ourselves, or would thrust upon others, any popular, or democratical church government, may it please the Christian reader to make estimate of both our judgment and practise. . . .

First, We believe, that the external government under Christ . . . is plainly aristocratical, and to be administered by some choice men, although the state, which many unskilfully confound with the government, be after a sort popular and democratical. By this it appertains to the people freely to vote in elections and judgments of the church. In respect of the other, we make account it behoves the elders to govern the people, even in their voting, in just liberty, given by Christ whatsoever. Let the elders publicly propound, and order all things in the church . . . let the people of faith give their assent to their elders holy and lawful administration.[1]

Non-separating Congregationalists, being even more conservatively minded, aggravated this emphasis. According to Jacob, the church, once organized, was "to be informed, directed, and guided by the Pastor chiefly, and also by the grave assistant Elders."[2] He intended that the members should be the source of elections and censures, but they were ordinarily to avoid acting upon their own initiative, striving rather "freely to consent to their Guides preparing & directing every matter."[3]

The crucial point in the system was excommunication. Whoever controlled that weapon would rule the church.

1, 130; Henry W. Clark, *A History of English Nonconformity*, I, 198.
1. Robinson, *Works*, III, 42–43.
2. Jacob, *The Divine Beginning*, sig. A3 verso.
3. Burrage, *op. cit.*, II, 160.

At first sight it would seem to have been the congregation's, for if the society was created by compact, then the signers of the compact should have the ultimate word about admitting or expelling members. This, the theorists admitted, was true; but, they continued, rejections had to be determined not by the whim of the crowd, but by concrete laws. Therefore those who were skilled in the laws, the ministers, were to direct the trial and make clear to the congregation how it should exercise its God-given power. The "right and power" of censure belongs to the brotherhood, said Ames, but the "administration" belongs to the elders.[1] The officers should consult together, "apart from the People," agreed Jacob, should cross-examine the accused, and prepare the case against him, "in such sort that the *People* may not neede to do ought afterward but only Consent with them." [2] The ideal of the discipline was compared by Robinson to a session of Assize, where the whole procedure is dictated by the law of the land, where, nevertheless, the jury's "power and sentence is of such force, as that the Lord Chief Justice himself and all the Bench with him, cannot proceed agaynst it," yet where "the Bench governeth the whole action, and the Jury is by them, according to law, to be governed." [3] By some such counterbalancing of the governors and governed, through their mutual subjection to an explicit and all-sufficient code, Congregationalism had been attempting to work out a discipline in which the pre-

1. Ames, *Conscience*, bk. IV, pp. 88–89.
2. Jacob, *Reasons taken out of Gods Word*, p. 28.
3. Quoted in Ainsworth, *An Animadversion to Mr. Richard Clyftons Advertisement*, p. 113.

scriptions of Christ could be realized while the social predilections of the age would at the same time be respected.

When the discipline was carried to America, it was put immediately to uses exactly opposite to those it had served in England. Instead of being the shield of an attacking party, it suddenly became the platform of a ruling oligarchy; instead of being invoked to delimit the sway of kings and prelates, it was now employed to rule a populace. Whereas the supporters of the polity had formerly stifled its democratic tendencies to preserve their respectability, they now were compelled to chain them to maintain their power. Consequently, though they carried over the idea of limitation of church officers by the fundamental law of God and by the corporate will of the society, they now had to make sure that such limitation would not prevent the ministers from holding the throttle. In England Congregationalists had confidently predicted that the loyalty of Christian congregations would keep them obedient to the law as expounded by the elders; confronted with the problem of ruling an actual and often cantankerous crowd of erstwhile dissenters, they realized this obedience had to be insured by more potent guarantees. If the clergy failed to control the internal affairs of their churches, then for all their attempts to maintain Non-separation and unity, their parishes would inevitably drift apart, divergences and schisms appear, and popular frenzies break out.

The New England divines, therefore, went over the whole framework of Congregational thought, tightening up the bolts of cohesion. They continued to characterize the government as mixed, or, as Davenport called it, "Aristocratico-Democratical." The essence of a church was still the covenant of the fellowship, and a church existed as soon as the covenant was taken, whether any officers were elected or not. Yet, the apologists hastened to add, a church without officers was not complete, and as soon as the compact was made, the members had no choice but to proceed to an election. This necessity, the *Cambridge Platform* declared, was by order of Christ "to continue to the end of the world, and for the perfecting of all the Saints." [1] Thus Cotton said that while he granted a covenanted brotherhood was essentially a church, still he himself never thought of a "particular church" without intending "a Congregation of Believers furnished with Officers." He insisted that the elders were given to the church, "not as meer adjuncts given to a Subject, but as Integral parts given to the whole Body of the Church, for completing the integrity and perfection of it." [2] Though a church properly began with the people, and though a ministry could not exist until the people had themselves ordained it, yet newly associated members could not linger to congratulate each other upon the power they had acquired, but immediately must subject themselves to the rule of proper superiors. They had a freedom as to *whom* they should choose, but no freedom to refrain from choosing at all. [3]

1. Chap. vi, pars. 1–2, in Walker, *Creeds and Platforms*.
2. *The Way of the Congregational Churches Cleared*, pt. ii, p. 20.
3. Even this freedom was seriously qualified by the requirement that the man chosen should possess a discernible "inner call"; the congregation, said Cotton, "cannot choose or ordaine whom they please, but whom they

Since a minister's election to office was dependent upon a congregation's call, to that extent he might still be said to derive his rank from the constituency. But the constituency had not created the office, and could not designate to an officer what his powers should and should not be; those were already determined by an altogether independent authority, by the Bible. This was a matter which Hooker warns us is "to be understood with a grain of salt, and requires a wise and wary explication." [1] The power of government might be said to be in the brotherhood "in that they design the persons unto office, who only are to act, or to exercise this power," [2] but not in that they invented the office itself. That was "the immediate institution of Christ, the gifts and power belonging thereto are from Christ immediately." The congregation could not "inlarge or straiten the limits of his office whom they do elect or ordaine, but as the Lord hath prescribed." [3] The minister's outward call was essentially "from Christ," although "by his Church"; and his election, therefore, no more made him "the servant of the Church, then a Captain (by leave of the Generall) chosen by the Band of Souldiers is the servant of his Band." [4] Christ alone bestowed upon individuals the graces and abilities which qualified them

see the Lord Iesus hath prepared and fitted for them " (*The Way of the Churches of Christ in New England*, p. 44). There are numerous instances of the authorities prohibiting the election of a minister because they felt his spiritual summons was faulty; the debarring of Williams at Salem, already referred to, was but the first instance of the sort.

1. Hooker, *Survey*, pt. 1, 187.
2. *Cambridge Platform*, chap. v, par. 2.
3. Cotton, *The Way of the Churches of Christ in New England*, p. 44.
4. Shepard and Allin, *A Defence of the Answer*, p. 130.

as ministers, and he alone, "out of his supreme and regal power . . . appoints the work, laies out the compasse thereof, the manner of dispensing, and the order and bounds of their dispensation." The church controlled the gateway to the office, but not the office, and its voluntary subjection permitted persons to enter upon the office, "to put forth their abilities and Ministerial authority over such a people." Thus congregations could ordain pastors, although the powers of the office never passed through their hands; they might "give a call and power to such and such to be Pastors, and yet themselves not Pastors." [1] There is no analogy between this system and American constitutional theory; the component elements of the society did not draw up the fundamental law or delegate to the government any sovereignty they originally held. On the contrary, an absolute monarch had laid down the law arbitrarily, and had chosen to formulate two kinds of prerogatives, each of which was to be traced directly to him and not one to the other. The congregations retained no "residual powers"; their existence simply was prerequisite to the ministers' opportunity "to do that which they themselves cannot do." [2] Both parties had certain prescribed obligations to fulfill, and neither of them could overstep its limits. Elders could come into being only by the call of a particular congregation, because it was physically impossible for a church to exist until the elect had gathered in one place. "Beleevers that are as scattered stones, and are not seated in a visible Church or Cor-

1. Hooker, *Survey*, pt. 1, pp. 190–191.
2. *Ibid.*, p. 187.

poration, as setled in the wall," could not be possessed of any coherent power.[1] Yet the primary condition of their becoming seated in a corporation was that they formally enslave their will to the revealed Word of God, and the revealed Word required them to nominate a fitting man upon whom Christ and not themselves should bestow the authority they were to obey.

Thus when the internal government of a Congregational church was perfected in New England, the ostensible result was a peculiar system of balanced, interlocking, and yet independent authorities. The elders administered and the congregations rendered judgments, each according to a set of rules devised for those particular functions: "*The power of judgement* and *power of office* are apparently *distinct* and different *one from another.*"[2] The assumption was that the two were complementary; the elders, said Hooker,

are superior to *the Fraternity* in regard of *Office*, *Rule*, *Act*, and *Exercise*; which is proper only to them, and not to the Fraternity. The people or *Church* are superior to the Elders in point of censure; each have their full scope in their own sphere and compasse, without the prejudice of the other.[3]

Cotton corroborated Hooker:

The Gospel alloweth no Church authority (or rule properly so called) to the Brethren, but reserveth that wholly to the Elders; and yet preventeth the tyrannie and oligarchy, and exorbitancy of the Elders, by the large and firm establishment of the liberties of the Brethren.[4]

1. *Ibid.*, p. 203.
2. *Ibid.*, pt. III, p. 45.
3. *Ibid.*, pt. I, pp. 190–191.
4. *The Keyes of the Kingdom of Heaven*, p. 12.

Shepard and Allin declared that if the rules were properly distinguished,

a dim sight may easily perceive how the execution of the Keys by the officers authoritatively may stand with the liberties of the people in their places *obedientially* following and concurring with their guides.[1]

The *Cambridge Platform* epitomized the theory by declaring that the power of the elders and the privileges of the brethren did not prejudice each other, but "may sweetly agree together"; hence all ecclesiastical conduct was the expression of a divine partnership, proceeding "after the manner of a mixt administration, so as no church act can be consummated, or perfected without the consent of both." [2]

This theory of dual authorities coöperating voluntarily in the advancement of Christ's kingdom was a triumph of ingenuity. It preserved the genuine Christian virtues that Puritanism opposed to the formalism of the Establishment, and projected a church system which followed the instructions of Christ, admitting members only upon profession of their faith and allowing them as Christians to exercise the privileges of the elect. At the same time, the theory provided a check upon human tendencies to go astray, a sure-fire method for maintaining law and order. On paper it served the purpose for which it was evolved: it proved that Congregationalism was not unduly democratic. "Tumultuous disorder" clearly was impossible where "the multitude of Brethren are governed by the Elders" and where "not the will of

1. *A Defence of the Answer*, p. 131.
2. Chap. x, pars. 10–11.

each man beareth sway, but the voice of Christ alone is heard." [1] But when the theory was put into practice it was not long in betraying an all-important catch. In spite of the delicate balancing of coördinate realms of activity, the really crucial power was in the hands of the elders. The reason, once more, was the fundamental assumption of the whole enterprise, that the discipline was derived out of the Word. For the ministers were the interpreters of the Word. Individual members were no match for those who devoted their days and nights to exegesis. As official expounders of the law, the elders took the lead in every action and laid down the principles upon which the congregation was to make its decisions. They were, in effect, the interpreters of the very rules by which they were supposed to be limited, so that it was only in flagrant cases that the democracy had much chance of disciplining them. "It was generally desired," at the Synod of 1643, "that the exercitium of the Churches power might onely be in the Eldership in each particular Church, unless their sinnes be apparent in their worke." [2] If a single member objected, the elders could easily go through the ceremony of "confuting" him; if he persisted he was "partial" and "factious," and "the Church ought to deale with such an one, for not consenting," else "they shall all be guilty of the sinfull dissent of such an one." [3] The elders interviewed candidates and determined their fitness for membership; though the whole church finally voted upon the

1. Cotton, *The Way of the Church of Christ in New England*, p. 100.
2. *A Reply of two of the Brethren to A. S.* (1644), p. 8.
3. Richard Mather, *Church-Government and Church-Covenant Discussed*, p. 58; Dexter, *op. cit.*, p. 429.

applicants, the officers were "to shew the Church the rule on which the Church is to receive them, and themselves are ready to admit them,"[1] a privilege which gave the officers a working control over the make-up of the organization. In the matter of censures they first prepared the indictment against an accused and demonstrated the rule by which he should be dealt with, so that the congregation's function as "the supream Tribunal in poynt of judgment" resolved itself in practice into a doing of what it was told:

the peoples discerning and approving the justice of the censure before it be administred, ariseth from the Elders former instruction and direction of them therein: Whereunto the people give consent, in obedience to the will and rule of Christ.[2]

Complaints against members could not be made before the church, but only to the elders. In fact, all business upon which the whole body had to vote was prepared beforehand by the officers.[3] We "bring as few matters as possible, into the Assembly," declared Weld, "rather labouring to take all things up in private, and then make as short work in publique, (when they must needs come there) as may be." [4] This meant, of course, that the congregation's decision was always dependent upon the way evidence was submitted to it; Roger Williams, for instance, accused the elders in Boston of holding back public letters from the body of the church.[5] Finally, in

1. Shepard and Allin, *A Defence of the Answer*, p. 194.
2. Cotton, *The Keyes of the Kingdom of Heaven*, pp. 14–15.
3. Hooker, *Survey*, pt. I, pp. 134, 135; pt. III, p. 36; Lechford, *Plain Dealing*, pp. 20, 31.
4. *An Answer to W. R.*, p. 41.
5. Williams, *Letters*, p. 72.

the conduct of meetings the elders were moderators, and exercised an overwhelming influence both as the wielders of the gavel and as interpreters of parliamentary procedure. They had power "from Christ" to restrain "any mans speech, whilest another is speaking; and to cut off any mans speech that groweth either impertinent or intemperate." [1] The original intention of Congregationalism had been, as Williams expressed it, that an apprehension of the mind of Christ be returned "in solemn seeking of God's face by the whole Church." [2] In the New England Way the "guidance" of the elders constantly minimized the congregation's share in the search. The Synod of 1637 frowned upon the custom of asking questions from the floor after a sermon,[3] so that Richard Mather proudly boasted, "A man may now live from one end of the year unto another in these Congregations, & not hear any man open his mouth in such kind of asking Questions." [4] The *Cambridge Platform* summarized the development by informing the members that they might not

oppose nor contradict the judgment or *sentence* of the Elders, without sufficient & weighty cause, becaus such practices are manifestly contrary unto order, & government, & in-lets of disturbance, & tend to confusion.[5]

In addition to the powers the elders possessed by virtue of their office, they exacted respect and obedience from the imponderable influences of their social posi-

1. Cotton, *The Way of the Churches of Christ in New England*, p. 100.
2. Williams, *op. cit.*, p. 73.
3. Winthrop, *Journal*, 1, 234.
4. *Church-Government and Church-Covenant Discvssed*, p. 79.
5. Chap. x, par. 8.

tion, their learning, and the tradition in which the
people had been reared. The Middle Ages and the Reformation had inculcated the virtues of submission to
authority so thoroughly that Shepard was conscious of
no incongruity when he declared that the "liberty" of a
Congregational people was exercised most appropriately
"in a way of subjection, and obedience" to their elders.[1]
The supposedly more liberal Hooker, though stressing
the congregation's right to censure a transgressing elder,
still salvaged the almost irresistible influence of the
minister by instructing the people that "they must give
way while he delivers the mind of Christ out of the
Gospel, and acts all the affairs of his Kingdome, according to his rule; and as it suits with his mind."[2]
"The work and duty of the people," concluded the
Cambridge Platform, "is expressed in the phrase of obey-
ing their Elders, and submitting themselves unto them
in the Lord."[3] The difference between an elder and a
member, said Richard Mather, was the difference between a steward over a house and one of the house-
maids.[4] In spite of the fact that the congregation called
the officers to their position, it could not remain in command; a queen, said Cotton, could summon her mari-
ners and instruct them to carry her to such and such a
place, but

they being called by her to such an office, shee must not rule them in
steering their course, but must submit her selfe to be ruled by them,

---

1. Shepard and Allin, *op. cit.*, p. 13.
2. Hooker, *Survey*, pt. 1, p. 192.
3. Chap. x, par. 7.
4. Mather, *op. cit.*, p. 60.

till they have brought her to her desired Haven. So is the case between the Church and her Elders.[1]

The voyage upon which the church had embarked was for
life, and the latitude and longitude of the destined haven
had been determined by Christ; consequently, although
a congregation launched a church, thereafter any attempt it might make to mount the bridge and displace
the navigators was mutiny on the high seas of religion.
The Christian liberty of the common man, which
had looked so tremendous when preached by Robert
Browne, had shrunk by the time of the *Cambridge Platform* to little more than his liberty to enter a church
covenant if he could prove he possessed the faith. The
perfect characterization of the whole system was that of
Hooker's colleague, Stone, when he described it as "a
speaking *Aristocracy* in the face of a silent *Democracy*." [2]

* * *

In English Congregationalism there had existed the
rudiments of another feature which the proponents of
the system had advanced as an aid to uniformity.
Synods were permitted as long as they were to be "de-
liberative and persuasive" rather than "ruling," as long
as they were to lend advice and counsel but not to impose decrees upon particular churches by force. Because
Congregationalists at that time were combating the centralized systems of both Presbyterianism and Anglicanism, they took more pains to delimit synods than to define them. Yet both Separatists and Non-separatists

1. *The Keyes of the Kingdom of Heaven*, p. 23.
2. Cotton Mather, *Magnalia*, 1, 437.

had dimly perceived their value. A synod's determinations, said Jacob, "are most expedient and wholesome alwayes," [1] and the Confession of the London-Amsterdam church in 1596 declared that though congregations should be distinct bodies, "every one as a compact Citie in it selfe," they were still "by all meanes convenient to haue the counsell and help one of another in all needfull affayres of the Church." [2]

Once more, when the platform of an English opposition became a system of control in New England, the emphasis was inevitably shifted.   Congregationalists had glibly predicted that the instructions of the Bible were explicit enough to keep autonomous organizations facing in the same direction; but when they at last set up a number of such churches, they realized that interpretations might vary more than they had imagined. Little by little they came to rely upon periodic consociations of elders from the various churches to make sure that they were all continuing in substantial agreement. The Bible and their tradition prevented the clergy from ever acknowledging that their sessions did more than give mutual advice and criticism, but in the close confinement of a frontier community the agreement of a majority acquired practically an irresistible weight. A lone dissenter or a single dissenting church would be socially almost isolated. The more disagreements appeared, the more was the device employed, until by the time of the *Cambridge Platform* its function in the system was formally recognized.

1. *Reasons taken out of Gods Word*, p. 31.
2. Walker, *Creeds and Platforms*, p. 71.

The ministers evidently began very early to get together for the discussion of matters "of moment"; Williams objected to the custom in 1633, fearing it "might grow in time to a presbytery or superintendency." The ministers at once denied the possibility, and assured Williams that they held that "no church or person can have power over another church." [1] Still, the effectiveness of consociation as a means of control had already been demonstrated. In July, 1631, a ruling elder at Watertown, one Richard Browne, broached the intolerable opinion that the Church of Rome, like the Church of England, was "in substance" a true church. Winthrop, Dudley, and Nowell visited the town twice; they told the congregation that it had to decide first of all in what capacity they were appearing, whether as magistrates, or as members of a neighboring church come to offer "advice." The church decided in favor of the latter rôle, whereupon the visitors "advised" against Browne, and the ultimate resolution of this trouble proved that in the voluntary consociation of churches the colony possessed a weapon of social pressure all the more effective for not being frankly mandatory. [2] Other advantages of the practice were revealed in 1634, when John Eliot criticized the magistrates for making a peace with the Pequods "without consent of the people." Cotton, Weld, and Hooker were sent to deal with him, that he might "be brought to see his error, and heal it by some public explanation of his meaning; for the people began to take occasion to murmer against us for it." The emi-

1. Winthrop, *Journal*, I, 112.
2. *Ibid.*, pp. 66, 71, 83, 95.

nent pillars of society succeeded, by way of "advice," in
showing the Apostle to the Indians his "error." [1]
Thenceforward there are numerous evidences of the associated ministers being called upon to deal with a
lengthening list of matters, their survey soon including
a goodly part of the internal workings of individual
churches. In March, 1635, several elders went to Saugus
to iron out difficulties between the minister and his
flock.[2] People at Lynn, in the next year, attempted to
found a church, and the elders of the Bay, dubious about
the orthodoxy of the town, hastened to examine the
candidates; after two days of investigation, they approved the pastor and six members, "but with much
ado." [3] The Charlestown church quarrelled with its
pastor, James; the neighboring elders were summoned,
decided James was in fault, and "advised" the church
to dismiss him.[4] Shepard and Mather both paid obei-
sance to the consociation by inviting representatives
to the formation of their respective churches.[5] Hugh
Peter, in dealing with the remnants of the Williams
faction at Salem, called in other churches for advice,[6]
and he wrote into the revised covenant of the church a
clause binding it to use the counsel of "our sister
Churches." [7] Within a decade it had become the established custom of the colony to require the presence of
neighboring ministers at the covenanting of new organizations, at the election of all officers, or at the deposi-

1. *Ibid.*, p. 142.   2. *Ibid.*, p. 148.
3. *Ibid.*, p. 199.   4. *Ibid.*, p. 176.
5. *Ibid.*, pp. 173, 177.
6. *Ibid.*, p. 179.
7. Walker, *Creeds and Platforms*, p. 117.

tion of erring ones, and to refer to outsiders for the arbitration of all parish quarrels.[1]

The two great crises in the colony's existence found the consociation of churches playing a major rôle in the maintenance of uniformity. Cotton says that he spent the summer of 1635 seeking "by word and writing" to satisfy Williams's various scruples.[2] In April the assembled elders heard his objections to the oath, "and very clearly confuted" him.[3] When Williams perceived the drift of these tactics, he wrote a circular letter to all the churches, urging that the magistrates and deputies be reproved for a "heinous sin";[4] it was a foolhardy attempt to convert the consociation of churches into a weapon against the very power it was designed to subserve. Cotton at once requested the civil power to forbear until Williams could be dealt with "in a church way," and Cotton, Hooker, and others debated with him.[5] When he still remained obstinate, the church at Boston sent a public admonition to Salem, giving a list of Williams's errors and declaring them "confuted."[6] By August Williams separated completely from his church; Hooker once more disputed with him and demonstrated to the satisfaction of everyone but Williams that he was wrong.[7] At this point consociation had done its duty and cleared the track for the civil government:

1. *Cambridge Platform*, chap. viii, par. 8; chap. x, par. 6; Lechford, *Plain Dealing*, p. 15; Weld, *Answer to W. R.*, p. 37.
2. Cotton, "A Reply to Mr. Williams," p. 76.
3. Winthrop, *Journal*, 1, 149.
4. *Ibid.*, p. 154; Cotton, *op. cit.*, pp. 14, 50.
5. *Ibid.*, pp. 50, 62; Nathaniel Morton, *New England's Memorial* (5th edition, 1826), p. 153.
6. *Ibid.*, p. 155.   7. Cotton, *op. cit.*, p. 52.

But now he having refused to heare both his own Church, and us
. . . we have now no more to say in his behalfe, nor hope to prevaile
for him. Wee have told the Governor, and Magistrates before, that
if our labour was in vaine, wee could not helpe it, but must sit
downe.[1]

Mere gatherings of various elders, however, failed
several times to untangle the Antinomian knot,[2] and at
last a formal Synod was gathered at Cambridge. The
immense success of this body made the synod an abid-
ing resource of American Congregationalism; English
Independency never enjoyed anything like the same
opportunity to dominate a community, and therefore
did not perfect the device of consociation.[3] This Synod
rendered incalculable service to the establishment of a
uniform orthodoxy by drawing up a list of eighty-two
errors, which it declared condemned by the Word of
God. Many of these were not attributed to Anne and
her friends, but were recollected from European experi-
ences with heresies of her type, and were added to serve
as guides for ferreting out future apostates.

The various uses of consociation were soon completely
rationalized. Though a gathering of ministers or a synod
still could not impose its decrees, yet it could "clear up
the truth dogmatically," [4] could determine "that which
is *evidently expressed, or infallibly collected* out of the
Word." As far as any human decisions ever could be,
the counsels of a Congregational synod were apt to be

1. *Ibid.*, p. 64.
2. Winthrop, *Journal*, I, 196, 203, 210.
3. Walker, *A History of the Congregational Churches in the United States*,
   p. 143.
4. Richard Mather and William Thompson, *A Modest & Brotherly Answer
   to Mr. Charles Herle*, p. 9.

"no other then *Gods Commands*"; they smacked of "a Divine Authority which is now by them discovered, and *in his Name applied* to the particulars under hand." [1] The particulars coming under a synod's hand were understood by 1648 rather extensively: an assembly was designed, declared the *Cambridge Platform*,

to determine controversies of faith, & cases of conscience; to cleare from the word holy directions for the holy worship of God, & good government of the church; to beare witness against mal-administration & Corruption in doctrine or manners in any particular Church, & to give directions for the reformation thereof.[2]

Of course, if a synod ruled anything contrary to law, or "prejudicial to the intireness of the Churches Power, within it self," then the particular church still had a theoretical right to resist; [3] on the other hand, if the assembled churches found a congregation obstinately nursing "the Gangreene of Heresie" or "the Leprosie of sin," though they had "no power to deliver them to Sathan, yet they have power to withdraw from them, the right hand of Fellowship, and no longer to hold them in the Communion of Saints, till they approve their Repentance." [4] Hooker defended this sort of "separation or rejection" as being quite different from "excommunication," but he was speaking somewhat equivocally, for if the procedure did not deliver a congregation to Satan, it gave them to something which, for the time being, was worse—to social ostracism and isolation. Hence Richard Mather could advise the Presbyterians of England that

1. Hooker, *Survey*, pt. IV, p. 3.
2. Chap. xvi, par. 4.
3. Davenport, *The Power of Congregational Churches*, p. 153.
4. Cotton, *The True Constitution of a particular visible Church*, p. 13.

if they would faithfully follow the course of voluntary consociation, they would find it an ideal means

to settle one unanimous consent in the thing, or at least to preserve peace in the Church by the dissentors submission to the judgement of the Major part, though they see not light sufficient to warrant them to act in the businesse.[1]

Cotton attributed the successful career of the New England Way largely to the employment of consociation:

Mutual conference between Godly, ingenuous, and selfe-denying Christians is a notable meanes sanctified of God for the instruction & edification one of another, till wee all come to be of one minde in the Lord.[2]

Consequently, the *Cambridge Platform* signalized the effect upon Congregationalism of eighteen years of successful use of consociation by emphasizing the rôle of this principle far beyond anything that had ever been done in European sketches of the polity. It proclaimed the moral duty of a church to carry its troubles to the ministers of other congregations, and stigmatized a refusal to do so as "a matter of just offence both to the Lord Jesus, & to other churches." The deliberations of a synod were to be received with "reverence and submission," not only because they were necessarily gathered out of the Word, but also "for the power wherby they are made, as being an ordinance of God appointed thereunto in his word."[3] This was about as far in the direction of centralization as Congregationalism could go without abandoning its basic premises. In synods the

1. *Church-Government and Church-Covenant Discussed*, p. 62.
2. Cotton, *The Bloudy Tenent Washed*, p. 185.
3. *Cambridge Platform*, chap. xv, par. 2; chap. xvi, par. 5.

New England Way found an instrument for "the conviction of errours, & heresyes, & the establishment of truth & peace in the Churches," [1] and it made the most of them.

*   *   *

In its original formulation, Congregationalism had appealed to many earnest Englishmen because it held out the exalted possibility of identifying the visible church with the invisible. It rushed in where Calvin had feared to tread, and had the courage of its predestinarian convictions. Yet even the most zealous Separatists had realized that it was supremely difficult to tell who in this world actually were elected, and had admitted that hypocrites might conceivably pass even the most rigorous requirements for admission to a church. The more circumspect Ames accepted this risk as inevitable in a sinful world. Faith, he said, was that which made the mystical Church, but the external profession of faith was necessarily that which made a visible church. Since faith "cannot be wrought by constraint" there would be every reason to presume that those who voluntarily professed it had been sincerely wrought upon; still, we had constantly to bear in mind that an appearance was not the thing in itself. The most we could say with assurance was that believers by profession were members of the Church "as touching the outward state." Concerning the "inward or essentiall state" no man was qualified to speak, either concerning himself or others. [2] Yet even granting all this, the Congregational idea of

1. *Ibid.*, chap. xvi, par. 2.
2. Ames, *Conscience*, p. 9; *The Marrow of Sacred Divinity*, pp. 137–140.

purifying the Church by admitting only those who at least strove to believe made the system all the more effective as a protest against the formalism and worldliness of the Establishment.

Once again, however, the task of dominating a new environment called upon the system to subordinate the radical insistencies of its youth to the responsibilities of a vested interest. The duty of the Church was no longer to hold aloft a barely attainable ideal of Christian virtue, but rather to train up law-abiding members. As long as the leaders had been attacking English bishops and their minions, they had been able to contemplate purification of God's house by an unlimited expulsion of the profane, but in America they had to call a halt to the process lest they should completely empty the churches. Yet their theology still held the world to be a world of sinners, and they knew that if they stopped short of the most rigorous standards for admission to membership, if they accepted evidences of reformation rather than made sure of reformation itself, they would have either to confess their system a failure, or else frankly to admit it to be at least as much concerned with external goodness as with real holiness. By this inevitable shift in emphasis the principle of restricted church membership was subtly transformed from a flashing scimitar drawn to sever the limbs of Satan into a net that caught up the substantial citizens.

As long as New Englanders remained Congregationalists, their textbooks perfunctorily rehearsed the old idea that church members possessed two "adjuncts," "who in respect of their Spiritual and Internal Estate (to wit, their Faith) are Invisible: but in respect of their External condition (to wit, the Profession of Faith) are Visible." [1] Cotton began his significant treatise, *Of the Holiness of Church-Members*, by insisting that it was "the duty of all the members of the particular visible Church ... to be truly regenerate." [2] But more and more the clergy began to realize they could not tell whether members had really lived up to their duty: "its certain, you can neither see, nor know, for truth of grace is invisible to man." [3] Therefore, whether or not the members actually had experienced regeneration, if Congregational churches were to operate at all, they had to operate on the affirmative assumption. "Christ believed on, is the Foundation, or Rock, of the Catholick invisible Church: But Christ believed on and confessed, is the Rock whereupon a particular visible Church is built." [4] There, precisely, was the danger. As Davenport warned, "in these places and times, where Church-fellowship is an honour, and drawes after it sundry out-ward and worldly advantages," [5] many men would surely desire membership who had not been "converted," or who were incapable of living perpetually on the lofty emotional plane supposedly natural to the elect. But since the gestures expressive of the true internal state were not difficult to imitate, at least well enough to pass inspection, clever men were sorely tempted to go through the motions. Noyes of Newbury, who never liked the restricted mem-

---

1. Cotton, *The Way of the Congregational Churches Cleared*, pt. II, p. 11.
2. *Of the Holiness of Church-Members*, p. 1.
3. Hooker, *Survey*, pt. I, p. 37.
4. Davenport, *The Power of Congregational Churches*, pp. 9–10.
5. *Ibid.*, p. 17.

bership, scored a telling point when he wrote that "the Churches may become impure, notwithstanding any thing we yet do, gifted men do easily learn the language of the pure ones." [1] Events more than justified such observations. Cotton Mather at the end of the century regretfully confessed that the "prodigious and astonishing scandal given by the extraordinary miscarriages of some that have made a more than ordinary profession of religion" had laid an "incredible temptation" before the multitude.[2] The facts were too patent to be ignored. Though officers and members might do all they could to examine carefully those who offered themselves to the fellowship, still, Davenport declared, "close Hypocrites will creep in." [3] Some saints, said Hooker, are so in truth, some in charity. "*Saints* according to *charity* are such, who in their practice and profession . . . *they savour so much, as though they had been with Jesus . . . These* we call *visible Saints* (leaving *secret things to God*)." [4] Cotton was less temperate: to say church members were in reality regenerate was, he declared, to speak of what they "ought to be *de jure* . . . rather than what they are, or are want to be *de facto*." [5] Shepard was downright pessimistic: "It is clearer then the day," he wrote, "that many who are inwardly, or in respect of inward Covenant, the Children of the *Devil*, are outwardly, or in respect of outward Covenant, the Children of God." [6]

1. James Noyes, *The Temple Measured*, p. 66.
2. *Magnalia*, II, 493.   3. Davenport, *op. cit.*, pp. 11–12.
4. Hooker, *Survey*, pt. I, pp. 14–15.
5. Cotton, *A Defence of Mr. John Cotton*, p. 71.
6. Shepard, *The Church-Membership of Children*, pp. 1–2.

These were damaging admissions. They certainly expose an anomalous predicament. Here was a Church which excluded a majority of the people from communion with the Saviour because they could not produce evidence of his having called them, and yet admitted that evidence of the sort was so tricky that beyond all doubt an indefinite proportion of the ostensible elect were in reality children of the devil. The clergy of New England did not lack courage when called upon to reconcile many facts with their preconceived ideas, but none of them quite had the effrontery to plead for this situation purely upon the basis of any correspondence to spiritual realities. They who formerly scorned the social and ethical arguments of the Anglican Church were reduced to defending Congregationalism on those very grounds; the erstwhile rebels against formalism came finally to rest upon a formality. The important thing, they were bound to admit, was the profession; they knew that it was desirable for examiners to test the sincerity of a profession, but the externality of the act was after all its essential aspect.

The meaning is not as if we allowed none to be of the Church, but *real Saints*, and such as give demonstrative evidence of being members of the invisible Church; for we profess . . . that it is not *real*, but visible faith, not the inward being, but the outward profession of faith . . . that constitutes a visible Church.[1]

After acceptable professions had been uttered, whether in sincerity or not, the professors were made

partakers of the covenant, and all the priviledges outwardly belonging thereto; yea, though they have not saveing faith, but be

1. Shepard, *Two Questions*, p. 5.

hypocrites; and so themselves, and all that ever proceed from them, continue in the same state, parents and children successively, so long as the Lord continues the source of his dispensation; nor can any alteration befall them, whereby this estate is dissolved, but some apparant act of God breaking them off from him.[1]

Only public offenses could come within the purview of the church; "As the Church judgeth not of hidden crimes, so neither do the Faithfull judge of the Churches by their hidden hypocrisie, but by their open scandals in Doctrine, or life." [2]   In fact, as long as hypocrites remained publicly obedient, they were for all practical purposes just as good as the truest believers. "The Spirit giveth many Gifts to the edification of others . . . which often does not reach to the Regeneration of him that Receiveth them." [3] Sir Richard Saltonstall, made wiser by the Civil Wars, told Cotton that he thought compelling men to outward conformity created hypocrites; and Cotton's reply indicates the long road official thought in the colony had travelled: "If it did so, yet better to be hypocrites than prophane persons. Hypocrites give God part of his due, the outward man, but the prophane person giveth God neither outward nor inward man." [4] Cotton had actually become convinced that good hypocrites should be allowed the keys of church power, if not for the reality of their faith, at least for the truth of the words "which they do profess in common with sincere Believers"; he deliberately argued that however "non-regeneration evidently known"

1. George Phillips, *A Reply to a Confutation*, pp. 125–126.
2. Cotton, *The Way of the Congregational Churches Cleared*, pt. II, p. 40.
3. Cotton, *A Defence of Mr. John Cotton*, p. 71.
4. Hutchinson, *Collection of Papers Relating to the History of Massachusetts Bay* (Prince Society, 1865), II, 132.

might be a cause for holding a man out of the Church, it was "not a just cause of casting him out of the Church, after he be received." [1] In unguarded moments the New England divines came perilously close to admitting that they were concerned more with the letter than the spirit: "But if it should be asked," wrote Shepard, "how charity may know the reality of this profession, we answer: so long as the rule be attended, we leave every one to the wisdome of Christ." [2]   Church members were saints, peremptorily declared the *Cambridge Platform*, "though perhaps some or more of them be unsound, & hypocrites inwardly." [3]   At this rate, the real question was no longer were you a believer, but could you pass for one among your neighbors? "Hypocrites in outward profession and appearance, go for faithful and godly." [4]

*   *   *

Anomalous though this situation was, another inherited principle of Congregationalism was gradually creating an even more peculiar dislocation in the New England churches. The original assumption of the polity had been that since only believers were entitled to the sacraments, only the children of believers could be baptized. "We doe administer baptisme only to such infants as wherof ye one parente, at ye least, is of some church." [5]   It was, as a matter of fact, difficult to find any rational excuse for baptism at all when the sole discernible basis for church membership was adult conver-

1. Cotton, *Of the Holiness of Church-Members*, p. 56.
2. Shepard, *op. cit.*, p. 11.   3. Chap. iii, par. 1.
4. Cotton, *The Way of the Congregational Churches Cleared*, pt. II, p. 41.
5. Declaration of Robinson's church, 1617, Walker, *Creeds and Platforms*, p. 91.

sion, but the Bible commanded the rite and so it had to
be. Congregationalists explained the ceremony as a
symbol of a sort of spiritual apprenticeship: it delivered
the "seals" to those who in all probability would some
day become converted and take the full church covenant. Baptized persons, it might be said, were proba-
tionary members of the church, though they still could
not be admitted to Communion "unlesse there doe first
appeare an increase of Faith." [1] The difficulties of this
arrangement had not become apparent in Europe, for
those who had been Congregationalists long enough to
raise up children had generally lived in so surcharged an
atmosphere that their offspring were emotionally prepared to experience definite conversions in early adoles-
cence. While Congregationalists lived the stirring life of
English Puritans, their sons went almost automatically
from baptism to profession.

The practice of baptism and religious apprenticeship
was, of course, continued in America. It was the only
way Congregationalism could assure itself of a future.
"Churches are propogated by continuall succession." [2]
Hence infants, said Shepard, "may be in Gods account
professors of ye Faith parentally, as well as personally." [3]
The children of Massachusetts church members therefore received baptism, "the seal of righteousness of
faith." But it was still understood to be merely an "offer
of righteousness from God"; it could not in itself make
the recipients "partakers of that grace offered." [4] When

1. Ames, *The Marrow of Sacred Divinity*, p. 140.
2. Phillips, *A Reply to a Confutation*, p. 4.
3. Shepard, *The Church-Membership of Children*, p. 26.
4. Phillips, *op. cit.*, p. 9.

the baptized came of age they were expected to "hold forth publickly their personal confession of Faith"; otherwise "they may not be owned for Members." [1] But once the colony was successfully established, it provided children with an entirely different environment. Instead of living in an atmosphere of continuous religious excitement, they grew up in comparative security, with the greater part of their energies directed to the physical tasks of frontier life. Under these conditions the emotional convulsion, which was understood to be conversion, simply did not arrive. [2] As Cotton Mather tells us, among the sons and daughters of the first generation of settlers there were a number of sober persons, who were eminently moral and reputable, who sincerely desired to renew their baptismal covenant, yet who "could not come up to that experimental account of their own regeneration, which would sufficiently embolden their access to the other sacrament." Calvinistic theology attributed conversion to the arbitrary condescension of God; environmental influences did not count. Therefore, if the original philosophy had been strictly observed, there could have been only one conclusion: these persons had not been called. Then if they were not regenerate, *their* children ought not even to be baptized, a contingency which "the good old generation could not, without many uncomfortable apprehensions, behold." Were the churches to retain their pristine insistence upon the reality of spiritual life as the sole basis for

1. Davenport, *The Power of Congregational Churches*, p. 22.
2. Cf. Frank Hugh Foster, *A Genetic History of New England Theology*, pp. 27 ff.

church life, and watch the membership dwindle, or were they to loosen the requirements and retain the unconverted but baptized members on the basis of their mundane behavior and their family affiliations? As Cotton Mather phrased it,

to make no ecclesiastical difference between these hopeful candidates . . . and Pagans, who might happen to hear the word of God in our assemblies, was judged a most unwarrantable strictness, which would quickly abandon the biggest part of our country unto heathenism.[1]

There is observable in the New England writings of the 1640's a decided tendency to evade this question. Richard Mather put off the curiosity of English Puritans in 1637 by telling them that because "of the Infancy of these Churches, we have had no occasion yet to determine what to judge or practise one way or other." [2] With the passing of years and the multiplication of children, the issue became more urgent. Many of the divines began to feel that the system must be modified to suit the obstinate facts. Shepard, for instance, preached that "the children of godly parents, though they do not manifest faith in the Gospel, yet they are to be accounted of Gods Church, untill they positively reject the Gospel." [3] He defended their participation in church government, even if they could not communicate, on exactly the same grounds on which he and his colleagues defended the existence of hypocrites within the church; he did not mean that non-converted but

1. *Magnalia*, II, 277.
2. *Church-Government and Church-Covenant Discussed*, p. 20.
3. Shepard, *op. cit.*, p. 20.

baptized members "enjoy the inward and saveing bene-
fits of the Covenant," but he did feel they could still
be "in external, and outward Covenant, and therefore
outwardly Church Members."[1] Cotton also felt they
should be continued as members on that basis "untill
they justly deprive themselves of the priviledge of that
Fellowship."[2] The clergy clearly were putting out of
mind some of their early fervor, and were becoming
filled instead with a determination to keep the pillars of
society within the ecclesiastical structure. Phillips of
Watertown rationalized the whole thing as an instance
of human inability to know anything about subjective
religious life, or to judge of anything save appearances.
The faith of a parent was, he said, sufficient grounds to
think a child belonged to God, "which though I may be
mistaken and my judgement in this case is not infallible,
yet it is as much as I can have of any man of yeeres, of
whose state I cannot judge infallibly."[3] It was altogether possible, according to this reasoning, not only for
a church to become entirely constituted of hypocrites,
but for it to be perpetuated by the hypocritical children
of hypocrites. If the clergy were not careful, the element
of conversion and profession, which had been the corner-
stone of their system, would be entirely dropped out.
The churches within two or three generations would
become closed societies, made up of formally baptized
but dubious Christians, holding their membership by

1. *Ibid.*, p. 2.
2. *Of the Holiness of Church-Members*, p. 1.
3. Phillips, *op. cit.*, p. 8.

hereditary right. Then, of course, it would be difficult to explain to the many who were excluded for just what reason they were kept out.

It was primarily to avoid such an eventuality that the General Court was moved in 1646 to call a Synod. The churches, struggling against a congenital weakness, were obviously incapable of curing themselves. Some of them, the Court recorded, were baptizing only children of members, some were already baptizing grandchildren, and some "do thinke that whatever be ye state of ye parents, baptisme ought not to be dispensed to any infants whatsoever." [1] This difficulty was the most serious threat to uniformity the New England Way had yet encountered, for it was a problem in which parental emotion clearly clashed with the Bible, social expediency with religious tradition. The distress call of the Court was inspired, as will appear in the sequel, by a particular disturbance among the non-members; but by the time the Synod convened, in 1648, the immediate danger had passed; unless compelled, the elders hesitated to stir up more trouble by taking too emphatic a stand on the question of children of believers. The *Cambridge Platform* skirted the problem gingerly, barely affirming the conventional theory that only children of members were entitled to baptism, and that these should manifest their faith by open profession when they came of age. This did not solve the riddle, and the Synod's failure on this score was the Achilles' heel in the otherwise complete success of the *Platform*. Within a few years the "half-

1. *Massachusetts Records*, II, 155.

way covenant" was being openly agitated, and a voluminous controversy was joined which for the rest of the century disturbed the peace of the churches.

*   *   *

The final problem confronting the New England Way was one that had been completely unforeseen by its English forerunners. When they had preached restricted membership, they had never considered what, in a completely Congregationalized nation, should be done with those who were not admitted. They simply asserted that all Christians "ought to frame the Visible Church wherin they live to this only true forme, or els betake themselves vnto some suche Church so formed."[1] They assumed that the technique of examination would be sufficiently accurate to make no mistakes in separating the sheep from the goats, and they dismissed the shadowy non-members from their speculations as persons of no ecclesiastical importance. If those not joined to a visible church, said Ames, "doe obstinatly persist in their carelessenesse, whatsoever they doe otherwise professe, they can scarce be accounted for believers truly seeking the Kingdome of God."[2]

While Congregationalists were concentrating their energies in England on proving the truth of the churches there, "in substance," they became altogether habituated to disregarding the profane; but in New England the unregenerate were an ever-present reality. The majority of the populace were expected to live quietly

1. Jacob, *The Divine Beginning*, sig. A4 recto.
2. *The Marrow of Sacred Divinity*, p. 143.

under a church system which not only held them without
the pale, but insinuated that they were in all probability
damned. That certainly was conduct difficult for many
Englishmen to comprehend. A friend of Winthrop's
wrote in 1637 that men in England were hearing with
amazement how one half the people in Massachusetts
were shut out from communion: "Ther is now so much
talke of yt, & such certeyne truth of yt, & I know of
many of worth, for outward estate & ability, for wisdome & grace, are much danted from comeing." [1]
Thomas Lechford, a lawyer who was imprudent enough
to try for three years to make a living in Massachusetts,
published abroad the fact that "three parts of the people
of the Country remaine out of the Church," and called
attention to what the leaders themselves must have
realized was something of a problem:

> The people begin to complain, they are ruled like slaves, and in
> short time shall have their children for the most part remain un-
> baptized: and so have little more priviledge then Heathens, unlesse
> the discipline be amended and moderated.[2]

This was, however, a problem for which the Congregational system admitted no real solution. There could be
no churches without covenants, and there could be no
covenants without professions of faith; if the mass were
not able to make professions satisfactory to what were
considered "charitable" standards, there was nothing
the churches could do about them. "Church priviledges
do not belong to Believers, as such, but onely to such as
withall are Members of some particular Church." [3]

1. *Mass. Hist. Soc., Coll.*, Series 4, VII, 11.   2. *Plain Dealing*, pp. 89, 151.
3. Richard Mather, *Church-Government and Church-Covenant Discvssed*,
   p. 11.

Hooker, confronting the augmenting problem of the non-members and recognizing that the process of admission was clearly taking in many whom a more perfect technique would reject, was compelled to conclude that probably some were being excluded who were better Christians than many who managed to gain admission. There were times when he very much wished "that such persons (many whereof we hope are godly) might enjoy all such priviledges, which might be usefull and helpfull to them and theirs"; but his protracted meditation only convinced him that any other system was impossible, "and the main pillar principle which fortifies the judgement against all approaching assaults, is the nature and truth of *Church-Covenant.*" [1] He concluded that those "who by God are *excluded* from *his covenant* . . . as *unfit, they* are *not fit* to have *communion* with the *Church.*" [2] The system was making enemies abroad and creating a disinherited and possibly rebellious class within the colony, but the Massachusetts churches had set out to prove that the principle of restricted church membership would work. They had to stand to their guns, although in the face of their own admission that hypocrites abounded in the fold and the patent fact that baptized children were failing to become converted, they were finding it increasingly difficult to explain upon what basis "many persons liveing in ye country who have bene members of ye congregations in England" were still "not found fit to be received at ye Lords table here." [3]

1. Hooker, *Survey*, pt. III, p. 12.
2. *Ibid.*, pt. I, p. 17.
3. *Massachusetts Records*, II, 155.

The best the divines could do was to rehearse the dogmas of Ames, and intimate that anyone who complained because he was rejected had only himself to blame. Believers, said Davenport, were in duty bound to join a church, "and if they persist in that neglect, they can hardly be accounted Believers truly seeking the Kingdom of God, what profession of Religion soever they make otherwise." [1] We do not refuse admission to any man "of approved piety," said Cotton, "if he be willing to accept it." [2] If, however, a man was willing, and yet was blackballed, he obviously had not exhibited approvable piety.

The fear of God, and Faith of those men, may be justly doubted, whose setled abode is in a place where Churches are gather'd and order'd according to Christ, and yet are not after a convenient time joyned to them.[3]

The system might creak, but being that of Christ, it could not fail. If there were but few church members in the colony, "That is the fault of people, not of the rule, nor of the way; If the Saints be thin sowen, who can helpe it?" [4] And if men were not religious, "no not so much as in profession," why, Cotton asked, "should it be accounted a grievous absurdity, not to receive them into the Church?" [5] There was, Davenport concluded, every reason to eliminate them: "The same Spirit of unrighteousness and enmity against Christ, worketh and bears rule in an unconverted Christian, as doth in an

1. *The Power of Congregational Churches*, p. 58.
2. *Of the Holiness of Church-Members*, pp. 29–30.
3. Davenport, *A Discourse about Civil Government*, p. 21.
4. Weld, *An Answer to W. R.*, p. 15.
5. *The Way of the Congregational Churches Cleared*, pt. I, p. 73.

unbaptized Heathen." [1] The *Cambridge Platform* once
again summarized the matured conviction of the years
by repeating the clergy's dogged defense of the restricted
membership in spite of all foreign criticism and domestic
threats:

> We conceive the receiving of them into our churches would rather
> loose & corrupt our Churches, then gain & heale them. A little
> leaven layed in a lump of dough, will sooner leaven the whole lump,
> then the whole lump will sweeten it. Wee therefore find it safer, to
> square rough & unhewen stones, before they be layed into the
> building, rather then to hammer & hew them, when they lye un-
> evenly in the building.[2]

The churches, by themselves, could do no more. If
"those without" still refused to see the justice of their
relegation, then it was up to the civil government to
convince them. Meantime, the churches had achieved
an ecclesiastical "due form." They had proved that the
colony was not Separatist, and was therefore religiously
legitimate; they had demonstrated that the discipline
was divinely ordained, and had perfected methods for
maintaining uniformity; they had developed the system
so that only responsible persons should control it, even
though they had largely transformed the nature of the
polity in the process; finally, they had provided machinery for keeping out those who could not be trusted
with a voice in the direction of affairs. The churches had
solved one half of the old Puritan dilemma, by showing
how a discipline gathered out of the Word could subserve the political ideals of civil supremacy and national
unity. In order that the other half of the dilemma also

1. Davenport, *op. cit.*, p. 21.
2. Preface, Walker, *Creeds and Platforms*, p. 200.

might be disposed of, in order that the polity might have an opportunity of showing just how effectively it could coöperate with the secular office, the magistrates had to do their share. The politicians had to create in Massachusetts a civil government equally in accord with the best Puritan conceptions of what should constitute a "due form."

VII

THE SUPREME POWER POLITICKE

THE secular leaders of the Massachusetts enterprise did not have to be told what was expected of them. Winthrop recognized at once that the task of the Great Migration involved as much a problem of civil as of ecclesiastical government. Behind his statement lay the century-old Protestant endeavor to harmonize State and Church, and to him a proper civil rule was one which would contribute to the erection of that spiritual Utopia which Puritans had long preached to unheeding royal ears. If Massachusetts was to be the cynosure of all Protestant eyes, the shining example of the Christian commonwealth, then its civil government had to assume the duties and responsibilities of a civil supremacy.

The accomplishment of this design required, however, that the government first prove its ability to stand squarely upon its own political feet. It could hardly rule in accordance with Puritan ideals unless it had first demonstrated it could rule at all. To protect the Church, it must become capable of enforcing its decrees; to suppress heresy, it must become competent to meet emergencies; to preserve orthodoxy, it must become strong enough to resist foreign domination or domestic revolt. The colony had, in short, to meet the twofold task of effecting a practical freedom from English interference and of establishing a firm control over the populace before it could render the Church the service implied in the possession of a "due form."

From the charter itself the leaders took their cue for dealing with the first aspect of the problem. Before leaving England, the Company had informed Endecott that the patent conferred upon it an absolute authority over such of the King's subjects as might inhabit the jurisdiction. Lawyers have learnedly doubted whether the colony was legally entitled to the extensive powers it assumed, but over fine points the leaders themselves were not inclined to be punctilious. They were satisfied that because a residential requirement had been omitted from the patent, they had a perfect right to become a corporation upon the place if they chose. They certainly did not hesitate to act upon that assumption. Straws proclaim the way winds blow, or as Thomas Dudley put it, "small things in the beginning of natural or politic bodies are as remarkable as greater in bodies full grown." [1] The Massachusetts chiefs indicated at once that in their view the charter had invested them with a sovereign dignity. Endecott began the wreck of Thomas Morton's hilarious station at Merry-Mount, and Winthrop banished the roisterer "because the habitation of the wicked shall no more appear in Israel." [2] The Court of Assistants, in September, 1630, declared that no persons should be permitted to settle in the colony without the consent of the magistrates,[3] and the

1. Dudley, "Letter to the Countess of Lincoln" (1631), Young, *Chronicles of Massachusetts Bay*, p. 329.
2. Thomas Morton, *New English Canaan* (Prince Society, 1883), p. 311; Winthrop, *Journal*, 1, 53.
3. *Massachusetts Records*, 1, 76.

following June added that neither could they travel out of the patent without official leave.[1] Thomas Gray, for "dyvers things obiected against him," was expelled in the fall of 1630;[2] on the first of March, 1631, six men were sent back to England as "persons vnmeete to inhabit here,"[3] and the next month the picturesque Sir Christopher Gardiner was invited to follow.[4] May saw Thomas Walford and his wife banished "for his contempt of authoritie & confrontinge officers";[5] and June witnessed Ratcliffe's whipping, the loss of his ears, and his banishment "for uttering mallitious & scandulous speeches against the gouernment & the church of Salem."[6] The months thereafter were punctuated with such instances of summary justice, the most significant of which was the sentencing of Thomas Knower to the bilboes in April, 1632, "for treateing the Court that, if hee should be punist, hee would haue it tryed in England whether hee was lawfully punished or not."[7] If the charter allowed no appeal from the determinations of the colonial government, then to all intents and purposes the government was indeed sovereign, and could perfectly keep step with an established Church.

The position suggested by these decrees was more frankly avowed in December, 1633. The Quixotic Roger Williams then became suddenly obsessed with a peculiar sympathy for the Indians, and circulated "a large Booke

1. *Ibid.*, p. 88.   2. *Ibid.*, p. 77.
3. *Ibid.*, p. 83.
4. Winthrop, *Journal*, 1, 63.
5. *Massachusetts Records*, 1, 86.
6. *Ibid.*, p. 88; Winthrop, *Journal*, 1, 64.
7. *Massachusetts Records*, 1, 94.

in Quarto," maintaining "that we have not our Land by Pattent from the King, but that the Natives are the true owners of it, and that we ought to repent of such a receiving it by Pattent." [1] Williams's high moral stand caused the elders some anxious moments as they turned the pages of their Bibles to find parallels between the Israelites' occupation of Canaan and the Massachusetts settlement, but Winthrop spoke more to the purpose when he told Endecott that an aspersion upon the royal grant might "haue provoked our Kinge against us, & putt a sworde into his hande to destroye us." [2] For the colony to have permitted the patent to be called into question "had subverted the fundamentall State, and Government of the Countrey." [3] The all-important pretense to legitimacy, without which the Puritans could never have ventured the colonial solution of their peculiar dilemma, depended solely upon this one sheet of parchment:

By that Patent it is, that we received allowance from the King to depart his Kingdome, and to carry our goods with us, without offence to his Officers. . . . . By the Patent, certain select men (as Magistrates, and Freemen) have power to make Lawes, and the Magistrates to execute Justice. . . . By the Patent we have Power to erect such a Government of the Church, as is most agreeable to the Word.[4]

As long as the officials of the Bay kept the document safely on their own side of the Atlantic Ocean, their

1. Williams, "Mr. Cottons letter lately printed" (1644), *Publications of the Narragansett Club*, I, 324.
2. Charles Deane, *Roger Williams and the Massachusetts Charter*, p. 6.
3. Cotton, "A Reply to Mr. Williams," *Publications of the Narragansett Club*, II, 47.
4. *Ibid.*, p. 45.

autonomy was assured.   An overburdened and dis-
tracted Laud could not contest the interpretation of a
charter which had been whisked into another hemi-
sphere; anyone on the spot who disputed the magistrates'
version could receive no more support from a distant
and none too solvent English government than did
Thomas Knower when he found himself in the bilboes
for threatening an appeal to London. If the governors
could only keep hold of the charter, they were safe, and
rather than part with it they demonstrated themselves
capable of going to considerable lengths. In 1634 Sir
Ferdinando Gorges convinced the Privy Council that
the insolence of the Puritan colony must be chastised.
Gorges had become an implacable foe because he believed that the Company had obtained its patent from
the Council for New England under false pretenses, and
that the grant overlapped one which had been issued to
his son Robert. In 1632 he had presented a petition
against the charter, and seen the Privy Council disregard it, as Winthrop says, "through the Lord's good
providence, and the care of our friends in England." [1]
But two years later the Council was learning the true
state of affairs, and readily entertained a second petition. Gorges declared that the charter had made the
settlers "a free people," who were now laboring "for no
other cause save onely to make themselves absolute
Masters of the Countrey"; he requested that a governor
be appointed "neither papistically nor scizmattically
affected." [2] Sir John Banks instituted *quo warranto* pro-

1. Winthrop, *Journal*, i, 99, 101.
2. *Records of the Council for New England*, p. 125.

ceedings, charging the patentees with various political offenses, such as the assumption of the right to admit and discharge the King's subjects at will, the claim to sole government over persons in the jurisdiction, the use of martial law, and the making of laws contrary to the laws of England.[1] Good Matthew Craddock was ordered to write for the document.

The colony's response was electric. The magistrates replied to Craddock, but sent "no answere or excuse" to the Council. When Craddock again applied for the charter, the magistrates continued their Fabian tactics, pleading that it could not be shipped until the General Court could meet in September, and on July 29, after consulting with "divers of the ministers" took measures to fortify Boston harbor.[2] In September, instead of doing anything about the charter, the General Court reaffirmed the acts of the magistracy, made provision for training troops and gathering arms and munitions, required all towns to be equipped, prescribed new oaths for the militia officers "suteable to their places," and even authorized employing Indian mercenaries "to shoote with a peece."[3] Meantime word was received that the old Council for New England had voluntarily surrendered its charter, and that affairs of the region were to be regulated thereafter by a royal commission with Laud at the head, which information, Winthrop

1. Hutchinson, *A Collection of Papers*, 1, 114–117; *Mass. Hist. Soc., Coll.*, Series 2, viii, 97; Gideon Delaplaine Scull, "The *Quo Warranto* of 1635," *New England Historical and Genealogical Register*, April, 1884, pp. 209–216.
2. Winthrop, *Journal*, 1, 129, 130.
3. *Massachusetts Records*, 1, 123–128.

says, only "occasioned the magistrates and deputies to hasten our fortifications."[1]   Before adjourning, the Court left an order on the books that Winthrop, Haynes, Humphrey, and Endecott "shall haue power to consulte, direct, & giue command for ye manageing & ordering of any warr that may befall vs for the space of a yeare nexte ensueing."[2]   In January the elders unanimously agreed that if a royal governor were sent over "we ought not to accept him, but defend our lawful possessions (if we were able); otherwise to avoid or protract."[3] The committee was reorganized in March and given all the powers of martial law:

. . . to imprison or confine any that they shall iudge to be enemyes to the commonwealth, & such as will not come vnder commaund or restrainte, as they shalbe required, it shalbe lawful for the said commissioners to put such persons to death.[4]

Freeman and non-freeman alike were not only taxed [5] but were required under compulsion of the constable to contribute a due quota of physical labor on public works.[6]   These works were, of course, fortifications against England.   Beyond this there was but one possible step — actual independence.   Had Laud or Gorges been free to give military support to the *quo warranto* summons, there seems no doubt that rather than sur-

1. Winthrop, *Journal*, I, 135.
2. *Massachusetts Records*, I, 125.
3. Winthrop, *Journal*, I, 145.
4. *Massachusetts Records*, I, 138, 147.
5. So heavy was the taxation for this year that when the wealthy Haynes was elected governor he waived his salary, because "he observed how much the people had been pressed lately with public charges, which the poorer sort did much groan under" (Winthrop, *Journal*, I, 150).
6. *Massachusetts Records*, I, 124, 139.

render the leaders would have taken a chance on resistance, and a monument on Bunker Hill might have commemorated an earlier date.

Because neither Gorges nor Laud was able to project an invasion across the Atlantic, the crisis did not materialize, and the colony, by staving off the loss of its charter, became a practically independent power. The elders in 1644 considered the General Court a sovereign parliament:

> Ye Generall Cort . . . is ye chiefe civill power of this common wealth, & may act in all things belonging to such a power concerning counsell & iudicature, namely, for making lawes, receiving appeales, quaestioning & sentencing ye highest officers, & consulting about ye weightiest affaires of this commonwealth, & in all other cases which in their wisdome they thinke fit to take cognisance of.[1]

Wheelwright was told that he could not appeal his sentence to England, "for by the king's grant we had power to hear and determine without any reservation." [2] Winslow, as the agent for Plymouth, in 1635 petitioned the Council on Plantations for permission to withstand the Dutch and French; but Massachusetts had already assumed that the colonies could make war or peace as they chose and demurred, lest "such precedents might endanger our liberty, that we should do nothing hereafter but by commission out of England." [3] The momentum of controversy had carried the Puritan band into exile with a deep determination to lose nothing that they gained by their removal; at the same time their

1. *Ibid.*, 11, 95; Winthrop, *Journal*, 11, 216.
2. *Ibid.*, 1, 240; *Antinomianism in Massachusetts Bay*, p. 147; *Plain Dealing*, p. 64.
3. Winthrop, *Journal*, 1, 164.

religious philosophy had imbued them with a sense of invincible rectitude; and though they would make immense efforts to keep up a semblance of loyalty, they deliberately intended it should be no more than a semblance. Even that much they would repudiate before again submitting to the bishops. So audacious had the colony's conduct become that by 1636 it had ceased to fly the King's colors in the harbor. For this reason a sailor on an English ship called the townsmen traitors, and though his captain brought him to apologize, all the skippers then in the harbor besought the magistrates to display the standard at least once, "in regard they should be examined upon their return, what colors they saw here." Winthrop, Dudley, and Cotton decided this request was no more than reasonable, since the fort was openly maintained in the King's name. Thereupon they were embarrassed to discover there was not a single royal ensign in the Bay, and they had to borrow one from a ship so that the crews might truthfully swear they had seen the King's banner afloat in Massachusetts! [1]

The second half of the governmental task was not so easily achieved. The leaders knew that to preserve the integrity of the venture those men who had conceived the ideals to which the commonwealth was dedicated must remain in power. Yet the colony attracted many immigrants, some of them not noticeably godly, persons whom John White called "the very scum of the earth." [2] Furthermore, even good Christians, becoming absorbed

1. *Ibid.*, I, 181–182.
2. *Cal. St. Pap., Colonial, America and West Indies*, I, 155.

in the material tasks of a new world, might allow lesser and more selfish considerations to dim the original vision. From the leaders' point of view a domestic upheaval spelled ruin as distinctly as any possible interference of Laud. The internal problem in the State paralleled that in the churches, and in their respective spheres magistrates and elders alike strove to hold a decisive influence. Where the elders combated the dissidence of seventeenth century dissent, the magistrates sought to bridle the political assertiveness of seventeenth century Englishmen.

It might have seemed as though the magistrates were fighting against the stars in their courses. Englishmen of that era evidently had an amazing propensity for seizing as much self-government as they could get their hands on. Just as in Virginia the precocious House of Burgesses gathered with hardly so much as an "if-you-please" to the nominal rulers of the commercial enterprise in England, or just as in Lord Saye's plantation at Barbados "godly men were unwilling to come under other governors than such as they should make choice of themselves,"[1] or just as the restless settlers in the Carolinas made a mockery of John Locke's feudal constitution, so in Massachusetts the people displayed political impulses with which the leaders had always to reckon. In 1643 the magistrates refused judgment to Goody Sherman when she accused Robert Keayne of killing her sow. Keayne had made himself unpopular by profiteering from the then current financial depression, and the deputies insisted upon reviving the already much con-

1. Winthrop, *Journal*, I, 334.

tested case. "Neither the judgment of near all the magistrates, nor the concurrence of the elders and their mediation . . . could prevail with them to let such a cause
fall." [1] The reason for this persistence, Winthrop continues, was not only the deputies' desire for victory, but
their cognizance of the fact that their constituencies
were not yet satisfied, which seemed plainly to show
their "democraticall spirit." In England Winthrop and
his associates had been heart and soul in the struggle
against unlimited prerogative; in New England, when
they were called upon to preserve a state dedicated to
peculiar and rarified ideals, they found themselves
anxiously seeking opportunities to avoid the very limitations they had wished to impose upon the King.

In a purely political respect, however, the magistrates
had little opportunity to acquire an absolute sway. In
more ways than one Massachusetts had a government
founded upon fundamental law. It was, in the first
place, designed by the charter. Though the machinery
of commercial regulation which this document unwit-
tingly bestowed upon the State needed various extra-
legal supplements, the form of the government was un-
changeably designated, and the power of legislation
was placed in a General Court of all the citizens. To
that extent the charter was an irrevocable constitution,
a law of the land, and as such the magistrates had to
abide by it.

Furthermore, the colony was an offshoot of Puritanism, and therefore was founded not only upon its patent,
but upon the eternal laws of the Bible, which Puritans

1. *Ibid.*, II, 118.

had been contending were adequate guides for most departments of life. Even when Puritans had granted that there might be some cases not specifically covered by the Word they had held that deductions from the Bible could reasonably be made to cover such "indifferent matters." In 1635 the ministers reminded the Court that it was the duty of the magistrate "in all lawes about indifferent things, to shew the Reason, not onely the Will, to shew the expediency, as well as the indifferency of things of that nature." Such demonstrations were to be according to "the Rules of Expediency set downe in the Word." [1] Accordingly the next General Court ordered that in administering justice the assistants were to proceed according to the laws then established "& when there is noe law, then as neere the lawe of God as they can." [2] Saltonstall wrote in 1642 that in a religious commonwealth there should exist no power, administration, or authority "but such as are commanded and ordained of God"; this principle the assembled elders solemnly endorsed, with the added provision that God might command "either expressly or by consequence, by particular examples or by general rules." [3] On this score, also, the leaders had to be careful. They had to respect the limits of the charter, and they had also to be ever prepared to show authorization for their actions in the Bible, "either expressly or by consequence," and to explain away what scriptural passages the democracy might quote against them.

1. Quoted in Williams, *The Bloudy Tenent of Persecution*, ed. Samuel L. Caldwell, *Pub. Narragansett Club*, III, 255.
2. *Massachusetts Records*, I, 175.
3. Winthrop, *Journal*, II, 86–87.

Besides being a Puritan enterprise, Massachusetts was specifically a Congregational one, and for better or worse was saddled with the social philosophy inseparably connected with the ecclesiastical polity. We have already noted that the social compact was a peculiar tenet of Congregationalism; the prophets of the Way had invariably posited it as the basis of the State as well as of the Church. For ministers to assume their calling, Browne had said, there must first be an agreement of the Church; so "for ciuil Magistrates, there must be an agreement of the people or Common welth."[1] Penry had held "it is the crown and honour of princes . . . to be in covenant with their subjects,"[2] and the Separatists aboard the *Mayflower* had found in a covenant the obvious answer to the problem of political organization. Jacob had pointed out that a covenant was basic to the existence of a church, and had added, "By such a free mutuall consent also all Civil perfect Corporations did first beginne."[3] Even before the migration had reached America, Winthrop declared the emigrants had entered into a compact not only with each other but with God:

It is by mutuall consent, through a speciall ouervaluing providence . . . to seeke out a place of cohabitation and consorteshippe under a due forme of Government both ciuill and ecclesiasticall. In such cases as this, the care of the publique must ouersway all private respects. . . . For this end we must be knitt together, in this worke as one man. . . . We are entered into a Covenant with Him for this worke. . . . We have professed to enterprise these and those ends, upon these and those accounts.[4]

---

1. Walker, *Creeds and Platforms*, p. 25.
2. Dale, *History of English Congregationalism*, p. 158.
3. Burrage, *Early English Dissenters*, II, 157.
4. *Mass. Hist. Soc., Coll.*, Series 3, VII, 45–47.

The actual creation of the Massachusetts State by the deliberate assemblage of the people dramatized the theory, and it became a fixed idea in New England's sociology. Those who "come together into a wilderness," Winthrop declared in 1642, "where are nothing but wild beasts and beastlike men, and there confederate together in civil and church estate," such people do, "implicitly at least, bind themselves to support each other, and all of them that society, whether civil or sacred, whereof they are members." [1] John Cotton defended the church compact because it was evident "by the light of nature, that all civill Relations are founded in Covenant"; he could see no other way whereby a people could become "one visible body." [2] One result of this reasoning, as a certain elder once put it, was that if the uniting of freemen under a civil bond created the commonwealth, then those freemen were "the first subject of ciuill policy and power." [3] And in Massachusetts more than lip service had to be paid the popular origin of the State, for in the republican government provided by the charter the people were always capable of asserting themselves as "the first subjects" of power. The actions of the magistrates, the elders admitted, "are to be limited by ye Generall Cort, as ye supreme counsell." [4]

Finally, because the emigrants were almost entirely men who had contended against, or at least resented, the King's refusal to accept parliamentary limitation —

1. Winthrop, *Journal*, II, 83.
2. *The Way of the Churches of Christ in New England*, p. 4.
3. *Mass. Hist. Soc., Proc.*, XLVI, 280.
4. *Massachusetts Records*, II, 92.

because they believed their migration had been precipitated by precisely that refusal — the colony could never afford publicly to disown the imperishable principle for which the brethren in England were still striving and suffering. Puritans had thoroughly learned their lesson, and even the mouthpiece of the Massachusetts theocracy, John Cotton himself, preached that it was unwholesome to give officers in Church and State unconditional authority:

> It is necessary therefore, that all power is on earth be limited, Church power or other. . . . It is counted a matter of danger to the State to limit Prerogatives; but it is a further danger, not to have them limited. . . . It is therefore fit for every man to be studious of the bounds which the Lord hath set: and for the People, in whom fundamentally all power lyes, to give as much power as God in his word gives to men: And it is meet that Magistrates in the Commonwealth, and so officers in Churches should desire to know the utmost bounds of their own power.[1]

"If you tether a Beast at night," he said, with a grimness that carries us back to Pym and Hampden, "he knows the length of his tether before morning." [2]

Therefore, when the secular leaders in Massachusetts set out to keep the populace facing in the right direction, when they undertook to prove to the world that a government which endorsed Congregational churches could just as surely reckon with social problems as one which coöperated with an episcopal hierarchy, they labored under a handicap. They were subject to several inescapable restrictions, they could easily be compelled to toe various marks, and the possibility of their being

1. *An Exposition upon the Thirteenth Chapter of the Revelation*, p. 72.
2. *Ibid.*, p. 77.

ousted by a popular uprising was always imminent. They had, constitutionally speaking, hardly room to turn around in; yet it was from within these narrow confines that they had to wield sufficient influence to direct the colony to those ends to which it had theoretically pledged itself.

The political conflict of the oligarchy and the freemen has been variously chronicled, and our purposes do not require a detailed narrative. But one or two aspects deserve comment if we are to understand the emergence of a government capable of supporting a uniform orthodoxy. In general, the deputies were on the democratic side of the fence, and all but one or two of the assistants on the other. The latters' attitude was their natural heritage. Bishops had called Puritans demagogues, and in their rebuttals the insulted champions of reform had asserted their utter abhorrence of all democratic ideas. Cotton declared that his inculcation of subjection was no idle gesture, for the godly of Massachusetts had practised what they preached; they had been obedient to whatever magistrates they had ever lived under, "Orthodox or erroneous, just of our Consciences, or unjust against them." [1] He was teaching in America nothing that he had not taught in England; it had always been his settled conviction that churches should obey the authorities, "in patient suffering their unjust persecutions without hostile or rebellious resistance." [2] Since the officers of the colony had been consistently obedient and reverent to magistrates, when they had been the

1. Cotton, *The Bloudy Tenent Washed*, p. 119.
2. Cotton, *The Keyes of the Kingdom of Heaven*, p. 52.

citizens, they could see no reason now that they themselves were magistrates why their subordinates should not treat them accordingly. Though their decisions might conceivably be unjust, the citizens should abide by them precisely as they themselves had formerly obeyed the unjust edicts of James and Charles. When the Boston congregation moved to censure Winthrop for his abrupt measures against the Antinomians, he wrote them a little treatise, concluding "that though their magistrates did oppresse & iniure them, yet they should praye for them, & commende them, & seeke to winne them by gentlenesse. . . . A man may not say to a king, thou art wicked; nor call princes ungodly." [1] In 1639 the Court reduced the representation of each town from three to two deputies, whereupon some freemen protested. Winthrop invoked the Reformation's philosophy of government to bring them to their senses, pointing out that the precepts of subjection applied in a republic no less than in a monarchy:

When the people have chosen men to be their rulers, and to make their laws, and bound themselves by oath to submit thereto, now to combine together . . . in a public petition to have any order repealed, which is not repugnant to the law of God, savors of resisting an ordinance of God; for the people, having deputed others, have no power to make or alter laws, but are to be subject; and if any such order seem unlawful or inconvenient, they were better prefer some reasons, etc., to the Court, with manifestation of their desire to move them to a review, than peremptorily to petition to have it repealed, which amounts to a plain reproof of those whom God hath set over them, and putting dishonor upon them, against the tenor of the fifth commandment. [2]

1. Robert C. Winthrop, *Life and Letters of John Winthrop*, II, 213.
2. Winthrop, *Journal*, I, 303.

As Cartwright had long before predicted, a Puritan government would be no friend to "a lewd and licentious liberty."

Inspired by such ideals, the magistrates naturally set their faces against the persistently democratic deputies. They permitted no mistake about the matter. "Democracy," Cotton wrote to Lord Saye and Sele, "I do not conceyve, that ever God did ordeyne as a fitt government eyther for church or commonwealth. If the people be governors, who shall be governed?"[1] Winthrop defended the magistrates' claim to a negative voice lest otherwise the government be brought "from a mixt Aristocratie to a meere Democratie. . . . A Democratie is, among most Civill nations, accounted the meanest & worst of all formes of Government."[2] In spite of all limitations which the patent, the Bible, or the social covenant laid upon them, magistrates who spoke in these accents were determined that by fair means or foul they would let none of the "inferior sort" stand between them and the successful erection of the Puritan orthodoxy they had left England to create.

It is a tribute to the political genius of the English race that when the means employed by the magistrates were too patently foul, they failed. Whenever the assistants clearly transgressed the limits of the fundamental law, whenever they ran counter to English political tradition, they were blocked. They attempted at the beginning of the settlement to secrete the charter and disregard it. It had legalized the migration to a happier

1. Hutchinson, *History of the Colony of Massachusetts Bay*, I, 497.
2. Robert C. Winthrop, *op. cit.*, p. 430.

ecclesiastical clime, where, once arrived, the magistrates were willing to forget its specifications in order to make sure the venture should not miscarry for lack of their personal direction. The assistants themselves were the only officially enrolled freemen in the colony in 1630; at the first session of the "General Court," in October, they, as the people, before any other freemen had been admitted, voted to themselves, as the assistants, the sole powers of choosing the governor and enacting legislation.[1] The charter had clearly vested these functions in the whole number of the freemen; now the right of electing the assistants was all that was to be left to such as the assistants would enfranchise.[2] In the spring of 1631 the magistrates further declared, "in regard the number of Assistants are but fewe, & some of them going for England," that a mere majority of them might hold a Court, although the charter specifically stated that seven constituted a quorum.[3] Though the patent required four General Courts a year, none was called between May, 1631, and May, 1632. "When I came into the Country . . .," wrote Israel Stoughton, "the gouernment was solely in the hands of the assistants."[4] But by 1634 the citizens became suspicious. A delegation called on Winthrop and asked to view the charter. He attempted to evade, explaining that the assistants had assumed the power of legislation because the freemen had now grown too numerous to work together. If the citizens wished to participate in the government

1. *Massachusetts Records*, I, 79.   2. Winthrop, *Journal*, I, 74–75.
3. *Massachusetts Records*, I, 84.
4. *Mass. Hist. Soc.*, *Proc.*, LVIII, 452.

they would have "to have a select company to intend that work, yet for the present they were not furnished with a sufficient number of men qualified for such a business." [1]   The freemen, however, had their own opinions; they selected delegates from each of the towns, who appeared at the General Court of May, 1634, and at one fell swoop effected a constitutional revolution. They deposed Winthrop and elected Dudley, although Cotton, informed of their intentions, had preached at the opening session that a magistrate should not be turned out of office without just cause, his incumbency being in the nature of a "freehold." [2]   A comprehensive declaration was entered on the books that by the charter only the whole Court could choose and admit freemen, make and establish laws, elect officers, prescribe their duties, raise money or taxes, and dispose of land. Thereafter four General Courts were compelled to assemble every year, at each of which the freemen were to be adequately represented by their deputies.[3]   Truly, as Winthrop admitted, "many good orders were made this Court." [4]

The magistrates made one other notable move to subvert the charter, and once more were checkmated. During the hysteria of the Antinomian crisis, "upon the advice and solicitation of the elders," [5] a standing council for life was created, to which Winthrop, Dudley, and Endecott were appointed, with the possession of full magisterial powers whether they were chosen as assist-

1. Winthrop, *Journal*, I, 122.   2. *Ibid.*, p. 124.
3. *Massachusetts Records*, I, 117–119.   4. Winthrop, *Journal*, I, 125.
5. *Ibid.*, II, 60; *Massachusetts Records*, I, 167, 174.

ants or not. When the panic blew over, the freemen realized that this council was neither constitutional by the patent nor amenable to their vote. At the first attack the magistrates surrendered, and the Court rendered the council innocuous by declaring that no councillor could perform any magisterial act unless he were annually elected an assistant, "according to the tenure of the patent." [1] Winthrop pointed the moral of the episode:

Here may be observed, how strictly the people would seem to stick to their patent, when they think it makes for their advantage, but are content to decline it, where it will not warrant such liberties as they have taken up without warrant from thence.[2]

"I see the spirits of the people runne high," Nathaniel Ward wrote about this time, "& what they gett they hould." [3]

Ward was referring to a recognizably English desire for what Dunning has called "the security inherent in the appeal to recorded grant, to custom, to precedent." [4] The deputies eminently demonstrated their desire for that security in a long contest. During the first summer of the colony, the assistants had commissioned themselves justices of the peace, "to haue like power that justices of peace hath in England for reformation of abuses & punishing of offenders." [5] A year previous the Company had instructed Endecott to mete out punishment "(as neere as may be) according to the lawes of this

1. *Ibid.*, p. 264; Winthrop, *Journal*, I, 304.
2. *Ibid.*, p. 305.
3. *Mass. Hist. Soc., Coll.*, Series 4, VII, 26.
4. William Archibald Dunning, *A History of Political Theories*, II, 194.
5. *Massachusetts Records*, I, 74.

kingdome"; [1] but when the leaders themselves arrived upon the scene, they became much less inclined to hunt for precedents in English law. They were bound too much as it was, and a discretionary judicial power was to them an invaluable asset. Very soon they deliberately repudiated English examples, arguing that as the garments of a grown man would oppress or stifle a child, so "the Lawes of *England*, to take the body of them, are too unweldy for our weake condition." [2]   But the freemen began to grow apprehensive. If their judges were not bound by English statute, they were not bound at all, and the people naturally "thought their condition very unsafe, while so much power rested in the discretion of magistrates." [3] Israel Stoughton, deputy for Dorchester, wrote a paper in 1634 to prove that in the administration of justice the magistrates could do naught by their own wills, "but they must eie and respect generall courts, which by patent consist of the whole company of freemen." [4] His booklet aroused the ire of Winthrop, who caused him to be suspended from public office for three years, but the cause for which Stoughton argued was, in an English community, irresistible. The magistrates evaded codifying the laws as long as they could, but by 1641 Nathaniel Ward's *Body of Liberties* was adopted, and thereafter the government was bound to respect not merely "ye Lawes of God" and "ye patent," but also "ye fundamentall lawes & liberties established in ye commonwealth." [5]

1. *Ibid.*, p. 393.   2. Winslow, *New-Englands Salamander*, p. 23.
3. Winthrop, *Journal*, 1, 323; cf. p. 151.
4. *Mass. Hist. Soc., Proc.*, LVIII, 455.
5. *Massachusetts Records*, II, 95.

As long as the contest between the magistrates and the freemen was purely political, as long as the matters in dispute had to be settled upon bare constitutional grounds, the magistrates were apt to wage a losing fight. However clever they were, they could not by mere secular weapons overcome prejudices rooted in centuries of experience. Certainly they made the effort to do so. They took advantage of every opportunity. They were unable to deny that they were perennially bound by the terms of the charter, and they were unable to withstand the citizens' demand to know precisely by what laws Englishmen were governed; but in the conception of social compact they did see a small chance to exercise their ability as casuists and to interpret one of the fundamental laws to their own advantage. What the magistrates attempted to do with this theory came to light most clearly in the stand which Winthrop took against Harry Vane in 1637. During the hysteria of the Antinomian affair, the Court passed an order that no stranger should be offered hospitality until he had been approved by two of the magistrates. Vane called this tyranny, and as usual Winthrop was spokesman for the defense.

The first consideration, Winthrop said, was what constituted a state. He conceived it to be "the consent of a certaine companie of people, to cohabite together, under one government for their mutual safety and welfare." Otherwise no government could ever come into being:

It is clearly agreed, by all, that the care of safety and wellfare was the original cause or occasion of common weales and of many familyes subjecting themselves to rulers and laws; for no man hath lawfull power over another, but by birth or consent, so likewise, by the law of proprietye, no man can have just interest in that which belongeth to another, without his consent.

Now if Massachusetts was such a corporate society, she had a right to admit whomsoever she pleased, and conversely, "we may lawfully refuse to receive such whose dispositions suite not with ours." No one denied this privilege to the churches; "why then should the common weale be denied the like liberty?" [1]

Vane at once perceived the drift of this argument. If the magistrates could view the Massachusetts colony as an independent corporate society, and if they could subordinate the conception of binding, fundamental law to that of a covenanted purpose, they would then be in a position to insist that the social compact be interpreted according to their own notions. Settlers would be constantly surprised to learn that by their very participation in the colony, they had "implicitly" taken a covenant to uphold whatever the magistrates took it into their heads to declare should be upheld. Vane, therefore, took issue with Winthrop upon the basic position. Massachusetts, he declared, was not built upon a compact; it was founded first upon the Bible, and then "upon the grante also of our Soveraigne." The government could be only such a one as Christ would allow and as "the grante requires and permitts and in that manner and forme as it prescribes." Winthrop's reasons, "taken from the nature of a common-wealth, not founded upon

---

1. All the documents in this controversy are found in Thomas Hutchinson, *A Collection of Papers Relating to the History of Massachusetts Bay*, I, 79–113.

Christ, nor by his Majestyes charters," did not apply here, and "must needs fall to the ground." The commonwealth could only proceed as it had been authorized by God or King; it could not allow important matters to depend "upon such unlimited and unsafe a rule, as the will and discretion of men." Of course the colony could exclude proved undesirables, but it could do so only by concrete law and trial by jury; it could not pronounce sentence through "the illimited consent or dissent of magistrates." The analogy to the churches Vane dismissed by declaring that the churches did have a fundamental law, that they did not "receive or rejecte at their discretions . . . but at the discretion of Christ." The elders themselves often admitted this when they affirmed that the churches' power was purely "ministerial." The State should copy them, using its charter for a guide as the churches used Scripture. Otherwise, to give the magistrates power on the basis of some vague social theory "setts down no rule" for them, and was a tyranny, quite of a piece with the unauthorized taxation of a Stuart monarch.

Vane's paper is an epitome of the whole political temper which the magistrates in Massachusetts had set themselves to quieting. Winthrop's reply furnishes us with another tribute to the ingenuity of those who had learned their logic from William Ames. It was a clever attempt to reconcile the theory of constitutional limitation with that discretionary exercise of executive power which he felt was essential to a respectable state. There was, he hastened to declare, no reason why the laws of the Bible and the charter could not be the basis of a state which owed its existence to a compact. Vane's approach seemed to him limited; his own description of a state had been given in general, philosophic terms which Vane had not appreciated. "The definition or description of the genus may be applyed to all the species, reserving the specificall differences." Among these latter were both the charter and the religion; the patent was only an accidental circumstance, not the essence; the society came into being not when the charter was granted, but when, in order

to cohabite in the Massachusetts and under the government set up among us by his Majesty's patent or grant for our mutual safety and wellfare, we agreed to walke according to the rules of the gospell. And thus you have both a christian common weale and the same founded upon the patent, and both included within my description.

The commonwealth itself was the reality; both its charter and its Christianity were only the language in which its particular compact had been enunciated.

If, to begin with, the corporate society had expressed its will by adopting the form of government which happened to be described in the patent, then it could continue to dictate its desires as it saw fit; and what more rational than that it should express itself through the magistrates, who by their very offices represented the whole society? Vane's distinction between "a consent regulated, and a vast and illimited consent" was therefore "frivilous discourse." It was as though Vane came to borrow Winthrop's horse, and Winthrop refused him. "yet he may take him, because my dissent is unlawful . . . If this speed well, the next conclusion will be an anarchie." However much Winthrop had ever protested against royal absolutism, when he had assumed the task of government he, like the King, began to see in the resort to fundamental law a dangerous device whereby subordinates could find a way to appeal over the heads of their lawful superiors and to indulge their corrupt desires in the name of some easily fabricated inalienable right. According to his theology, man, perceiving such an opportunity, would surely abuse it.

As for Christ and not men determining in the churches, Winthrop called Vane's attention to the fact that Congregational theory recognized that the voice of God could be expressed only through the men composing the congregation, and that even they should be ruled. "Did he never heare, that our practise is, that none are propounded to the congregation, except they be first allowed by the elders, and is not this to admitt or reject by discretion?" In like manner the fundamental law in the State could not be administered "otherwise than as it is dispensed in the ministry of men." Since the exercise of authority had to be committed to some person, "to whom may it more properly than to the fathers of the common wealth?" The truth of the matter was that these fathers were sufficiently limited. They were church members and had taken the church covenant; they were freemen and had taken the freeman's oath; they were magistrates and had taken the magistrates' oath. They were triply bound "to square all their proceedings by the rule of Gods word." Therefore the magistrates could not be considered apart from the State; their every action was automatically an expression of the will of the State, and hence of the will of God.

"Whatsoever sentence the magistrate gives, according to these limitations, the judgment is the Lords, though he do it not by any rule particularly prescribed by civill authority."

Winthrop's argument was the peak of ingenuity, but the citizens found Vane's position more attractive, and the *Body of Liberties* signalized the magistrates' failure to retain the full discretionary powers for which Winthrop pleaded. In 1644 the deputies carried the assault still further, and objected to the magistrates' being left at liberty to vary penalties to suit their own conception of the gravity of offenses. The magistrates were angry, but they and the reverend elders once more bowed to the political wisdom of the race, and admitted that fixed penalties ought to be prescribed wherever possible. In the political sphere limitation by the fundamental law meant something the magistrates were compelled to respect. To this extent, then, we may recognize that they had no easy time of it, as did the clergy.

But politics in Massachusetts were the lesser half of life. The magistrates had other strings to their bow. If they were balked by English political traditions, they found succor in Puritan political principles. The assistants were not able to run the government with as unhampered a hand as they might have wished, but they were able to mould the commonwealth with the assistance of their clerical colleagues. It was to the co-operation of the Church that the Massachusetts leaders owed their final triumph. Though they lost important points in the constitutional struggle, they gained even more strategic ones by employing spiritual auxiliaries, whom they were then able to repay by contributing their share to the establishment of a uniform orthodoxy, such a one as had hovered for years before all Puritan visions.

The partnership of State and Church operated in Massachusetts precisely as Puritans had expected it would where a government could be induced to accept the qualified supremacy. The Puritan plea for distinct yet coöperating departments was thoroughly vindicated. Jacob had written that Church and State were "distinct and cleerlie severed the one from the other: albiet each doth ayd & succour the other."[1] Davenport continued in the same strain: the two were not to be

set in opposition as contraries that one should destroy the other, but as coordinate States, in the same place reaching forth help mutually each to other, for the welfare of both, according to God.

The two realms were not to be confused,

either by giving the Spiritual Power, which is proper to the Church, into the hand of the Civil Magistrate . . . or By giving Civil Power to Church-Officers, who are called to attend onely to Spiritual matters, and *the things of God*.[2]

Cotton even declared that for a magistrate to follow uncritically any mistaken advice of the clergy would be for him to make a "beast" of the church itself.[3] The two agents did not often overstep the limits of their respective jurisdictions. "The Magistrates and Church leaders," said Lechford, "labour for a just and equall correspondance in jurisdictions, not to intrench one on

1. Jacob, *Reasons taken out of Gods Word*, p. 26.
2. Davenport, *A Discourse about Civil Government*, pp. 7, 8.
3. Cotton, *An Exposition upon the Thirteenth Chapter of the Revelation*, p. 18.

the other." [1] During the Antinomian affair the Court passed a law requiring excommunicated persons to be dealt with in a civil way within six months of their sentence, but the clergy caused its repeal. Cotton condemned it:

It is dangerous to bring civill authority immediately upon the Churches censure. . . . It is good to have these two States so joyned together, that the simplicity of the church may be maintained and upheld, and strengthened by the civill state according to God, but not by any simplicity further then according to the word. [2]

In 1639 the Court tried to reduce the number of midweek services, — which seemed to be cutting into working hours, — but gave over the attempt as soon as the elders remonstrated. [3] The magistrates were annoyed once more during the period of the Civil Wars because the clergy called for repeated days of humiliation; still "they would not contend with the elders about it, but left the churches to their liberty." [4] But when the clergy trespassed upon the political bailiwick, the magistrates did not hesitate to object. Some of the Boston congregation moved to censure Winthrop for his treatment of their Antinomian brethren, but he promptly informed them that "a church hath not power to call any civill Magistrate to give account of his juditiall proceedings in any court of Justice." [5] In 1640 certain elders wanted the Court to forbear proceeding against any politically offending church member until he could be dealt with in a church way, but the magistrates in-

1. *Plain Dealing*, p. 35. 2. Cotton, *op. cit.*, p. 30.
3. Winthrop, *Journal*, I, 326–327.
4. *Ibid.*, II, 91.
5. *Ibid.*, I, 256; Robert C. Winthrop, *op. cit.*, II, 211.

dignantly refused to agree; and when a Boston constable acted on the assumption that the elders had won their case, he was promptly committed.[1] At times the elders' propensity for putting their fingers into political pies seems to have become a bit exasperating. Winthrop complained that in the disputes of 1644 the elders did no good office "through their misapprehensions both of the intentions of the magistrates, and also of the matters themselves, being affairs of state, which did not belong to their calling."[2] But in the main the partnership operated without friction, and the magistrates would have put up with even more serious clerical officiousness in order to preserve the relationship. Greater things were at stake, because as Winthrop unblushingly admitted,

The elders had great power in the people's hearts, which was needful to be upheld, lest the people should break their bonds through abuse of liberty, which divers, having surfeited of, were very forward to incite others to raise mutinies and foment dangerous and groundless jealousies of the magistrates, which the wisdom and care of the elders did still prevail against; and indeed the people themselves, generally, through the churches, were of that understanding and moderation, as they would easily be guided in their way by any rule from scripture or sound reason.[3]

Within the first year of the experiment, the magistrates hit upon a device which practically guaranteed that the "people" should become amenable to the rules of Scripture and sound reason. In the spring of 1631, when the assistants were casting about for some means of improving upon the inadequate charter, one hundred

---

1. Winthrop, *Journal*, II, 15, 40.   2. *Ibid.*, p. 190.
3. *Ibid.*, I, 326–327.

and eight Englishmen confronted them with an ominous petition for citizenship. If the community was to hang together, these men could not be denied, and yet for the assistants to throw open the franchise indiscriminately could only spell the eventual passing of their control. The leaders urgently required some basis for selection which would at once insure the desired security and yet not be repulsive to the populace. At that moment they beheld a hitherto unsuspected utility in the Congregational principle of restricted membership. The petitioners were admitted regardless of their ecclesiastical affiliations, but "to the end the body of commons may be presued of honest & good men," the magistrates decreed "that for time to come noe man shalbe admitted to the freedome of this body polliticke, but such as are members of some of the churches within the lymitts of the same." [1] When the deputies enacted their constitutional revolution in 1634, they had already become so well schooled to viewing church members as the only assuredly honest and good men that though they overturned all the other presumptuous legislation of the assistants, they left the religious qualification of the electorate untouched. Thus at the outset the magistrates more than halved the problem of domestic rule, and transformed the republican government of the charter into a sort of religious soviet. Even a picked body of freemen offered difficulties, but they were at least Congregationalists, and therefore had some glimmering of what the leaders aimed at. If their political obstinacy could not be overcome in the council chamber,

1. *Massachusetts Records*, I, 87.

it could be softened in the meeting-house. We can, consequently, thoroughly understand why the churches were compelled to insist more and more upon the restricted membership, however much the exclusion failed to accomplish all the spiritual purposes for which it had been designed, and also, why they were driven to devise some excuse for regarding the unconverted children of substantial citizens as working members. The question before the churches was no longer one of approximating the make-up of the invisible Church; it was one of controlling the Massachusetts electorate. "Whereas the way of God hath alwayes beene to gather his Churches out of the world; now the world, or civill state, must be raised out of the churches." [1] In 1636 Lords Saye and Brooke toyed with the notion of migrating, and they asked whether such "gentlemen" as they might bring with them could be admitted to citizenship. Cotton wrote the official response, wherein he paid the respects of the colony to rank and title, but he could promise no exception to the qualified franchise. He denied that this provision in any way entailed the subversion of the State to the Church, for the magistrates were not chosen by the Church, "nor doe governe by directions from the church, but by civill lawes . . . in all which, the church (as the church) hath nothing to do: onely, it prepareth fitt instruments both to rule, and to choose rulers." Therefore, he could conscientiously conclude the qualification "to be a divine ordinance." [2] Davenport, who rigorously applied the ordinance to his colony at New

1. Hutchinson, *A Collection of Papers*, I, 101.
2. Hutchinson, *The History of the Colony of Massachusetts Bay*, I, 493–497.

Haven, defended it at length in his *Discourse about Civil Government*. "Members fitly chosen out of the Church," he declared, were the best material for citizenship in a religious commonwealth, because they were bound "unto all Faithfulness in all things to God and man." Unfortunately, "the like assurance cannot be had in any other way, if this course be neglected." [1] The magistrates and clergy frequently warned the freemen against permitting zeal for their own constitutional liberties to betray them into championing the cause of the unfranchised. Shepard preached to the General Court of 1638 in a hortatory mood:

> Maintayne the privilege to death. Whomsoeuer you shall choose let him be one from among yourselues; a member of some church; he yt is shut out of the fellowship of churches will be an enemy vnto the strictnes of churches; & ruine church you ruine state; & Christ also.[2]

The advantage of a qualified electorate, according to Davenport, was that since it meant that both electors and elected were in covenant with God, then "men of God are consulted with in all hard cases and matters of Religion." [3] That the State should take counsel of the clergy had, as we have noted, been definitely advocated by the Puritans. Yet they had hardly intended that appeals should be made in other than purely religious affairs. But when a state had actually assumed the Bible as its fundamental law, there soon appeared to be very few occasions upon which that book had nothing to say. In 1632 Winthrop and Dudley quarreled, and the

1. Davenport, *A Discourse about Civil Government*, pp. 12, 22.
2. *New England Historical and Genealogical Register*, xxiv, 366.
3. Davenport, *op. cit.*, p. 15.

ministers were asked to interpose. Their "advice," supported by scriptural citation, healed the breach.[1] In the next year a French attempt at Fort Royal threatened the colony; before adopting a policy the Court consulted with the elders to see if by any chance the Lord had foreseen such an emergency. It seemed that he had,[2] and thereafter all contingencies, military and diplomatic as well as ecclesiastical, were met in the same manner. "The rulers of the people," Cotton preached in 1637, "should consult with the ministers of the churches upon occassion of any war to be undertaken, and any other weighty business, though the case should seem never so clear." [3]

By referring governmental questions to the elders the magistrates not only received direction from the Word of God; they soon discovered that by this means the deputies could be given such advice as would not be taken from themselves, advice always bolstered with unanswerable biblical demonstrations to which the citizens, being church members, could not object. If the election sermon which Shepard preached in 1638 is, as I suppose, a sample of the political doctrine constantly inculcated by the elders, we may easily understand how they turned the balance of the constitutional struggle. You, the people, Shepard frankly delivered, are apt "to desire & accept of change of gouernment," even though you have "the beste gouernment of god." You are inherently corrupt, unstable, "apt to be led by colours like birds by glasses & larkes by lures, & golden pre-

1. Winthrop, *Journal*, 1, 84–91.
2. *Ibid.*, p. 97.   3. *Ibid.*, p. 231.

tences which Innouators euer haue." You should therefore understand that innovators of any sort, in Church
or State, are taking advantage of you; "if they can come
in by your faction, you will then find them to be indeed
brambles; ambitious, base, & bloody." [1] This was no
mere idle oratory. Good Christians could not demur
when the ministers all agreed that the will of Christ had
such and such political implications. In 1634 the citizens
of Newtown petitioned for permission to remove to Connecticut. A majority of the deputies were favorable,
but a majority of the magistrates were not, and they
claimed that by the charter and the laws of God they
possessed a negative voice. Once again the leaders confronted a crisis. In those instances in which the deputies
gained their way, the victories had no greater effect than
to bind the whole State to a more meticulous observation of some basic law; in this case, however, a triumph
of the deputies would have meant that by numerically
dominating a uni-cameral legislature they could practically shoulder the assistants out of the government.
Before the next Court convened, the magistrates, "considering how dangerous it might be to the commonwealth, if they should not keep that strength to balance
the greater number of the deputies," once more pressed
John Cotton into service. He preached at the opening
session, explaining the divine philosophy of Congregational rule, the Calvinistic theory of "mixed government," and applying it conclusively to the case in hand:

He laid down the nature or strength . . . of the magistracy,
ministry, and people; viz — the strength of the magistracy to be

1. *New England Historical and Genealogical Register*, xxiv, 362–364.

their authority; of the people, their liberty; and of the ministry their purity; and showed how all of these had a negative voice, etc., and that yet the ultimate resolution, etc., ought to be in the whole body of the people.

"Mr. Cotton," Hubbard tells us, "had such an insinuating and melting way in his preaching, that he would usually carry his very adversary captive after the triumphant chariot of his rhetoric." [1] He had failed to captivate the deputies when he had attempted to persuade them that Winthrop had a divine right to reëlection, because they then stood upon good constitutional grounds; but when their case was not so well founded, and when he assured them he was the last person in the world to deny the peoples' "duty and right to maintain their true liberties against any unjust violence," then his pontifical rendering of the Word was effective. "It pleased the Lord so to assist him," and the magistrates retained their veto. [2]

Once again, however, the issue came up. In 1643, when the magistrates refused judgment to Goody Sherman, the people cried out upon the negative voice. The magistrates defended it with "many arguments from scripture, reason, and common practice"; they pointed out that it was "of great concernment, even to the very frame of our government." To all this the deputies, activated by a "democratical spirit," paid no heed. Then the magistrates played their trump card: they offered to accept the arbitration of the elders. Concerning the motive Winthrop is delightfully frank: "It was

1. *Mass. Hist. Soc., Coll.*, Series 2, v, 175.
2. Winthrop, *Journal*, 1, 133–134.

the magistrates' only care to gain time, that so the peoples' heat might be abated, for then they knew they would hear reason, and that the advice of the elders might be interposed." As might have been expected, the elders only rehearsed Cotton's arguments; they proved the superiority of a "mixed forme of Government . . . from scripture, Reason, and Experience," and they quoted Calvin, "famous both for diuinity and law." Enlightened by these learned disquisitions, a better informed people "let the case fall." [1]

They could, indeed, do nothing else. The combination of magistrates and ministers dominated the restricted horizon of the frontier community. As Winthrop, in another of his candid moments, succinctly expressed it, "the Ministers haue great power with the people, whereby throughe the good correspondency between the Magistrates & them, they are the more easyly gouerned." [2] The magistrates alone might be opposed, but the magistrates in correspondency with the elders, furnished with a bristling array of biblical citations, were irresistible. Thus with the political régime sufficiently intrenched, the State was ready to play the part assigned to it in Puritan theory, was prepared to repay the clergy by taking over the protection of orthodoxy and the enforcement of uniformity.

The magistrates had displayed an early disposition to do their share, but in the still undeveloped condition of the church system they were not certain just how to go about it. In 1635 the Court, confronted with the radical

1. *Ibid.*, II, 66, 120–121; *Massachusetts Records*, II, 91–94; *Mass. Hist. Soc., Proc.*, XLVI, 276–285.   2. *Robert C. Winthrop, op. cit.*, II, 460.

assertions of Roger Williams, requested the elders to frame "one vniforme order of dissipline in the churches" and then to decide "how farr the magistrates are bound to interpose for the preservation of that vniformity." [1] The clerical opinion seemed to be that the time was not yet ripe for publishing an official platform, but a few of the ministers (Cotton later insisted he was not one of them) drew up a tentative statement of principle on the subject of uniformity.[2] The major part of this document was a reiteration of the conventional Puritan doctrine that civil government, in its dealing with the Church, was limited by the Word of God to a concern with only "outward order, as in Rites & Ceremonies for uniformities sake," and that its means should remain purely political.[3] But they hazarded the suggestion that the magistrate should *allow* the churches to assemble in synods, "as the meanes appointed by God, whereby he may mediately reform matters amisse in Churches, which immediately he cannot nor ought not to do." [4] Consociation proved a complete success as an instrument of discipline both in the Williams episode and in the Hutchinson affair, and the moral of these events was not lost upon the leaders. Cotton saw in the events of 1637 an ideal illustration of the partnership of Church and State:

The Neighbour Churches . . . took a right course (according to the principles of the Independent Government) to gather into a

---

1. *Massachusetts Records*, I, 142.
2. Samuel L. Caldwell, Preface to Williams, *The Bloudy Tenent of Persecution*, p. viii.
3. Quoted in Williams, *The Bloudy Tenent of Persecution*, pp. 261, 247–248, 226.   4. *Ibid.*, p. 391.

Synod with the consent of the civill Magistrates: and in the Synod to agitate, convince and condemne the Errors, and the offensive carriages then stirring. Whereat the Magistrates being present, they saw just cause to proceed against the chief of those whom they conceived to have bred any civill disturbance: and the Churches saw cause to proceede against their Members, whom they found to bee broachers or maintainers of such heresies.[1]

Thereafter it became the accepted tenet in Massachusetts that the supreme magistrate should summon synods and strengthen their decisions "either by his meer Authoritative suffrage, assent, and testimony, (if the matter need no more) or by his authoritative Sanction of it by Civill punishment, the nature of the offence so requiring." [2] Yet all the time these decisions were supposed to be the fruit of friendly consultation and the synods were to impose nothing by force. Johnson, in one of his most charming pages, boasted that Presbyterian coercion would never be so effective as Congregational "brotherly love":

Could your eyes but behold the efficacy of loving counsell in the Communion of congregationall Churches . . . you would never stand for Classicall injunctions any more. . . . Verily its more universall then the Papall power. . . . Yea, and it may be added, because civill Government is like to turn nurse.[3]

Lechford properly retorted that even if the determinations of a synod were reached "by way of love, and friendly advice,"

Were not the counselled bound to receive good counsell? If they would not receive it, was not the Magistrate ready to *assist*, and in a manner ready, according to duty, to *enforce* peace and obedience? [4]

---

1. *The Way of the Congregational Churches Cleared*, pt. i, p. 84.
2. Cotton, *The Result of the Synod*, p. 65.
3. *The Wonder Working Providences*, p. 105.   4. *Plain Dealing*, p. 127.

But with the successful Synod of 1637 in mind, magistrates and ministers could afford to ignore such comments. They saw nothing incongruous in a civil power "nursing" a people into orthodox uniformity, when the uniformity was precisely that which Christ had commanded.

In the "Modell" of 1635, the program drawn up by certain of the elders in response to the request of the Court, it was stated briefly that one aspect of the magistrate's duty involved the forbidding of idolatrous and corrupt assemblies.[1] This remark seemed to insinuate that if the government had been on its toes a little earlier it could have prevented Salem from calling Williams in the first place. The authorities now decided to take official measures which would prevent the recurrence of any such situation. In March, 1636, having found "by sad experience" that much trouble had been caused both "the church & civill state by the officers & members of some churches, which haue bene gathered . . . in an vndue manner, & not with such publique approbation as were meete," the Court ordered that thereafter all companies about to join in church fellowship should beforehand notify not only the neighboring elders but also the magistrates, "& haue their approbation herein."[2] Thus when five or six men of Saugus, at the instigation of the troublesome Mr. Batchellor, attempted to establish a second congregation there, the church appealed to the government; the magistrates, "forseeing the distraction which was like to come by this course," forbade Batchellor to proceed until the

1. Williams, *op. cit.*, p. 278.   2. *Massachusetts Records*, I, 168.

elders could talk to him. When he rebelled, "the marshall was sent to fetch him." [1]

Thereafter, whenever the churches assembled, either at the covenanting of new societies or at the election of new ministers, some or all of the magistrates were present. Often, as at Weymouth in 1644, the magistrates and visiting elders, "finding upon trial, that the persons appointed were not fit for foundation stones, they advised them not to proceed," which, naturally, "they obeyed." [2] The Dedham congregation, fresh from England in 1638, feared that this practice would infringe the Christian liberty they had sought in the wilderness, but the officials at once explained that the law of 1636 did not imply that a church privately gathered was not a true church,

but ye scope was this, yt if any people of unsound judgment or eroneous way, etc. . . . should privately sett up churches amongst them ye commonwealth would not so approve them as to communicate yt freedome & other priviledges unto them which yei did unto others or protect them in ther government if they saw ther way dangerous to the publike peace.[3]

Congregational peoples did indeed secure in America a "liberty" to follow Christ according to his laws; but they certainly secured no liberty to follow him in any other fashion.

English Congregationalists had glibly assumed that though the masses would be excluded from church membership, they could still be expected to attend

1. Winthrop, *Journal*, I, 169.
2. *Ibid.*, II, 179.
3. *The Records of Baptisms, Marriages, and Deaths . . . in the Town of Dedham*, pp. 9–10.

church services. But it is not surprising to find that many who were excluded on the assumption that they were damned should not have been enthusiastic about listening to a weekly description of their plight. In the "Modell" of 1635 the ministers took occasion to remind the Court that the civil magistrate had a legitimate power "to compell all men within his grant, to heare the Word, for hearing the Word of God is a duty which the light of Nature leadeth even Heathens to." [1] The Court responded at once, and declared that since it had been found "that dyvers persons within this jurisdiction doe vsually absent themselues from church meeteings vpon the Lords day," hereafter any two magistrates should have power to punish "all misdemeaners of that kinde committed by any inhabitant." [2] Those without the churches, boasted the *Cambridge Platform*, are "invited by counsel" to come to meeting, "& required by wholesome lawes to attend." [3]

This much the government could do and still remain well within the Congregational tradition. But it also seemed reasonable that the reprobates should pay for the invaluable privilege of witnessing Christ's ordinances. Here, however, was a difficult problem, for the polity had clearly intended that contribution, like profession, should be voluntary. As Jacob emphatically put it,

For preserving due freedome in the Congregation, sincerity in Religion, and sanctity in the whole stock, the Congregations voluntary & conscionable contribution for their Pastors sustenance, and

1. Williams, *op. cit.*, p. 279.   2. *Massachusetts Records*, I, 140.
3. Walker, *Creeds and Platforms*, p. 200.

maintenance is doubtless the safest, and most approved, nay it seemeth, the onely way.[1]

But it had been one thing for the ministers to preach voluntary payment when they were attacking the tithes exacted by a hostile Establishment, and another to do so when they expected livelihood. It speedily became apparent that "many of those who are freemen, nor members of any church, do take advantage thereby to withdraw their helpe in such voluntary contributions as are in vse";[2] the godly began to feel that "the burthen grew too hevy upon church members."[3] The ministers who wrote the "Modell" of 1635 were already concerned about the problem, and ventured to suggest to the Court that maintenance of the churches should arise "from all those who are ordinarily taught thereby"; they were willing to conclude that "hence it is the dutie of the Civill Magistrate to contend with the people . . . who doe neglect and forsake the due maintenance of the Church of God, and to command them to give such portions for the maintenance of Church officers, as the Gospell commandeth."[4] The Court, which had at once adopted the "Modell's" suggestion on the oversight of new churches, was yet unwilling to embark upon this departure from the pristine theory without more warrant from the clergy than a private memorandum. It therefore made a point of asking the Synod of 1637 what should be done, but the elders did not wish to take the decision upon themselves, "lest it should be said that

1. Jacob, *A Confession and Protestation*, pp. 30, 32.
2. *Massachusetts Records*, I, 240.
3. Hutchinson, *A Collection of Papers*, II, 6–7; cf. *Magnalia*, II, 491.
4. Williams, *op. cit.*, pp. 291–292.

this assembly was gathered for their private advantage." [1] The next General Court took the hint, and upon its own initiative ordered that thereafter such persons as did not freely and willingly contribute to churches "shalbee compelled thereto by assessment & distress to bee levied by the cunstable, or other officer of the towne, as in other cases." [2] Nothing more strikingly signalizes the transformation of the English heterodoxy into the New England orthodoxy than this complete reversal of the original position. Jacob's statement makes an odd contrast to the dictum of the *Cambridge Platform*. "All that are taught in the word," that document reads, should contribute to the church, and if, "through the corruption of men," the church does not obtain sufficient revenue, then "the magistrate is to see [that the] ministry be duely provided for." [3]

These various laws were obviously specific applications of contemporary conceptions of supremacy and uniformity. The comparatively easy creation of an established order in New England is explicable only when we understand how the people had been fully prepared to accept it. When elder Browne caused a flurry at Watertown in 1632, and Winthrop, Dudley, and Nowell came up from Boston to offer their mediation, they asked the Watertown congregation whether they were to figure as members of a neighboring church or as magistrates, "their assistance being desired." [4] The congregation decided on the first rôle, but that the other was considered ready for use at this early date is extremely

1. Winthrop, *Journal*, I, 235; *Massachusetts Records*, I, 240.
2. *Ibid*.   3. Chap. xi, par. 4.   4. Winthrop, *Journal*, I, 71.

significant. After the Hutchinson affair the leaders were resolved that even though a definite platform could not be formulated, they should be empowered to act with a free hand whenever necessary. The deputies refused to permit the assistants a discretionary power in purely civil or criminal matters, but in the light of their religious training they could not object to giving officials a large freedom in dealing with religious offenses. Thus, at the trial of Wheelwright, the Court and elders agreed that though doubtful opinions should be referred to the church for judgment, "in some cases of religious natures, as manifest heresie, notorious blasphemy, etc., the Civill power may proceed *Ecclisia inconsulta.*" [1] With that prerogative secured, the magistrates were assured of the success of their experiment. Whatever they lost in the political contest did not ruin their prestige; it only made them observe certain legal forms. But any serious threat to their power was bound to have religious ramifications. If on that ground they could lead the action against offenders, either by themselves or better still with the aid of the elders, then they could accomplish that for which they had crossed the ocean.

At this point it may be worth noting, in view of the immense abuse that has been heaped upon the righteous heads of the Massachusetts leaders, that the officials were expected to exercise their ecclesiastical powers in accordance with what had been the most enlightened conceptions at the time they left England. The great principles which Puritans had invoked against the high-handed ecclesiastical courts were not forgotten. The

1. *Ibid.*, p. 210; *Antinomianism in Massachusetts Bay*, p. 192.

government of the colony could not employ "external violent means, as by Oathes *ex officio*, close Imprisonments, wracks, Strappadoes, and other preposterous wayes of Inquisition." Neither could it punish "a mere supposed Corruption in Religion, but that which is so really, and manifestly appearing from grounds of the Word." [1] The State claimed no surveillance over private opinions; it professed to deal only with the "outward man," when "either his mentall errours or hearts lust breake out into open expression and view, and become scandalous and spreading." [2] But magistrates in a biblical commonwealth could freely admit such qualification upon their procedure without sacrificing an iota of their power. They applied rules which Cotton declared were "so fundamentall, and palpable" that anyone who persisted in an offense after one or two admonitions thereby condemned himself. [3] The magistrates, said Cobbet, "do restrain and punish that only, which if others had any conscience, (as we say) they would refrain from." [4] Heresy, in other words, was understood to be as concrete a crime as murder, and though the guilty one refused to recognize his offense as such, society nevertheless had a right to judge him. Just as in the Church the clergy themselves determined when an obstinate heretic deserved excommunication, so, when the magistrates dealt with him, they too could legitimately decide at what point they should cease persuading and deliver a just sentence.

1. Thomas Cobbet, *The Civil Magistrates Power In matters of Religion*, pp. 15, 14.   2. Cotton, *The Result of a Synod*, pp. 15–16.
3. Cotton, *The Bloudy Tenent Washed*, pp. 9, 101.
4. Cobbet, *op. cit.*, p. 37.

The civill Magistrate is to informe and convince, and not to proceed suddenly till all just means are used to leave him convinced, of which it is more meet for the Magistrate than for the offending person to judge, who it may be will never say he is convinced.[1]

Thus it was that in Massachusetts the political theory of English Puritanism was at last vindicated. We could multiply citations from the colonial apologists indefinitely; the only difference between them and such passages as we have quoted from English Puritans would be a difference in tense and mood. English dissenters had told what ought to be; the New Englanders described what was. They had successfully limited the magistrate by the Word; he did not attempt to impose whatever form of worship he pleased, "as *Erastus* and some others since him affirm," [2] but he accepted that which God had decreed. In dubious matters he called for "the counsell of the churches," and considered himself "bound in conscience to follow what they according to God do clear up to be his mind." [3] But this qualification had proved itself no hindrance to the enforcement of uniformity; the civil government enjoyed an incontestable supremacy: "the head of the Church under Christ is the Civill Magistrate." [4] Therefore Hooker could argue that Independency was an utter misnomer for Congregationalism, at least in New England, for certainly no undue freedom was permitted a particular church when it was

subject unto, and under the supreme power politicke in the place where it is; so that the *Magistrate hath a coactive power* to compel the Church to execute the ordinances of Christ, according to the order

---

1. Cotton, *The Result of a Synod*, p. 7.
2. Cobbet, *op. cit.*, p. 51.   3. *Ibid.*, p. 67.
4. Cotton, *A Briefe Exposition of . . . Canticles*, p. 210.

and rules of Christ . . . and in case she swerves from her rule, by a strong hand to constraine her to keepe it.[1]

Rathband thought that in New England a magistrate was held to have nothing to do with matters of religion, but Weld disabused him at once: "All the Churches with us doe abhorre that vile opinion." [2] Much to the contrary, they expected him to be an active participant in the religious sphere, "to draw on the people to holy duties, by all meanes he can, by his Proclamation, Lawes, and Examples." [3] "Zeal of God in sharp punishing of such like corruptions stood very well with Christs Dove like Spirit; none so meek as he, Yet none so zealous this way." [4] The noblest object of a magistrate's endeavor was "that a right opinion and worship of God should be openly professed within the territories and jurisdiction of a State." It was his duty to study the Word, with the assistance of his synods, that he might "inquire and judge of professions and Religions, which is true, and ought to be maintained, which is false, and ought to be rejected." [5] The magistrate, concluded Cobbet,

is a political Minister of God, in his civil way, and by his Civil means, of the subjects spiritual good; so he is to improve his Authority, that the liberty, purity, and peace of Gods own instituted worship, and wayes, wherein their spiritual good, externally, doth much lye, be maintained and defended against all Infesting, infringing, Impugning or Impairing principles.[6]

It was, Cotton preached, only "a carnall and worldly, and indeed, an ungodly imagination" that would con-

---

1. Hooker, *Survey*, pt. II, p. 80. 2. Weld, *An Answer to W. R.*, p. 67.
3. Cotton, *op. cit.*, p. 21. 4. Cobbet, *op. cit.*, p. 42.
5. Hooker, *Survey*, pt. IV, p. 57. 6. Cobbet, *op. cit.*, p. 25.

fine "the Magistrates charge, to the bodies, and goods of the Subiect," and would "exclude them from the care of their soules." [1]

New England divines could afford to speak in confident tones, for within a decade of the migration the colony did seem to be a success. Puritans had long been of the opinion that even in this world the elect would be rewarded, and Jacob had predicted that if a nation would only adopt the true polity, "God will crowne his owne worke, and blesse his owne ordinance, and sanctify his owne way." [2] Winthrop promised aboard the *Arbella* that a sign of God's favor would be prosperity. After the system had lasted out the Antinomian convulsion, whatever else one might say about it, the indisputable fact remained that it worked. "Thus God delivered his people out of the snare of the Devil," ejaculated pious old Roger Clap, "then had the churches rest, and were multiplied." [3] "God hath at once subdued the proud Pequats and the proud opinions that rose up in this Land." [4] Presbyterians only let themselves in for crushing rebukes when they insinuated that Congregationalism would fail to secure uniformity. "For ought we know," said Richard Mather, "there is no materiall point, either in constitution, or government, wherein the Churches in *N. E.* . . . do not observe the same course." [5] When Rathband said that popular government in New England had proved a cause of schism, Weld promptly came back with:

1. *The Bloudy Tenent Washed*, p. 68.   2. *An Attestation*, p. 154.
3. Young, *Chronicles of Massachusetts*, p. 360.
4. W. Hooke, *New Englands Teares*, p. 8.
5. *Church-Government and Church-Covenant Discvssed*, p. 82.

Blessed be God, that under that Government of ours (which you call or rather miscall Popular) the very neck of Schisms, and vile opinions, (brought to us from hence) was broken; When here amongst you where there is not such a Government, they walke bolt upright amongst you and crowe aloud.[1]

The moral of New England history by 1648 was simply, according to Cotton, the very point Congregationalism had tried to make in England, and failing there through no fault of its own, had set out to prove in America:

That government, which by the blessing of Christ, doth safely, speedily, and effectually purge out such grievous and dangerous evills, as threaten the ruine of Church and State, that government is safely allowed, and justly and wisely established in any civill State.[2]

1. *An Answer to W. R.*, p. 66.
2. *The Way of the Congregational Churches Cleared*, pt. 1, p. 84.

VIII

TOLLERATING TIMES

FROM the standpoint of the English government, the most prominent fact about the New England Way was its independence. Gorges had prophesied that New Englanders would soon "wholly shake off the Royall Iurisdiction of the Soveraigne Magistrate," [1] and Laud's agent, Burdett, reported in 1639 that "it was not discipline that was so much aimed at, as sovereignty." [2] Lechford, who had been in a position to know, informed the English world in 1641,

> They themselves say, that in the generall and quarter Courts, they have the power of Parliament, Kings Bench, Common Pleas, Chancery, High Commission, and Star-Chamber, and all other Courts of England, and in divers cases have exercised that power upon the King's Subjects there.[3]

These were facts Laud could not for ever disregard. In 1638 the Lords of the Council bestirred themselves once more, and wrote to Boston asking what had happened to the charter which in 1634 they had wished to lay their hands on. Once more the General Court procrastinated. The comic interlude was played through again the next year, the Court simply pretending this time that it never received the Council's communication. The test upon the colony would undoubtedly have

1. Baxter, *Sir Ferdinando Gorges*, II, 60.
2. Winthrop, *Journal*, I, 285, 300.   3. *Plain Dealing*, p. 63.

come very shortly had it not been that "concernments
of an higher nature intervening in that juncture of time,
gave a supersedeas to that design and intendment." [1]
On July 23, 1637, a woman known to fame as Jenny
Geddes threw a three-legged stool at the Bishop of
Edinburgh in the great Church of St. Giles; she missed
the bishop, but she started a riot. Thereafter did Scotland "so take up the king and council, that they had
neither heart nor leisure to look after the affairs of New
England." [2] The First Bishops' War of 1639 demonstrated the bankruptcy of the Stuart absolutism, and
when the King at last called for a Parliament in April,
1640, there were portents aplenty. John Tinker wrote
to Winthrop that in this year

there are like to come but a small quantyty of passengers ouer . . .
and the reason I conceiue to be the hopes of some reformation in
England, by the intended parliament, the which cann hardly bee
expected per judicious and wise men . . . but rather see troublesome
times aproaching, both within and without the kingdome. [3]

Charles justified the apprehension of the wise by pro-
roguing the Parliament within three weeks, after it gave
unmistakable evidence of being more interested in the
reformation of England than in the subjugation of
Scotland. But with the complete fiasco of the Second
Bishops' War even Charles realized the game was up. In
November the Long Parliament began its momentous
sessions.

This collapse of Laud's régime meant that Puritanism
was out in the open. The lid was off. Whatever that

1. Hubbard, "General History of New England," *Mass. Hist. Soc., Coll.,*
Series 2, V, 271.   2. Winthrop, *Journal,* I, 271.
3. *Mass. Hist. Soc., Coll.,* Series 4, VII, 220.

persistent movement really stood for was to be demonstrated at last. But though it was a foregone conclusion that Parliament would attempt some sort of reformation, that body nevertheless inserted in the *Grand Remonstrance*, amid a zealous arraignment of episcopal abuses, a significant protest:

We do here declare that it is far from our purpose or desire to let loose the golden reins of discipline and government in the Church, to leave private persons or particular congregations to take up what form of Divine Service they please, for we hold it requisite that there should be through-out the whole realm a conformity to that order which the laws enjoin according to the Word of God.[1]

All parties to the dispute, at the beginning, were as thoroughly given over to the assumptions of a state church and an enforced uniformity as Laud himself had been, and on that score saw eye to eye with Massachusetts.

John Tinker and the wise men expressed dread in 1640 because they foresaw a controversy between the King and the "Root and Branch" Puritans. However discouraging a prospect this had seemed, it had after all presented a simple dualism, with the issue clearly defined on each side. But in the course of a very short time, there began to appear intimations of yet a further division. Hitherto, Thomas Shepard said, it had been "doubted not but if the Prelates were downe, all would agree in one";[2] but that canny Scotsman, Robert Baillie, coming to London in November of 1640, understood that Saye and Sele, with Brooke, in the Lords, and some leading men in the Commons, were supposed to be

1. Gardiner, *The Constitutional Documents of the Puritan Revolution*, p. 229.
2. Shepard and Allin, *A Defence of the Answer*, p. 16.

inclined to the Separatists. He feared for a moment that they "would divide from the Presbyterians, and so weaken the party opposite to bishops." However, he did not expect them to muster any considerable strength, and he predicted that they would be silent, "upon hope either of satisfaction when we get more leisure, or of toleration, on their good and peaceable behaviour." [1] But he little reckoned how far the teachings of Ames and Bradshaw had permeated English Puritanism. Several London ministers, aware of the fatal cleavage, wrote to the Scottish Assembly on July 12, 1641, saying that since God had "raised our hopes of removing this yoke of Episcopacy . . . sundry other forms of Church-government are by sundry sorts of men projected to be set up in the room thereof." One of these forms was the Congregational, and what, the ministers asked, should they do about it? The Kirk replied without hesitation: its "unanimous judgment and uniform practice" had ever been to put all power in the hands of the officers of the Church, who exercised it in "subordination unto greater Presbyteries and Synods, provincial and national." Any other arrangement seemed unscriptural.[2]

But even at that moment Burton was bringing the split to public notice with his *Protestation Protested*; he was soon joined by the five Independents from Holland and by Hugh Peter, Weld, and others from New England. Together they presented a formidable bloc, representing a growing and energetic opinion. In their

1. Baillie, *Letters and Journals*, Letters 20, 23.
2. David Masson, *Life of Milton*, ii, 288–290.

party manifesto, the famous *Apologeticall Narration*, the five brethren gave a significant history of their position; they told how in Holland they had been able to take warning from "the fatall miscarriages and shipwracks of the Separatists." They specifically declared that their conceptions of Church polity owed much to New England:

We had the recent and later example of the wayes and practices (and those improved to a better Edition and greater refinement by all the forementioned helps) of those multitudes of godly men of our own Nation, almost to the number of another nation,

who had settled New England "merely to worship God more purely." [1]

Presbyterians mustered their best strength and brains against the movement; Thomas Edwards passed from paroxysm to paroxysm of abuse:

Satan is now transforming himself from an Angell of darknesse into an Angell of light . . . so that he will now labour to do that by correcting and building up, which hee did before by persecuting and pulling downe. . . . One extremitie hath caused another, the Tyrannie of Episcopall government in some Bishops hath brought forth the Democracie and Independencie, the violent pressing of some pretended orders hath set many against all order. . . . Independencie will bring againe what now it would cast out, namely libertinisme, prophanenesse, errors, and will by some removes bring many men to be of no religion at all. [2]

These charges were precisely those which New Englanders had been repelling, and the Independents defended English Congregationalism by duplicating their arguments. The five brethren denied that they ever had

1. *An Apologeticall Narration*, pp. 5 ff.
2. Thomas Edwards, *Reasons against the Independent Government*, sig. B2.

been Separatists, and assured the world that they gave to the magistrates "as much and (as we think) more, then the principles of the Presbiteriall government will suffer them to yeeld." [1] Burton insisted there could be no danger of Independency infringing upon uniformity when all congregations were to be adequately disciplined by the Bible and by consociations;

and if at any time such a thing should fall out, which cannot grow but from some roote of apostacy, particular or generall: if the offence doe reflect also upon the Laws of the Civill state, which are made against knowne Heresie, or blasphemy, or Idolatry, and the like, the offenders are obnoxious to the civill power. So little feare there is, that any independent congregation, or any member thereof, should be exempt from Condign Censure, where just cause is given either Ecclesiasticall or Civill.[2]

He prophesied that the Independent way would function ideally as a state religion: "Where such Congregations are erected and allowed of by a Civil State, they are both a strength and beauty, and procure many blessings unto it." [3]

In its first formulation, this conflict between Independent and Presbyterian disciplines was a typical Reformation battle between absolutes; each claimed an exclusive divine authorization, and neither of them could see any possibility of tolerating the other. For a time it looked as though Presbyterianism would win. Parliament needed the aid of Scotland, and the Scotch would not respond until Parliament swore to the Solemn League and Covenant. The English negotiators

1. *An Apologeticall Narration*, p. 19.
2. *The Protestation Protested*, sig. C4 recto.
3. *Ibid.*, sig. C1 verso.

were desirous that this league might be phrased in such a fashion as would keep "a door open in England to Independency," but against this the Scotch were "peremptor." [1] For them the aim of the covenant was "the propogation of our Church-discipline in England and Ireland," [2] and by accepting it Parliament committed itself unreservedly to Presbyterianism. The Scotch army entered England in January, 1644, following the advent of the masterful Scotch commissioners to the Westminster Assembly. The resolute resistence of the Independents failed to convince Presbyterians that they were "but an imperfect representation of contemporary English opinion." [3] Step by step the Assembly forced through its platform, and in the first months of 1644 the men of Scotland seemed to be within easy grasp of the goal to which Laud had aspired: the establishment of a religious uniformity throughout England and Scotland.

But by this time another unforeseen factor had entered into the situation. One of the chief Presbyterian arguments against Independency had been that it would stimulate the rise of other sects. Now, either because the Independents blocked the complete success of Presbyterianism, or simply because the turmoil of civil war gave centrifugal religious forces a long-sought opportunity, by the year 1644 the constant appearance of new and fantastic sects became a scandalous but insurmountable fact. "In the time of this anarchy, the divisions of people does much increase: the Independent party grows; but the Anabaptists more; and the Anti-

1. Baillie, *Letters and Journals*, Letter 36.
2. *Ibid.*, Letter 37.   3. Masson, *op. cit.*, II, 24.

nomians most," [1] moaned Robert Baillie; he and his colleagues found their hands full in attacking not only the Independents but a lengthening catalogue of "gangraena."

The overwhelming importance of this development was that it led both the Independents and the sects, being minority parties, to realize that the claim of any one polity to an absolute sanction and a uniform maintenance was absurd. The idea of toleration, which before 1640 had lurked only among the despised Baptists in Helwysse's congregation, [2] or had been tentatively suggested in the sophisticated pamphlets of Hales and Chillingworth, suddenly found large expression. As Troeltsch has put it, "it was now at last the turn of the stepchildren of the Reformation to have their great hour in the history of the world." [3] The idea was first taken up by the Independents in a limited form. Burton suggested in 1641 that there might be liberty left to such congregations, "as whereof the spirituall Commonwealth of Israel consisteth," to practise their way peaceably, even if the nation as a whole were Presbyterianized. [4] This amazing notion the Presbyterians attacked with their customary vehemence. "A Toleration," shrieked Edwards,

will spoile any Church and government; if Presbyteriall government be setled, and a Toleration given in this Land, that will marre

---

1. Baillie, *op. cit.*, Letter 40.
2. Herbert Hensley Henson, *Studies in English Religion*, pp. 218 ff.; cf. *Tracts on Liberty of Conscience and Persecution* (Hanserd Knolleys Society, London, 1846); Burgess, *John Smith, the Se-Baptist*, p. 255.
3. *Protestantism and Progress*, p. 124.
4. Burton, *The Protestation Protested*, sig. C3.

all. . . . I humbly beseech the Parliament seriously to consider the
depths of Satan in this designe of a Toleration, how this is now his last
plot and designe, and by it would undermine and frustrate the whole
work of Reformation intended.[1]

The Independents realized only the more clearly that
this "designe" was the one way out for them, and the
authors of the *Apologeticall Narration* proposed it anew.
Then in 1644 Roger Williams came to England; *The
Bloudy Tenent of Persecution* appeared, followed closely
by the publication of *A Reply of two of the Brethren to
A. S.*, a volume attributed to John Goodwin. "A
mighty faction is arisen," proclaimed Baillie, "to prefer
liberty of conscience for all sects." [2] The Independents
became definitely pledged to the movement, and began
to agitate for a toleration which was, of course, in its
first form relative, but which could only lead by implica-
tion to an ultimate separation of Church and State, to
the principle of voluntaryism, and to liberty of conscience in the completely modern sense. Within four
years advanced opinion in England had taken some
titanic strides in the history of thought; the "two
brethren" suddenly had escaped from the medieval
philosophy of coercive Church and State, and in the
might of their new vision hit upon the root of all previous religious agonies in a single sentence:

But that *coercive power in matters of Religion*, for the suppressing
of errours, schismes, heresies, etc., was never attributed to the civill
Magistrate by any Christian, but only by those that were very confident, that it would be used for their turns, and to effect their desires.[3]

---

1. Edwards, *Antapologia*, p. 303.   2. Baillie, *op. cit.*, Letter 56.
3. *A Reply of two of the Brethren*, p. 61.

The old appeals to scriptural warrant and political necessity were now, in the crucible of England's civil commotion, stripped of their pretensions and shown in their true character as the trappings of selfish ambition and class domination.

But even the opposition presented by the alliance of the Independents and the sects might have been overborne by the Presbyterians had not another surprising development settled the business outside the Assembly. The sects, being the most zealous and pugnacious Puritans, entered the army in great numbers. By April of 1644 Baillie himself admitted that they constituted a good two thirds of the fighting men, "and these of the far most resolute and confident." [1] Upon this purely practical basis the Independent officers became advocates of toleration and gave the numerous sects their first recognized footing. When a subordinate objected to promoting a soldier because he was an Anabaptist, Cromwell stormed:

Shall that render him incapable to serve the public? . . . Sir, the State in choosing men to serve it takes no notice of their opinions. Take heed of being sharp . . . against those to whom you can object little but that they square not with you in every opinion concerning matters of religion.[2]

By 1647 the Independents, professing toleration for all law-abiding Protestants, completely dominated the army.[3] Williams's *Bloudy Tenent* was burned by the Presbyterians, but when he continued his argument in *The Bloudy Tenent Yet More Bloudy*, his book

1. Baillie, *op. cit.*, Letter 51.
2. Thomas Carlyle, *Letters and Speeches of Oliver Cromwell*, Letter 20.
3. Charles Harding Firth, *Cromwell's Army*, p. 319.

was received with applause and thanks by the army, by the Parliament, professing that, of necessity, — yea, of Christian equity, —
there could be no reconciliation, pacification, or living together, but
by permitting of dissenting consciences to live amongst them.[1]

Sir Nathaniel Barnardiston wrote in disgust to Winthrop
that

noe opineones & blasfemy is so bad, but that our Independentes
heer generally will shelter & countenance, for all heresyes & sectes
wilbe Independantes vnder this notion, that none should be trobled
for ther contience though hurtfull to others.[2]

Finally, in 1647, the army leaders, in the long program
contained in *The Heads of Proposals*, demanded that
the Prayer Book and compulsory church attendance
be repealed, and that the taking of the Covenant be
not forced upon any "against their judgments or consciences."[3] The rank and file of the army itself, in
The Agreement of People, were even more decisive:

that matters of religion and the ways of God's worship are not at all
entrusted to us by any human power, because therein we cannot remit or exceed a tittle of what our consciences dictate to be the mind
of God without wilful sin.[4]

Thus, in the course of these teeming years the party in
England that had begun as the advocate of Congregationalism was swept by the rush of events into upholding
a policy which had been pronounced by the New England system to be eternally heretical in religion and
utterly intolerable in society.

The Civil Wars removed for the time being all danger

1. Williams, "Letters," *Publications of the Narragansett Club*, VI, 353.
2. *Mass. Hist. Soc., Coll.*, Series 4, VI, 550.
3. Gardiner, *The Constitutional Documents of the Puritan Revolution*, p. 321.
4. *Ibid.*, p. 334.

of the King's interference in Massachusetts, but created for the little Puritan state a delicate diplomatic problem. Its sympathies were all on the side of Parliament, and Parliament repaid that interest by quashing the *quo warranto* in 1641 and in 1644 by allowing goods to go to or from New England free of custom. The colony appreciated these overtures, but even gratitude did not cause it to lose sight of the autonomy for which it had labored. When the magistrates were importuned by certain "friends" in England to put the colony under Parliament, they betrayed their true disposition.

> If we should put ourselves under the protection of the parliament, we must then be subject to all such laws as they should make, or at least such as they might impose upon us; in which course though they should intend our good, yet it might prove very prejudicial to us.[1]

But the pretensions of the colony to loyalty towards England did seem to require that if it regarded itself as a part of England it should at least express a preference. As soon as the Court learned of the actual hostilities, it omitted King Charles "for the present" from the oaths of the magistrates, "seeing he had violated the priviledges of parliament." In 1644 a law was passed prohibiting anyone from disturbing "or peace, directly or indirectly, by drawing a party, under pretence that he is for the King of England, & such as adioyne with him against the Parliament." [2] When Captain Jennyson at Watertown seemed doubtful about the cause of Parliament he was at once haled before the Court; but the essential point as far as Massachusetts was concerned

1. Winthrop, *Journal*, II, 24.   2. *Massachusetts Records*, II, 69.

revealed itself when Jennyson was dismissed because, although he refused to affirm that if he were in England he would fight against the King, he did not hesitate to say that "if the King or any party from him should attempt anything against this commonwealth, he should make no scruple to spend estate and life and all in our defence against them." [1]

Massachusetts was compelled to avow its position more publicly in 1644, when a ship acting under a parliamentary commission seized a royalist craft in Boston harbor. The question was now raised whether the commission took precedence over the patent within the waters of the colony. To disallow the seizure might mean sacrificing parliamentary friendship. There was considerable debate about the question, some of the elders calling from the pulpits to "maintain the peoples' liberties," but the majority felt that Massachusetts could not escape acknowledging some allegiance somewhere without denying "the foundation of our government by our patent." Otherwise the State would have had to revise its whole theory and base its title to the land on a purchase from the natives, just as Roger Williams had held. At present that seemed a risky procedure; "if we stand upon this plea, we must then renounce our patent and England's protection, which were a great weakness in us, seeing their care hath been to strengthen our liberties and not overthrow them." However, the Court let it be understood that they had no intention of sacrificing to this loyalty any material advantage: "if the parliament should hereafter be of a

1. Winthrop, *Journal*, II, 178.

malignant spirit, etc., then if we have strength sufficient, we may make use of *salus populi* to withstand any authority from thence to our hurt." [1]

The most significant of the colony's initial reactions to the Civil Wars was its immediate assumption of the rôle of adviser. At last it seemed that the long-awaited chance had come, when New England was to lead England in the paths of righteousness. Weld and Peter were despatched in 1641, not only to look after certain interests, but to further "the work of reformation of the Church there which was now like to be attempted," and "to give any advice as it should be required, for the settling the right form of church discipline there." [2] Cotton wrote in 1645:

> We take not upon us . . . to prescribe unto our Brethren in England . . . what course to take in pursuing and perfecting the great work of Reformation in England. . . . Onely being absent in body, but present in spirit, we crave leave to bear witnesse to them, and with them; That if the Lord be pleased to prosper his worke amongst them, it is possible to reduce the estate of the Congregations in England, to such a reformation, as is sutable to the patterne revealed in the Gospel, according to the way of Primitive simplicity, described above.[3]

These fond expectations received their first setback with the apparent triumph of Presbyterianism. Cotton, Hooker, and Davenport were asked in 1643 to attend the Westminster Assembly, but by that time the New England colonies had realized that their hope of directing England was vain, and they once more assumed the defensive. "The maine busines for which they are

1. *Ibid.*, pp. 183–186.   2. *Ibid.*, pp. 25, 31.
3. *The Way of the Churches of Christ*, p. 111.

chiefly called," wrote Haynes, was "already sett in such a way that they who are trew to ther owne principles, may rather become a stumble then otherwis."[1] Meantime, the success of Presbyterianism abroad had encouraged the Presbyterians in New England; these derived further support from the smouldering sentiment against the restrictions on church membership. Noyes and Parker at Newbury became at last so intractable[2] that a Synod representing all the colonies was called at Cambridge, which, Winthrop tells us, "concluded against some parts of the presbyterial way."[3] Though the *Cambridge Platform* made some gestures of friendliness toward Presbyterianism, it still emphatically declared that the Gospel did not acknowledge mere civil cohabitation "a proper adjunct of Church-relation."[4]

As New Englanders were rebuffed by the Presbyterians, they naturally attempted to swing their support to the Independents, who, like themselves, were disciples of Ames and many of whom were their personal friends. Goodwin and Nye endorsed Cotton's *Keyes* in 1644 as a description of "That very Middle-way (which in our Apologie we did in generall intimate and intend)."[5] But when the Independents went over to the sects, and pleaded for liberty of conscience, the dazed New Englanders found themselves entirely out of the procession. Roger Williams returned to Massachusetts with

1. *Mass. Hist. Soc., Coll.*, Series 4, VI, 357.
2. Cf. position of Noyes in *The Temple Measured* (1647) and *Moses and Aaron* (1661).
3. Winthrop, *Journal*, II, 139; *A Reply of two of the Brethren*, p. 7.
4. Walker, *Creeds and Platforms*, p. 197.
5. *The Keyes of the Kingdom of Heaven*, sig. A4 recto; cf. Masson, *Life of Milton*, II, 598.

a charter for Rhode Island and a letter from various members of Parliament entreating the Court for "your utmost endeavors of nearer closing, and of ready expressing of those good affections."[1] A more impossible request from the orthodox viewpoint could hardly have been made. In the "anarchy" of the Civil Wars English Congregationalists had learned a new language, and their American brethren had no way of comprehending these novel accents. "They in New England," Baillie wrote, " are more strict and rigid then we, or any church, to suppress, by the power of the magistrate, all who are not of their way"; but, he continued,

The Independents here, finding they have not the magistrates so obsequious as in New England, turn their pens . . . to take from the magistrate all power of taking any coercive order with vilest hereticks.[2]

Astute as this observation was, the analytical powers of a certain Mrs. Katherine Chidley had, in 1641, hit even more precisely upon the moral of the story, which, as she saw it, was simply that the migration had left England too early and the settlers had lost touch with the more recent advances. It might be true, as the Presbyterians claimed, that the magistrates in New England took upon themselves the same authority to bind men's consciences which the Presbyterians aspired to wield in England.

But if it have beene so, I think it was, because they had (here in *England*) taken upon them an oath of conformity (as you have sometimes done;) and because the tyranny of the Prelats was so mighty, against all good men, that they were faine to go away privately, and so had not time or opportunity publikely to disclaime

---

1. Winthrop, *Journal*, II, 198.   2. Baillie, *op. cit.*, Letter 59.

this their oath; and then there might be feare, that upon complaint made for disorder there, which could not be admitted here, they might have beene sent for back by their ordinaries, and so have been committed to some stincking prison here in London; . . . and if they have banished any out of their Patents that were neither disturbers of the peace of the Land, nor the worship practised in the Land, I am perswaded, it was their weaknesse, and I hope they will never attempt to doe the like. But I am still perswaded, they did it upon the same ground, that having knowledge in themselves, that their former oath, might be a snare unto them, if they did not hold still some correspondencie with the practice of England, even till God should open a way or meanes for them to seeke free liberty for all, by the approbation of authority.[1]

Here is complete contemporary witness to the fact that the key to New England's thinking is to be discovered in the assumptions which all the emigrants had entertained in 1630, when they had unquestioningly accepted the oath of uniformity as a symbol of the supreme necessity for national religious unity; in her own person Mrs. Chidley represents the new liberal movements, with which New Englanders had had no contact and against which they were effectively quarantined by the Atlantic Ocean. Now that Massachusetts had succeeded in reproducing Elizabethan ideals on the frontier, she was not in a mood to understand an era which found no counterpart in her own experience. Already the "two brethren" were speaking of New England as having "miscarried for want of such light, as should have directed them in a better way," and were zealously vindicating the Independents from the charge of working to the same ends.[2]

1. Katherine Chidley, *The Ivstification of the Independent Churches of Christ*, pp. 34-35.
2. *A Reply of two of the Brethren*, pp. 104-105.

Presbyterians completed the isolation of Massachusetts by triumphantly adducing that colony as an example of what the Independents would bring about in England if only they had the opportunity. When the apologists attacked Presbyterian intolerance as "the fatal error to Reformation," Edwards scored a palpable hit by retorting that New England had indeed found the lack of it "fatal" and remedied the want "by banishment and imprisonement (under the names of disturbers of civill peace) many members of their Churches, for Familisme, Anabaptism, etc." [1]   The Independents could thereafter insure the coöperation of the sects only by disowning New England; colonial support was an embarrassment. Sir Richard Saltonstall wrote to Cotton and Wilson, telling the reports he had heard — reports which Cotton had deliberately been publishing abroad — and concluding,

We pray for you and wish you prosperitie every way, hoped the Lord would have given you so much light and love there, that you might have been eyes to Gods people here, and not to practice those courses in a wilderness, which you went so farre to prevent. [2]

Stephen Winthrop reported to his father from Cromwell's army in March, 1645, that "heere is great complaine agt vs for or severetye agt Anabaptists." [3]   And Sir Harry Vane wrote Winthrop in June that the miseries of England had taught men mutual forbearance,

which makes me hope that, from the experience here, it may also be derived to yourselves, least whilst the congregationall way amongst

1. Edwards, *Antapologia*, p. 83.
2. Hutchinson, *A Collection of Papers*, ii, 127–128.
3. *Mass. Hist. Soc., Coll.*, Series 5, viii, 200.

you is in its freedom, and is backed with power, it teach its op-
pugners here to extirpate it and roote it out, from its owne principles
and practices.[1]

Massachusetts replied to these criticisms by gathering
her holy skirts closer about her heels and proceeding on
her unlovely way alone. From this time forth the colony
turned aside from the main currents of English opinion,
refusing to admit any more progress in thought than
might be allowed by assumptions imported in 1630. In
November, 1644, the Court ordered the banishment of
all "Anabaptists," by whom were meant not merely
those who denied infant baptism, but such liberals as
denied the right of magistrates to punish breaches of the
first table.[2] It was this law, George Downing said,
"which makes us stinke everywheare,"[3] and in 1645
some citizens petitioned against it, because "of the
offence taken thereat by many godly in England."[4] As
soon as the elders heard of this, they hastened to the
Court, with the result that that body announced "yt ye
laws mentioned should not be altered at all, nor explained."[5] By this time there were books coming out of
England not only in defense of Presbyterianism, but "in
defence of anabaptism and other errors, and for liberty
of conscience"; the elders agreed that one sort was as
bad as the other, and commissioned various of their
number to write against both.[6] The isolation of the
New England Way was complete. Hugh Peter proved a

1. Hutchinson, op. cit., I, 153.
2. Massachusetts Records, II, 85; Winthrop, Journal, II, 177.
3. Mass. Hist. Soc., Coll., Series 4, VI, 537.
4. Winthrop, Journal, II, 259.
5. Massachusetts Records, II, 141. 6. Winthrop, Journal, II, 257.

great disappointment to his colonial colleagues, for once
he was in the thick of the fight he, like Cromwell, saw
the light. It was a light, however, that never gleamed in
New England. If Peter went astray it was not because
Thomas Shepard did not try to reclaim him:

> I see no more reason to beare with good men in their opinions
> then in their morall transgressions, for they commonly are coupled
> together. . . . I feare greater sorrowes attend England if they do
> not seasonably suppresse and beare publike witnesse agaynst such
> delusions. . . . I know there may be some connivance for a time
> while 'tis tumultuous and while the wars call all spirits thither, but
> toleration of all upon pretence of conscience I thanke God my soule
> abhors it.[1]

Cotton never even saw the point of Saltonstall's letter;
Sir Richard had evidently forgotten that the settlers
never dreamed of coming into a wilderness to cry an end
upon persecution. They had only fled from "mens inventions" to "Gods institutions," and the moral of their
experience, so far as Cotton could read it, was that

> if our native country were more zealous against horrid blasphemies
> and heresies than wee be, wee believe the Lord would looke at it as a
> better improvement of all the great salvations he hath wrought for
> them than to sett open a wide doore to all abhominations in re-
> ligion.[2]

The rococo pages of Nathaniel Ward's *Simple Cobler* in
1647 bristled with whole-hearted attacks upon the new-
fangled heresy of toleration; he dared to take upon himself to be "the Herauld of New England" to the extent
of telling the world that the only liberty the sects could

---

1. *American Historical Review*, IV (1898), 105; *Mass. Hist. Soc., Coll.*, Series
   4, VII, 277.
2. Hutchinson, *A Collection of Papers*, II, 132.

expect in America was "free liberty to keep away from us." [1] Clarke, coming over about this time from the triumph of modernism in England, epitomized the whole process on the title-page of his book: "While Old England is becoming new, New-England is become old."

Thus did the New England orthodoxy turn its back upon the greatest single religious advance of modern times, and exert itself to avoid making innovations in its thinking. The question now remained whether it could successfully maintain this reaction against the forces which in England had produced the revolution. In so far as Massachusetts embodied a political philosophy coeval with Laud, the State likewise had to confront the popular impulses he had striven in vain to stifle. Would the difference between a frontier environment and a complex society be sufficient for Winthrop and Cotton to succeed where Canterbury and Charles had failed, or where Parliament and the Presbyterians were even then coming to grief?

The first phase of the answer to this question centered about the person of Samuel Gorton. The opinions of this gentleman are difficult to define; some of them seem to be part and parcel of that lunatic fringe which at the moment was rampant in England. His own account is none too coherent, but it does reveal that among his heresies were certain of the recent liberal discoveries. Like the "two brethren," he had perceived the underlying psychology of the old belief in national uniformity. When the world, he said, had seen "troups of its ancestors go down to the grave" without having witnessed

1. *The Simple Cobler of Aggawam* (ed. David Pulsifer, Boston, 1843), p. 3.

the "glorious times of peace, ease, and exaltation" which religious prophets had promised, then the priests suffered from a reaction, which

works effectually for a transformation, to cast its worship of God into another form . . . and therefore must of necessity labour diligently as for life, to borrow a coercive power from the Civil Magistrate, to be transferred, turned over, and put into their hands, whereby they may subdue others, and compell them to follow their way, and to acknowledge their worship to be onely divine, yea the onely God of the world.

In the place of such spiritual husks he offered a sort of Antinomian mysticism, "a nearer and shorter cut to the Kingdom of God, then the common ministry of the world driveth at." [1]

In 1637 Gorton had come to Boston, which naturally had proved inhospitable; he had thereafter been successively expelled from Plymouth and from Portsmouth in Rhode Island. He settled in the vicinity of Providence, where he added to the worries of Roger Williams. In September, 1642, four citizens of Pawtuxet, who had enough of trying to live as Gorton's neighbors, petitioned Massachusetts to intervene, and the next spring two subordinate Indian sachems complained against their chief for having sold land at Shawomet to Gorton's band. The Court required all the petitioners to put themselves under the Massachusetts government, and then despatched an armed force to bring the ungodly crew before the bar. The machinery of Puritan inquisition was immediately put into action. Both the Court

1. "Simplicities Defense against the Seven-Headed Policy," Force, *Tracts*, IV, 6.

and the elders disputed with the Gortonists, but failed to make them see their manifold errors. The elders therefore concluded that they "deserved death by the law of God," and all but three of the magistrates agreed. The deputies, however, dissented, and the Court at last decided to imprison the men separately in various towns, because they were blasphemous enemies "of or Lord Jesus Christ & his holy ordinances, & also of all civill authority among the people of God, & perticulerly in this iurisdiction." [1]

This proved to be not a very satisfactory solution, because the Gortonists, even in chains, talked; and "we found that they did corrupt some of our people, especially the women, by their heresies." [2] In March, 1644, they were finally banished from the patent, upon pain of death. But the Court had gained what it wanted; it had gone on record against the sort of men who were creating the sects in England. The fundamental difference in the two points of view had been brought rather vividly to light when Gorton offered to submit his differences with the ministers to arbitration. To him this was altogether possible, but to the divinely authorized orthodoxy of Massachusetts it was utterly unthinkable. The elders responded with gusto: "Their blasphemous and reviling writings, etc., were not matters fit to be compounded by arbitrament, but to be purged away only by repentance and public satisfaction, or else by public punishment." [3] The colony had gone out of its way to attest its opinion of precisely such heresies as Cromwell

1. *Massachusetts Records*, II, 51; Winthrop, *Journal*, II, 148–149.
2. *Ibid.*, p. 149.   3. *Ibid.*, p. 141.

was beginning to look upon with favor, and by proclaiming the impossibility of a compromise announced a war to the death between its orthodoxy and the new thought.

The next ordeal of the government was more serious. It was inevitable that the deputies should derive encouragement from the course of events in England. They were still smarting from their defeat in the "sow case," and were only too susceptible to the revolutionary contagion. In the Court of June, 1644, they suddenly brought in a proposal to create a commission of seven magistrates, three deputies, and Nathaniel Ward, to displace the assistants as a council and as justices during the vacancy of the General Court. They justified the bill by saying that the magistrates held their judicial powers only by grant of the Court, and that the Court could dispose of that grant as it wished. Once again the magistrates were up in arms; they announced that their judicial power derived directly from the patent and that it could not be tampered with; whereupon one of the deputies roundly declared that if the assistants attempted to act as justices before the next Court, they would not be obeyed. But for all this bravado, the deputies surrendered again to the conventional tactics. Endecott, then governor, called for a council of the elders, and their report to the General Court of October confirmed the magistrates' claim to a constitutional authorization.[1] Most of the lower house gave in, but Winthrop noted that "some few leading men (who had drawn on the rest) were still fixed upon their own opin-

1. *Massachusetts Records,* II, 91; Winthrop, *Journal,* II, 212.

ions."[1] Winthrop had attempted to aid the elders by penning a treatise upon arbitrary government, another of his ingenious endeavors to explain the complex theory of Calvinistic political science, insisting that where the people could admit or reject their officers "& require the Rule by which they shalbe governed," there could be nothing arbitrary.[2] The deputies secured a copy of this work, and though some of them knew well enough who had written it, they pretended not to and branded it as false and dangerous. Bozon Allen, from Hingham, declared it "worse than Gorton's letters," and said that if any other person in the colony had written it "it would have cost him his ears, if not his head." Yet for these intemperate speeches the deputies showed no disposition to censure the Hingham delegate. The citizens were in an ugly mood.[3]

The fact that the man who so vociferously abused Winthrop's treatise was from Hingham was in itself significant. Trouble had long been brewing in that town, where the doughty Peter Hobart ruled his church in a "Presbyterial spirit" and in almost open defiance of his fellow ministers. In the spring of 1645 the town militia chose for their captain one Eames, but later changed their minds and picked Allen. It was an accepted rule in the colony that the election of all militia officers was subject to magisterial approval, and the leaders were naturally jealous of this power. When the local squabble was carried into the church, where Hobart was "very

1. *Ibid.*, pp. 170–172, 189, 217.
2. Robert C. Winthrop, *Life and Letters of John Winthrop*, II, 427–438.
3. Winthrop, *Journal*, II, 241–243.

forward" to have Eames excommunicated, the magistrates saw an opportunity to kill two birds with one stone, to assert their control over militia elections and pay off old scores with Hobart. Winthrop, then deputy governor, acting in the capacity which the last General Court had confirmed to the magistrates, ordered the Hobart faction to give bond for appearance at the quarter court, and when they refused committed them for contempt.[1]

Hobart was a man of passion, and now his blind rage played directly into the hands of the magistrates. Before the quarter court had met, the General Court assembled, and Hobart, at the head of ninety men of Hingham, presented to the deputies a petition craving of them to consider the charges against him and his friends. The lower house readily accepted the petition, thus confirming the magistrates' theory that democrats made foolish governors. For with the petition in their hands, they were at a loss what to do with it; finding themselves "at a stand for the present," they requested "or honnored magistrates yt they would send vs their thoughts & votes vpon ye whole case."[2] The magistrates saw at once that they had the deputies in a corner, and were determined not to let the people's spokesmen escape without rendering a strict account. They proceeded with what seems to have been calculated cruelty. Declaring that Eames was the properly elected captain, and that he now received their sanction, they pointed

1. Unless otherwise indicated, the citations concerning the Hingham episode are from Winthrop's narrative, *Journal*, II, 229 ff.
2. *Massachusetts Records*, III, 18.

out that the company was therefore mutinous, and had been justly committed. Hence the petition was "cawseless & iniurious" and should never have been entertained at all.

Immediately the whole question of the magistrates' position was again at stake: if the assistants permitted the petition to have a hearing and concurred in reëxamining the charges, even if they finally got Hobart punished, they would implicitly deny that Winthrop had possessed a right to indict the Hinghamites, and so would nullify the right of magistrates to act as justices. But the magistrates were equal to the occasion. Since the deputies insisted upon receiving the petition, they demanded that it should name a specific officer, and that the Court should then treat it as an accusation of illegal conduct. Then if the petition failed to prove its point, it would be nothing short of attempted revolution. The magistracy would be vindicated as a standing council, and the petitioners could be tried for such counts as Winthrop had legally drawn against them. Probably the instigator of this move was Winthrop himself; he says, at any rate, that he desired the case to have a public hearing because he knew how the magistrates had suffered "through the slanderous reports wherewith the deputies and the country about had been possessed." The Hinghamites fell into the trap, and laid "a chardge on ye Deputy Gouernor ffor illegal imprisoning of some of them & forcing the first with others to give bond with suertyes to appeare & answer at ye next Quarter Courte." [1] The assistants then graciously

1. *Ibid.*, pp. 17–18.

informed the deputies that though it was prejudicial to the authority and honor of the whole Court to call a magistrate to answer when he had done nothing but a duty which they themselves had allowed him, "yet if they would needs have a hearing, they would join in it."

When the Court assembled, Winthrop, coming in with the rest of the magistrates, "placed himself beneath within the bar and so sat uncovered." Many "both of the Court and the assembly were grieved at it," and begged him not to humble himself, but he pointed out that since he was accused, he "might not sit as a judge in that cause," nor would it be an advantage for him to be upon the bench, "for he could not take that liberty to plead the cause, which he ought to be allowed at the bar."

Having taken this "liberty," Winthrop did not mince matters. Pointing out again that strictly speaking there was no reason why he should answer at all, he declared that he was glad to waive that plea in order to face the charges "to the end that the truth of the case, and of all proceedings thereupon might appear to all men." He had done only what was the duty of his office; therefore the real issue was whether "the magistrates exercised too much power." He and his party, in opposition to the deputies, held "that authority was overmuch slighted, which, if not timely remedied, would endanger the commonwealth, and bring us to a mere democracy." He had acted "according to the equity of laws here established, and the custom and laws of England, and our constant practice here these fifteen years"; if at every flicker of popular sympathy the deputies were going to entertain groundless protests against the established order, then let them behold in the anarchy of England the future of the colony.

The magistrates were inexorable; the petition, they declared, must be pronounced scandalous, the petitioners censured, and Winthrop acquitted. The deputies by this time were demoralized. They could not bring themselves to censure their fellow citizens, and they struck out blindly, levying small fines indiscriminately, even on that part of the band that had been loyal and on Eames, who was neither plaintiff nor defendant. The magistrates promptly objected to this "manifest injustice"; however, they would let the guilty petitioners off with the amounts determined by the deputies if "ye Deputy Gouernor may be pronounced innocent in what hath binn chardged vpon him, & ye petitioners enioyned to make publicque acknowledgments for ye iniury donne him."[1]

Then the magistrates made an eloquent gesture. "If this may not be obtayned we then desire some indifferent arbitrators may be nominated, to whom ye cause for finall determination may be defferred." "Indifferent" is almost a comical touch, for what the passage meant was, as Winthrop says, that the deputies "join with them in calling in the help of the elders." The magistracy was invoking the familiar trick, and the deputies would rather lose honorably than be hoodwinked again, "for they knew that many of the elders understood the cause, and were more careful to uphold the honor and power of the magistrates than themselves well liked of."

1. *Ibid.*, pp. 24–25.

And so, "finding themselves now at the wall, and not daring to trust the elders with the cause," the deputies capitulated. Fines were exacted and censures ordered as the magistrates desired; Winthrop was formally acquitted of all that was "layd to his charge," and it was recorded upon the books of the lower house that "wee desire ye country will hereby take notice." [1]

It was a great victory, the best the magistrates ever won. Winthrop was too good a politician to let the occasion slip without collecting his full pound of flesh. The deputies, touchingly enough, had "by importunity" got the assistants to read the sentence of the Court, "without speaking any more," but when Winthrop returned to the bench, "he desired leave for a little speech." Considering the circumstances, this famous utterance can be compared to nothing less than the final twist of an inquisitorial thumb-screw.

He began by thanking God that the "troublesome business" had come to an end and pronounced himself satisfied. But something more, he felt, had to be said, "to inform and rectify the judgments of some of the people." There had been two questions involved in this case. The first concerned the authority of the magistrates:

It is yourselves who have called us to this office, and being called by you, we have our authority from God, in way of an ordinance, such as hath the image of God eminently stamped upon it, the contempt and violation whereof hath been vindicated with examples of divine vengeance. . . . The covenant between you and us is the oath you have taken of us, which is to this purpose, that we shall govern

---

1. *Ibid.*, p. 26.

you and judge your causes by the rules of God's laws and our own, according to our best skill.

When the people had elected a magistrate they had to choose as best they could, but once they had chosen, they "must run the hazard of his skill and ability" so long as he did not fail in faithfulness.

The second question was one of liberty. Confusion arose here from a lack of discrimination between the two sorts of liberty. The first sort was natural, and man possessed it in common with the beasts. "By this, man, as he stands in relation to man simply, hath liberty to do what he lists, it is a liberty to evil as well as to good. This liberty is incompatible and inconsistent with authority." It made men ultimately worse than beasts; it was that enemy to truth and peace which "all the ordinances of God are bent against, to restrain and subdue it." But the second sort of liberty was "civil or federal, it may also be termed moral, in reference to the covenant between God and man, in the moral law, the political covenants and constitutions, amongst men themselves." This liberty required authority, for it was a liberty to do only the good, just, and honest. Hence the people should defend authority with their lives; "whatsoever crosseth this, is not authority but a distemper thereof." And they who possessed it were to exercise it only in willing subjection, as the Church exercised her liberty by subjection to Christ, or a woman by subjecting herself to her husband. If the people would follow civil liberty in a social compact, and "cheerfully submit unto that authority which is set over you . . . for your good," then the magistrates would do their best, and would be willing to listen to advice. "So shall your liberties be preserved, in upholding the honor and power of authority amongst you."

Winthrop was not a vain man, but he could not fail to see what he had accomplished. He had done nothing less than avert the Civil Wars in New England. One of the saddest errors about the whole business, he said, was "that while we sympathize with our native country in their calamities," yet "we should be hastening by all our skill and power to bring the like miseries upon ourselves." The deputies, fearing an arbitrary government, were appealing to "extrema remedia, as if salus populi had been now the transcendent rule to walk by." They sought to make the magistracy "a ministerial office," so that "all authority, both legislative, consultative, and judicial, must be exercised by the people in their body representative." To this end they had labored at every stage of the game, in their attack on the negative voice, in their attempt to curtail the magistrates' judicial power, in their assault upon Winthrop's treatise. But the magistrates, by their expert strategy, had blocked the appeal to these dangerous justifications, and had salvaged, on a firmer basis than ever before, the original, static, legalistic structure of the government, in which authority was derived from God and obedience was a moral duty. The Reformation dictum that government was an ordinance of God survived intact in New England at the very time when England was discovering new implications in the social contract. The philosophy of civil rule in Massachusetts was paralleled to the ecclesiastical. The remote author of the constitution was

God; the magistrate derived his authority from God, even though elected by the people. He derived it, in fact, more clearly than the King had claimed to derive his, for he was the embodiment of the corporate will, and the corporate will had already contracted itself to be subject to the will of God. The magistrate could therefore demand an absolute obedience, so long as his administration did not offend against Revelation, and against Revelation, moreover, as it was authoritatively interpreted by the elders, his sworn partners in the task of government.

The final ordeal for the New England orthodoxy came within the next year; this assault combined the elements of both political and religious discontent and originated not among the freemen but the non-freemen. It was directed against the restricted church membership and the qualified franchise. The move owed something of its instigation to events in England. The elders in October, 1645, had felt apprehensive enough to ask for the calling of a great general Synod. In June the battle of Naseby had been fought, and in September the capture of Bristol assured the defeat of the King, who in May surrendered himself to the Scotch and not to the English army. The Scotch, of course, were in alliance with the Presbyterians. "It is thought ye warre is at an end," wrote Stephen Winthrop, "Only the Presbyterian Government is resolved on, & ye other are at a losse & cannot tell where they shall find rest." [1] There was apparently now a power in England equal to Laud's, which might resume his policy, fired by the hope of adding

1. *Mass. Hist. Soc., Coll.*, Series 5, VIII, 202.

New England to the Solemn League and Covenant. The Massachusetts divines girded their loins and began agitation for a Synod as a step to frank ecclesiastical independence.

Hobart put the match to the new train of powder by refusing to answer the marshall's summons, denying the warrant because it was not in the King's name, "and standing upon his allegiance to the crown of England, and exemption from such laws as were not agreeable to the laws of England." He was immediately brought before the Court, charged with "seditious practice and derogation and contempt of authority," because he held that the colony was but as any corporation in England and did not have power by the patent to "put any man to death, nor do divers other things which we did." [1] Massachusetts, freed by the Civil Wars from all but the merest shadow of dependence, was vaunting her autonomy in what seemed even to many New Englanders a flagrant fashion. Pynchon wrote in haste, advising moderation, but purely on grounds of expediency:

We are not a ffree state, neather do I apprehend that magistrates, elders, or deputies doe think we are a ffree state, neather do I think it our wisdome to be a ffree state; though we had our liberty, we cannot as yet subsist without England. [2]

But the magistrates were willing to take the consequences; they fined Hobart twenty pounds, at which, Winthrop says, "his spirits rose."

Other spirits followed suit. Sentiment against the exclusive church membership seems to have been gather-

1. Winthrop, *Journal*, ii, 265–266.
2. *Mass. Hist. Soc., Coll.*, Series 4, vi, 383.

ing weight. In March, 1644, a proposition had been
made in the General Court "for yielding some more of
the freeman's privileges to such as were no church members," but nothing had come of it.[1] William Vassal, who
lived in Scituate, close to Hingham, and who was a man
"always opposite to the civil governments of this country and the way of our Churches," gathered a group of
non-members and proposed to petition the Courts both
of Plymouth and Massachusetts, "and (if that succeeded not) then to the parliament of England, that the
distinctions which were maintained here, both in civil
and church estate, might be taken away, and that we
might be wholly governed by the laws of England."[2]
According to a letter from Winslow, of November 24,
1645, the petition in Plymouth asked also a "full and
free tollerance of religion to all men that would preserve
the civill peace and submit unto our government."
"You would have admired," he continued, "to have
seen how sweet this carrion relished to the pallate of
most of the deputies," but Bradford scornfully refused
even to put such a motion to a vote.[3]

Feeling that a crisis was imminent, the Court of Massachusetts acted upon the elders' recommendation and
on May 15, 1646, asked that a Synod be called, giving
an eloquent account of the reasons.

The right forme of church government & discipline being agreed
part of ye kingdome of Christ upon earth, therefore ye establishing
& settleing thereof by ye ioynt & publicke agreement & consent of
churches, & by ye sanction of civill authority, must needs greatly

1. Winthrop, *Journal*, II, 163.   2. *Ibid.*, p. 271.
3. Hutchinson, *A Collection of Papers*, I, 174.

conduce to ye honor & glory of or Lord Jesus Christ, & to ye settleing & safety of church & commonwealth, where such a duty is diligently attended & performed; & in as much as times of publike peace, which by ye mercy of God are vouchsafed to these plantations, but how long ye same may continue wee do not know, are much more commodious for ye effecting of such a worke then those troublesome times of warr & of publike disturbances thereby, as ye example of or deare native country doth witnes at this day . . . & considering withal yt, through want of ye thing here spoken of, some differences of opinion & practice of one church from another do already appeare amongst us, and others (if not timely prevented) are like speedily to ensue. . . .

Considering these things, the Court asked the elders to frame a platform of discipline, so that the orthodoxy of New England should know precisely where it stood.[1]

Within a week of this request, seven men, headed by Dr. Robert Child, appeared before the Court with a petition. These persons were, as Johnson said, "of a Linsi-wolsie disposition," [2] and were not agreed in their religious sentiments. Child and Burton were Presbyterians, Burton being from Hingham; Maverick was known to be an Anglican. But it was not the strength of this group that caused the alarm. The petition followed immediately after the Vassal one, shortly after the Hingham affair, and a half year after Gorton had landed in England petitioning Parliament for redress and reinstatement at Shawomet.[3] There seemed to be good cause to suspect Child of having been an agitator at Hingham; [4] at any rate, two of the votes refusing to fine him

---

1. *Massachusetts Records*, II, 154–155.
2. *The Wonder Working Providences*, p. 202; cf. Winslow, *New-Englands Salamander*, p. 3; Kittredge, *Dr. Robert Child, the Remonstrant*, pp. 23–28.
3. *Ibid.*, p. 25.
4. *New-Englands Salamander*, p. 5.

in November were cast by Hingham deputies, and in December Hobart and his townsmen refused to join in the fast ordered by the Court, because, some of them said, "they would not fast against Dr. Child and against themselves." [1] Winslow later declared that the petition was known and circulated in England, in all the colonies, in the West Indies, and even in New Amsterdam,[2] and at the moment he wrote to Winthrop entreating him

to be better prepared (at least to staue off prejudice against your Goverut in the Committee of Parliamt) in regard of the petitioners & many other who are very busie, who not onely threaten us as well as you, but grossly abuse us . . . & boast as if the victory were at-tayned before the enterprise is begun.[3]

The real reason for the government's fear of the petitioners was not their intrinsic strength, but the fact that they made a wide appeal to international as well as domestic sentiment, and threatened to upset the internal triumph the magistrates had secured in the Hingham case by calling in English Presbyterianism.

The text of the petition betrays its ultimate purpose. The ostensible requests would never have been willingly granted — that the fundamental laws of England be established in Massachusetts, that "civill liberty and freedom be forthwith granted to all truely English," and that "sober, righteous, and godly men . . . not dissenting from the latest and best reformation of England, Scotland, etc.," be given liberty to found their own churches. The point of the document is its conclusion that if these things could not be obtained, "we . . . shall

1. *Massachusetts Records*, III, 94; Winthrop, *Journal*, II, 321.
2. *New-Englands Salamander*, p. 6.
3. *Mass. Hist. Soc., Coll.*, Series 4, VI, 182.

be necessitated to apply our humble desires to the honourable houses of parliament, who we hope will take our sad conditions into their serious considerations." [1] The right of appeal to England was thus coming up for final trial, and Child was relying on a Presbyterian Parliament to see him through.

The authorities were in a bad temper, and were not mollified by the reception accorded their call for a Synod. There had been no doubt in their minds that they possessed a recognized right to summon such a body, but in order to forestall criticism they contented themselves with merely expressing a "desire" that the churches assemble. They expressly warded off all Presbyterian implications by directing that the Synod should reach its conclusions not "by way of power, but only of counsel from the word of God." [2] But at even so guarded an order the deputies balked, becoming suddenly much concerned for the independence of particular churches. The magistrates satisfied the scruples of the lower house by patiently pointing out the right, even the duty, of the civil authority to ask advice of general assemblies, since "the magistrate was bound by God to maintain the churches in purity and truth." [3] Hingham, for obvious reasons, made no attempt to be represented at the gathering; in Salem and Boston many of the congregations grew remarkably afraid they might "betray the liberty of the churches, if they should consent to such a synod." [4] The ministers resorted to something like

1. Hutchinson, *A Collection of Papers*, I, 214–223.
2. *Massachusetts Records*, II, 154–155.
3. Winthrop, *Journal*, II, 274.   4. *Ibid.*, pp. 278–279.

strong-arm tactics to bring these critics into line. But this opposition, Winthrop dryly comments, although it masqueraded in the good old Congregational spirit, was not simply an expression of anti-Presbyterianism; it arose rather from men who were pervaded with the new teachings, from men who had lately come from England,

> where such a vast liberty was allowed, and sought for by all that went under the name of Independents, not only the anabaptists, antinomians, familists, seekers, etc., but even the most godly and orthodox, as Mr. Goodwin, Mr. Nye, Mr. Burrows, etc., who in the assembly there had stood in opposition to the presbytery, and also the greater part of the house of commons, who by their commissioners had sent order to all English plantations in the West Indies and Summers Islands, that all men should enjoy their liberty of conscience, and had by letters intimated the same to us. . . .[1]

Winthrop's words are a significant comment upon the extent to which the New England Way had become an isolated faction; even the most godly and orthodox at home had, according to New England lights, gone utterly astray. Because of the obstructionist measures of the disgruntled, the Synod did not convene until well into the fall, and then disbanded for the winter without considering any of the things which the magistrates felt imperatively demanded settlement.

To make matters worse, the colony was treated at that moment to an intimation of what support Child might find in England when Randall Holden, one of Gorton's party, arrived with an order from the Commissioners for Plantations, giving him and his associates free passage to their land at Shawomet; this apparition

1. *Ibid.*, p. 279.

was soon followed by a notice that Gorton had been granted a charter. The Commissioners did this, Winthrop says, "partly for their adhering to some of their corrupt tenets, and generally out of their dislike of us for our late law banishing anabaptists." The elders and assistants realized that they had to yield, but they held themselves in reserve for new developments.[1] When the next session of the New England federation met at New Haven, the Massachusetts plenipotentiaries proposed, "vpon serious consideration of the spreading nature of Error . . . And vpon information of what petitions haue beene lately putt vp in some of the Colonies, against the good and straite waies of Christ," that greater rigor should be observed throughout the region, that candidates for admission to church membership be strictly examined, and that sects which opposed the Sabbath or other ordinances of God, or who "bring in and cry vp vnwarrantable Reuelations, inventions of men, or any carnall liberty, vnder a deceitfull colloure of liberty of conscience, may be seasonably and duly supprest."[2]

In November the Court and the elders considered Child's petition. When Hobart appeared among the divines, they decided that he had probably had a hand in the petition which Vassal was then carrying to England, and Winthrop asked him to withdraw.[3] The Court then gave its attention to the fundamental question involved in the petition, the question of "in what relation

1. *Ibid.*, pp. 282–284, 292–293.
2. *Records of the Colony of New Plymouth*, IX, 81.
3. Winthrop, *Journal*, II, 290.

we stood to the state of England; whether our government was founded upon our charter, or not; if so, then what subjection we owed to that state." The advice of the elders was asked, but the magistrates furnished their opinion in advance, "that the elders might have the better light":

> That though we owed allegiance and subjection to them, as we had always professed . . . yet by our charter we had absolute power of government; for thereby we have power to make laws, to erect all sorts of magistracy, to correct, punish, pardon, govern, and rule the people absolutely, which word implies two things, 1. a perfection of parts, so as we are thereby furnished with all parts of government, 2. it implies a self-sufficiency . . . and ergo should not need the help of any superior power . . . to complete our government.

The elders at once agreed. Massachusetts, of course, stood "in near relation, so also in dependence upon that state in divers respects," but "in point of government" the patent granted such full and ample powers "that no appeals or other ways of interrupting our proceedings do lie against us." For the present emergency, the ministers recommended sending an agent to England, who, if he found Parliament friendly, should secure a confirmation of "our just power." "But if parliament should be less inclinable to us, we must wait upon providence for the preservation of our just liberties." [1] Winslow was already going over for Plymouth, and he was accordingly asked to represent the Bay also.

The authorities then turned their attention specifically to Child. The elders condemned his remonstrance, but "they gave no advice for censure, etc., leaving that

1. *Ibid.*, pp. 293–294.

to the Court." Child, seeing the way things were going, lost his temper, and before the Court could levy an official charge, threatened an appeal to Parliament. Winthrop jumped at the chance thus offered, telling Child that no appeal was allowed by the charter and that by this "it appeared what their aim was in their petition; they complained of fear of perpetual slavery, but their intent was, to make us slaves to them and such as themselves were, and that by the parliament and commissioners." [1] An indictment was drawn up, accusing the petitioners of raising sedition "by insinuating into the people's minds, that there are many thousands secretly discontented at the government," of attempting to put the colony in a bad light by attributing to it such conduct "as is abominable to the parliament and that party in England," of saying "that our own brethren in England have just indignation against us," and of making an appeal before any sentence was given.[2] To make its position clear, the Court pointed out that the remonstrants entertained several mistaken notions about the colony; they claimed that the liberties of the charter belonged to all freeborn Englishmen, "whereas they are granted only to such as the governor and company shall think fit to receive into that fellowship"; they persisted in regarding the company as a corporation in England when it was one outside England and so definitely not subject to English laws in general; they held the colony obliged to the laws of England by the charter and oath of allegiance, but

1. *Ibid.*, p. 296.
2. *Ibid.*, pp. 297–298; *Massachusetts Records*, III, 90–92.

our allegiance binds us not to the laws of England any longer than while we live in England, for the laws of the parliament of England reach no further, nor do the king's writs under the great seal go any further.[1]

When the petitioners remained unconvinced by these *obiter dicta*, they were fined various amounts, Child being assessed fifty pounds.[2]

In view of such obstinacy, the authorities no longer had any doubts that the screws of discipline needed tightening. After the remonstrants were punished, the Court went in for an orgy of legislation. It made blasphemy punishable by death, prescribed fines for "notorious & violent heretics," rated "vaine swearing" at ten shillings an offense, and levied against anyone who contemptuously carried himself against any minister either a fine of five pounds or a sentence to stand for two hours upon a block on a lecture day, "with a paper fixed on his breast with this, A Wanton Gospeller, written in capitall letters." Persistently rebellious children, or church members who denied Scripture to be the Word of God, the Court judged to merit death, and it revived in a more stringent form the order compelling church attendance because hearing of the Word was not only the ordinary means to bring men to faith, "but also to civill obedience & allegiance unto magistracy." [3]

Child prepared to sail for England. The magistrates bided their time, and the day before he was to embark they seized his and Dand's papers. Among these they found a petition to the Commissioners that Massachu-

1. Winthrop, *Journal*, II, 297, 304, 301; cf. Winslow, *New-Englands Salamander*, pp. 9–10.
2. *Massachusetts Records*, III, 94.   3. *Ibid.*, II, 176–180; III, 98–102.

setts be given "settled churches according to the reformation of England," that English liberties be granted
and an English governor be imposed, and

that the oath of allegiance may be commanded to be taken by all,
and other covenants which the parliament shall think most convenient, to be as a touchstone to try our affections to the state of England and true restored protestant religion.[1]

The magistrates' suspicions were confirmed. Child was
aiming at nothing less than the subjugation of New
England to the Presbyterian discipline. The General
Court immediately took charge, "in regard the cause
was of so great concernment, as the very life and foundation of our government,"[2] and in May, 1647, levied
upon Child and his followers immense fines. The movement within the colony was effectively smashed. Child
soon departed for England, where he joined hands with
Vassall and the Gortonists against Winslow, and the
last act in the establishment of orthodoxy in Massachusetts was played out in London.

Winslow left Massachusetts equipped with a petition
to the Commissioners which frankly admitted that
appeals could not stand with the continuance of a successful government in the colony; the Commissioners were therefore asked "to confirme our libertyes
(graunted to vs by charter) by remitting delinquents to
our just proceedings."[3] When Winslow arrived in
London he found Gorton's *Simplicities Defense* already
on the stalls, to which he replied with *Hypocrisie Unmasked*. Dr. Child's brother then chimed in with *New-*

Englands Jonas Cast up at London, and Winslow had the last word in *New-Englands Salamander*.

Major John Child directed his appeal to Presbyterian prejudices. The various colonies in New England, he said, were ruled "by an Arbitrary government of their own, nor indeed can they endure the Laws of England." Independency had come from New England in the first place, and New England's government was like to follow; thereupon Wales, Ireland, and Cornwall would presume to act as independently as the New England states. He begged Parliament not to be deceived by the colonists' pretense of doctrinal agreement with orthodox England.[1] Winslow replied simply that New England could not be governed at all if the English government reserved the right to hear appeals. All that was required of Massachusetts by its charter "in the making of our Lawes and Ordinances, Offices, and Officers, is to goe as neare the Lawes of England as may be." Therefore, he concluded, in an uncannily prophetic paragraph,

If the Parliaments of *England* should impose Lawes upon us having no Burgesses in their house of Commons, nor capable of a summons by reason of the vast distance of the Ocean being three thousand miles from *London*, then wee should lose the libertie and freedome I conceived of *English* indeed.[2]

Interesting as these arguments were, events of more importance than a pamphlet warfare were to settle the destinies of Massachusetts. In June of 1647 Cornet Joyce, at the instigation of the army "Agitators," appeared at Holdenby House with his "commission" of a

1. *New-Englands Jonas*, pp. 116–120.
2. *New-Englands Salamander*, p. 24.

squad of well-armed cavalry. The King shrugged his
shoulders and rode off to the army's camp. On August 6
the army entered London, and the Presbyterian rule was
shattered. The next thirteen years were spent by the
victorious faction in attempting to remain in power, and
they had no time to look to New England; furthermore,
since they were attempting to formulate a policy of
toleration, they were content that Massachusetts should
go its own way. "Sir," wrote Thomas Harrison to Winthrop, "what cause haue we to wonder at that rich &
glorious grace, which hath wrought this. . . . That
golden apple, the ordinance for toleration, is now fairly
fallen into the lap of the saints." Although Harrison
added, "if any partake in this indulgence, besides the
orthodoxall party, 'tis noe matter of exultation to me at
all," [1] still it was enough for New England's "orthodoxall party" if it gained its point in England, no
matter in what company; such circumstances could be
rectified across the water.

This changing complexion of things won Winslow's
case. On May 25 the Commissioners delivered their
opinion on the petition. They placed the seal of their
approval on the colony's claim to absolute power within
its own jurisdiction, declaring that they did not intend

to encourage any appeals from your justice, nor to restrain the
bounds of your jurisdiction to a narrower compass than is held forth
by your letters patent, but to leave you with all that freedom and
latitude that may, in any respect, be duly claimed by you.[2]

With the triumph of Cromwell there was no longer a

1. *Mass. Hist. Soc., Coll.*, Series 4, VII, 436–439.
2. Winthrop, *Journal*, II, 337.

chance of this decision being reversed. He fought in the Second Civil War, as Masson says, with a halter around his neck, but when he lifted that halter from himself by the point of his sword, he placed the yoke of the New England Way upon the necks of everyone in those provinces. By forcing toleration upon Presbyterians in England, he insured the continuance of intolerance among Congregationalists in Massachusetts. No wonder Cotton wrote to him, "I am fully satisfied, that you have all this while fought the Lords battells," and that "in like frame . . . are the spirits of our brethren (the elders and churches of these parts) carried forth." [1] There was now nothing left for the Massachusetts leaders but to go on in peace, security, and righteousness, while Cromwell turned to the impossible task of enforcing a liberal régime by the most autocratic of rules.

The Cambridge Synod had assembled again in 1647, but an epidemic had forced a second adjournment.[2] Finally in the spring of 1648 it gathered once more, representatives from all orthodox colonies being present. When Mr. Allin of Dedham was preaching at the first session, a snake crawled into the building, upon which one Mr. Thomason of Braintree, formerly Wheelwright's congregation, trod "until it was killed." With more appropriateness than usually accompanied their allegorical divinations, the respectable elders agreed that the serpent signified the devil, and the Synod represented the churches of Christ; "the devil had

---

1. Hutchinson, *A Collection of Papers*, 1, 264.
2. Winthrop, *Journal*, 11, 324.

formerly and lately attempted their disturbance and dissolution; but their faith in the seed of the woman overcame him and crushed his head." Thus "the Synod went on comfortably," adopted the Westminster Confession of Faith, drew up an account of Congregational polity "according to the general practice of our churches," and "ended in less than fourteen days." [1] Although fourteen stubborn deputies continued to protest to the last, by 1651 the churches had all subscribed to the *Platform*, not, as Johnson said, because "a Synod hath said it, but because the Lord hath spoken it by his Spirit."

And there the *Platform* stands today, the consummation and the synthesis of this bit of human history. In a brief Preface is compacted a summary of all the historic features of the New England Way, beginning with a calm reassertion of its Non-separatist position, although Separation had ceased to be an issue in England. There is a conciliatory word towards Presbyterianism, which could be hazarded now that the danger from that quarter was past. Then the keystone of the system, limited church membership, is explained, and the whole organization advanced as an ideal method for a national church. There follows a detailed consideration of the various features, with the proper biblical authorizations appended to each. The next to the last chapter declares it lawful for magistrates to call synods "to counsell & assist them in matters of religion." The last chapter codifies the magistrates' function in the supervision of orthodoxy. There should be no opposi-

1. *Ibid.*, pp. 347-348.

tion between State and Church; the civil authorities do not "restrain" churches, but help and further them, and the churches should seek all opportunities to secure the magistrates' approbation. True, the State is limited, as Robert Browne had limited it; it cannot compel church membership, nor meddle with church censures, but it can enforce both tables and compel uniformity. The end of the magistrates' office "is not only the quiet & peaceable life of the subject, in matters of righteousness & honesty, but also in matters of godliness, yea of all godliness." Therefore

Idolatry, Blasphemy, Heresy, venting corrupt & pernicious opinions, that destroy the foundation, open contempt of the word preached, prophanation of the Lords day, disturbing the peaceable administration & exercise of the worship & holy things of God, & the like are to be restrayned, & punished by civil authority.

Hence if any should grow schismatical, rend themselves from the communion of churches, or walk obstinately in any "corrupt way of their own, contrary to the rule of the word; in such a case, the magistrate is to put forth his coercive power, as the matter shall require." [1]

Neither Winthrop nor Cotton long survived this crowning evidence of their success, but they should have died content. The contrast between the settled condition of their state and the turbulent confusion of kingless England probably brought to their lips more than one expression of gratitude to the Deity. "All is quiet," wrote Stephen Winthrop to his brother, in the hush that followed the execution of Charles, "but I know not how long it will last. . . . New England seems to be the only

1. Chaps. xvi, xvii.

safe place." [1] The purpose for which the orthodoxy had
labored was as much attained as any human purpose
ever can be in this world of imperfections, a purpose
expressed by the Court in 1646 when, in that dangerous
hour, it had turned to the Synod for a platform, asking
that the Lord being thus acknowledged the Judge, Law-
giver, and King of the colony,

he may be graciously pleased still to save us, as hithertoo hee hath
done, & glory may still dwell in or land, truth & peace may abide
still in these churches & plantations, & or posterity may not so
easily decline from ye good way.[2]

The magistrates and the elders conceived that they had
done their duty as John Cotton defined it: "It is for us
to doe all the good we can, and to leave nothing to those
that shall come after us, but to walke in the righteous
steps of their fore-Fathers." [3] Probably nothing could
have been told these gentlemen in those halcyon days
which would have puzzled them more than that some of
the most respectable of that posterity for whom they
exhibited such concern, while acknowledging that possibly the colony could not have survived had the orthodoxy not imposed its "due form" of government so
rigorously, would yet openly admire and venerate such
spirits as Williams and Anne Hutchinson, or find some
good even in Samuel Gorton. They would have been
equally astonished to find "those that shall come after
us" accounting it probably a misfortune that New
England escaped the calamities which befell old Eng-

1. *Mass. Hist. Soc., Coll.*, Series 5, VIII, 209–210.
2. *Massachusetts Records*, II, 156.
3. Cotton, *An Exposition upon the Thirteenth Chapter of the Revelation*, p. 77.

land. But least of all could they have believed that perhaps the greatest mind to be born of all the orthodoxy's numerous progeny, a lineal descendent of stalwart Peter Bulkley of Concord, would survey their handiwork and denominate the era inaugurated by the *Cambridge Platform* not that of "ye good way," but that of an "intellectual glacier."

BIBLIOGRAPHY

BIBLIOGRAPHY

Adams, Charles Francis
  Antinomianism in Massachusetts Bay, 1892
  Three Episodes in Massachusetts History, 1892

Adams, James Truslow
  The Founding of New England, 1921

Ames, William
  The Marrow of Sacred Divinity, 1643

Bailyn, Bernard
  The New England Merchants in the Seventeenth Century, 1955

Bradford, William
  History of Plymouth Plantation, edited by Samuel Eliot Morison, 1952

Burrage, Champlin
  Early English Dissenters in the Light of Recent Research, 1912

Costello, William T., S.J.
  The Scholastic Curriculum at Early Seventeenth-Century Cambridge, 1958

Cotton, John
  The Keyes of the Kingdom of Heaven and Power thereof, 1644
  The Way of the Churches of Christ in New England, 1645
  The Way of the Congregational Churches Cleared, 1648

Dexter, Henry Martyn
  Congregationalism of the Last Three Hundred Years, 1880

Foster, Frank Hugh
  A Genetic History of New England Theology, 1907

Haller, William
  The Rise of Puritanism, 1570-1643, 1938

Hanbury, Benjamin
  Historical Memorials Relating to the Independents or Congregationalists, from their Rise to the Restoration, 1839-1844

Hooker, Thomas
   A Survey of the Summe of Church Discipline, 1648

Hutchinson, Thomas
   The History of the Colony of Massachusetts Bay, edited by Law-
   rence S. Mayo, 1936

Knappen, Marshall
   Tudor Puritanism, 1939

Mather, Cotton
   Magnalia Christi Americana, 1702 (reprinted, Hartford, 1855)

Mather, Richard
   *An Apologie of the Churches in New-England for Church-
   Covenant*, 1643
   Church-Government and Church-Covenant Discussed, 1643

Miller, Perry
   The New England Mind: The Seventeenth Century, 1939, 1954
   The New England Mind: From Colony to Province, 1953
   Roger Williams, 1953
   The American Puritans, 1956
   Errand into the Wilderness, 1956

Miller, Perry, and Thomas H. Johnson
   The Puritans

Morgan, Edmund S.
   The Puritan Family, 1944
   The Puritan Dilemma: The Story of John Winthrop, 1958

Morison, Samuel Eliot
   Builders of the Bay Colony, 1930
   The Founding of Harvard College, 1935
   Harvard College in the Seventeenth Century, 1936
   The Puritan Pronaos, 1936, 1956

Murdock, Kenneth B.
   Literature and Theology in Colonial New England, 1949

Notestein, Wallace
   The English People on the Eve of Colonization, 1954

Norton, John
    The Answer (1648), translated by Douglas Horton, 1958
    The Orthodox Evangelist, 1654

Ong, Walter J., S.J.
    Ramus, Method, and the Decay of Dialogue, 1958

Palfrey, John Gorham
    A Compendious History of New England, 1858-1890

Schneider, Herbert W.
    The Puritan Mind, 1930

Shepard, Thomas and John Allin
    A Defence of the Answer, 1648

Simpson, Alan
    Puritanism in Old and New England, 1955

Sly, John Fairfield
    Town Government in Massachusetts, 1620-1930, 1930

Stearns, Raymond P.
    Congregationalism in the Dutch Netherlands, 1940

Stokes, Anson Phelps
    Church and State in the United States, 1950

Walker, Williston
    The Creeds and Platforms of Congregationalism, 1893

Winslow, Ola
    Meetinghouse Hill, 1952

Winthrop, John
    Journal, edited by James K. Hosmer, 1908

Winthrop, Robert C.
    Life and Letters of John Winthrop, 1869

Woodhouse, A. S. P.
    Puritanism and Liberty, 1951

INDEX

INDEX

NOTE. In the case of certain names that figure prominently throughout the book, such as Winthrop, Cotton, Ames, etc., only the more important references have been indicated.

INDEX

INDEX

OTHER BEACON PAPERBACKS OF INTEREST TO READERS OF THIS BOOK